The Coach's Mind Manual

CU00828535

The Coach's Mind Manual combines the latest findings from neuroscience, psychology and mindfulness research to provide an accessible framework to help coaches and leadership development specialists improve their awareness of the mind, enhancing their coaching practice. Syed Azmatullah explains how such knowledge can be used to guide clients on a journey of self-discovery, facilitating transformational changes and enriching their performance and personal lives.

- Part 1 considers the mind's management committee, the cerebral cortex, and how its contrasting functions can be accessed to improve problem solving skills.
- Part 2 considers the mind's middle management, the limbic system, balancing executive direction with our social and emotional needs, driving motivation around core values.
- Part 3 examines how the environment, via the body, influences our mental infrastructure at various stages in life, guiding the selection of interventions.
- Part 4 looks at interpersonal dynamics and how to maximise team performance.
- Part 5 considers the power of collaboration for generating the culture needed to improve the sustainability of our global community.

Each section contains self-reflection exercises and experiential role play to help clients derive benefit from their new personal insights. Coaches are encouraged to combine the broad range of concepts presented with their own experience, creating a contextually driven coaching process. By focussing on the mind as the target for coaching interventions, Azmatullah establishes a comprehensive framework for achieving transformational change.

The Coach's Mind Manual is ideal for all professionals engaged in adult development, including executive coaches, business coaches, human resource development professionals, leadership development professionals, management consultants and organisational development professionals.

Syed Azmatullah obtained a neuropharmacology PhD in 1983 and went on to lead global transformational change initiatives as a senior manager in the pharmaceutical industry. He pursued interests in executive coaching and psychotherapy at the London Gestalt Centre, The Grove and the Karuna Institute. He is a member of the Association for Coaching and is currently director of Kadak Consulting Ltd.

The Coach's Mind Manual

Enhancing coaching practice
with neuroscience, psychology
and mindfulness

Syed Azmatullah

Routledge
Taylor & Francis Group

LONDON AND NEW YORK

First published 2014
by Routledge
27 Church Road, Hove, East Sussex BN3 2FA

Simultaneously published in the USA and Canada
by Routledge
711 Third Avenue, New York, NY 10017

Routledge is an imprint of the Taylor & Francis Group, an informa business

British Library Cataloguing in Publication Data
A catalogue record for this book is available from the British Library

Library of Congress Cataloging in Publication Data
Azmatullah, Syed.
   The coach's mind manual: enhancing coaching practice with neuroscience,
   psychology and mindfulness/Syed Azmatullah.
   pages cm
   Includes bibliographical references.
   1. Cognitive psychology.   2. Neuropsychology.   3. Cognitive therapy.
   4. Personal coaching.   5. Executive coaching.   I. Title.
   BF201.A96 2013
   158.3 – dc23
   2013012031

ISBN: 978-0-415-82812-3 (hbk)
ISBN: 978-0-415-82813-0 (pbk)
ISBN: 978-0-203-50137-5 (ebk)

Typeset in Times New Roman and Gill Sans
by Florence Production Ltd, Stoodleigh, Devon, UK

MIX
Paper from
responsible sources
FSC
www.fsc.org   FSC® C013056

Printed and bound in Great Britain by
TJ International Ltd, Padstow, Cornwall

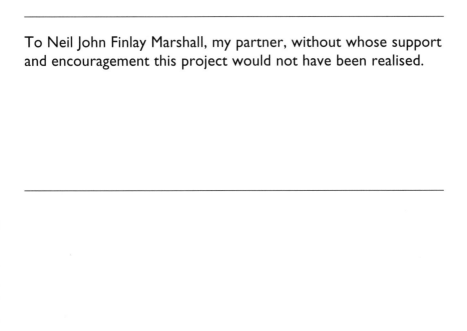

To Neil John Finlay Marshall, my partner, without whose support and encouragement this project would not have been realised.

Contents

Illustrations

Figures

Tables

Preface

When I decided to make a transformational career change from the world of pharmaceutical development into the world of professional coaching, I was struck by the rich diversity of possible coaching approaches. I was also struck by the apparent absence of any unifying concept. Perhaps because I was used to thinking in terms of therapeutic agents as having particular targets, I began to ask 'what is the target for coaching interventions?' Eventually the answer came: 'the mind is the target for coaching interventions'. Yet strangely there had been little mention of the nature of the mind in any of my training or coaching textbooks. Recently there has been increasing interest in coaching and the brain, but 'brain' and 'mind' are not synonymous. 'Mind' is a much more encompassing concept involving interplay between the brain, the body and the environment.

The mind is of course complex and I am reminded of a former CEO who once forbade me to use the word 'complex', informing me that my job was to overcome complexity and make things simple. In a sense this work is a meditation on the theme of evolving complexity and how it shapes human development. Complexity sciences point out the importance of initial conditions in determining the nature of the 'butterfly' effect which evolves according to simple underlying rules. It also puts forward the idea of self-similarity at different hierarchical levels. I am also reminded of 'Meditation XVII' of the English poet John Donne (1572–1631) who proclaimed 'No man is an island'. The sciences have now caught up with this notion and interpersonal psychology urges us to view ourselves as exerting a 'gravitational pull' on each other, influencing the disposition of each other's mind. We are innately social beings and it is our interactions that define us and enable us to develop. My hope for this book is that it will provide a valuable scientifically based framework for coaches and leadership development professionals to enrich their thinking about personal development.

Awareness of the potential of the human mind is improved by drawing upon insights from the neurosciences, psychology and mindfulness practices conveyed with accessible metaphors. With an enhanced awareness of the nature of the mind coaches and leadership development professionals are likely to engage in more insightful coaching conversations enabling more effective development. Their clients will then be more able to achieve transformational changes for themselves and those with whom they interact. I believe that effective coaching built upon an awareness of the nature of the human mind can play a vital part in enabling humankind to solve some of the most pressing problems facing us today.

Acknowledgements

I would like to acknowledge the following for their important influences on my mind: my parents, June and Saleem, for having the courage to bridge the cultural divide and demonstrate the power of love; my brother, Zia, for his encouragement; Prof. Lothar Lange, Dr Jens Preil and Maria Crudge for their ideas and personal support; Bernd Leygraf, Prof. Andrew Samuels, Prof. Susie Orbach, Prof. Renos Papadopoulos, Dr Ilona Eros and Chris Williams for their inspiring ideas; Rex Brangwyn and James Clifton for their tuition at the Integral College, Hove; Prof. Andrew Kakabadse for his guidance at Cranfield Business School; Carl Hodges for challenges at the Gestalt Centre, London; Maura and Franklyn Sills at the Karuna Institute, Devon for the insightful synthesis of Eastern and Western psychotherapeutic practices and Sir John Whitmore and Julio Olallo for their inspiring ideas about the future of coaching.

I would also like to express my thanks to David Rooke and Bill Torbert for their permission to use Table 8.2 and to Simon Heard at Sinage Design for his excellent illustrations. Finally I would like to thank Joanne Forshaw, Susannah Frearson and the team at Routledge for their support and help with this manuscript.

Abbreviations

The following abbreviations have been used:

ACC for anterior cingulate cortex
BIOS for basic input/output system
ANS for autonomic nervous system
CD for Creative Director
CEO for Chief Executive Officer
CMS for cortical midline system
COO for Chief Operating Officer
CPU for central processing unit
EBIT for Earnings before Interest and Taxes
EEG for electroencephalogram
fMRI for functional magnetic resonance imaging
GPM for Global Project Manager
HRD for Human Relationships Director
IWM for internal working model
MNS for mirror neuron system
PAG for periaqueductal grey
PASS for prolonged adaptive stress syndrome
PET for positron emission tomography
PFC for prefrontal cortex
REM for rapid eye movement (sleep)
SBU for Strategic Business Unit
SCMS for sub-cortical midline system
TA for Transactional Analysis
TQM for Total Quality Management
TV for television
WWII for World War II

Chapter 1

The nature of our minds

We all sit in the driver's seat of one of the most advanced pieces of equipment in the known universe, but it didn't get delivered with an owner's manual. Our vehicle has sophisticated functions developed and refined over thousands of years with a management system comprised of 100 billion neurons. Each one of these neurons can form connections with up to 10,000 others providing an unimaginably large number of possible wiring configurations. Much of the wiring at the back of the brain, close to the top of the spinal cord, controls the automatic functions, for example our heart and lungs. Many essential processes have become hard-wired to be automatic so that no conscious thinking is required, saving time and energy. Such hard-wired automatic functions evolved at a very early stage of our evolution and are even referred to sometimes as the reptilian brain, as reptile brains have similar functions. Further automation of non-essential routine processes is helpful when we need to perform repetitive tasks such as riding a bike. We don't want to relearn and rewire every time we sit on a bike and try to ride it, so once learned, the brain stores a relatively hard-wired circuit that can only be changed with active mental effort. Many of our daily activities follow this pattern. We don't actively need to think about brushing our teeth, getting dressed or travelling to work with our full level of conscious awareness unless something new happens. Then energy consuming effort is required to think through how we should respond.

As we age, much of our behaviour is driven by patterns that have become habitual, probably appropriate at the time we acquired the pattern, but then used without consciously questioning whether modifications are required. We may be reluctant to change these habits, not wanting to invest in the mental effort required, telling ourselves that such habits are hard-wired in our brains and we can do nothing about it. But using habitual processes without review may take its toll. One of the most important discoveries in recent years, the concept of *neuroplasticity*, shows just how much of our brain can be rewired. Apart from the circuits for our basic functions such as breathing and some of our basic frameworks and processes, we don't need to accept the ways in which we are currently configured for many aspects of our performance. Recent advances in the neurosciences and psychology have shown us that our brains are constantly reconfiguring themselves throughout life and with the right skills we can, to some extent, direct the way in which important parts are reconfigured. We can assert our *self-agency*, taking responsibility for consciously remodelling important functions within our brains. Coaches familiar with the functioning of the mind can facilitate this process by selective role play and, as we shall see later, encouraging personification of the various thinking modes available to us.

In our contemporary corporate business world, in addition to basic survival skills and specialist knowledge, well-developed social skills and emotional intelligence are needed to thrive. Many thousands of years ago humanity evolved into social groups of hunter-gatherers using more advanced parts of the brain for managing social interaction and coordinating group activities. Our social and emotional brain (limbic system) evolved to control reptilian instincts for easy quick wins according to the opportunities of the moment, enabling shared goals to be achieved by specialists working in teams. Hunting parties learned verbal and silent communication using gestures and facial expressions. Automated scanning systems were enhanced to observe and analyse threats and opportunities in the field of vision. Eye-gaze detection evolved to alert us to when we are being eyed-up as potential food or a target for sex. Visceral sensations were monitored more closely, contributing to an awareness of *our embodied selves*, our gut feel and what our sensory systems were picking up. Experiences were captured and indexed for future reference, particularly experiences suffused with emotional undercurrents so that we may quickly predict what a particular mix of sensory input, evoked feelings and emotions is likely to mean. An early warning defence mechanism developed, sharpening our get away (flight) or fight response, improving survival. But we also learned to override our basic instincts by enhancing our 'toward' response to socialise with each other so that we can engage in joint ventures with shared goals and shared longer-term rewards. Synergistic cooperation with others maximises our potential.

As social animals we do not only communicate verbally. The amount of information we receive or give away through facial expressions is surprisingly high. Paul Ekman, a psychologist in California, has led years of research into trying to understand the language of facial expression and has developed a Facial Action Coding System defining 44 unique action units: combinations of muscle contraction associated with different emotions such as sadness, fear, guilt, flirtation or disgust. His research also indicated that people learn to censor these expressions but usually there is a short delay, just time for the micro-emotion to leak out and be seen before the intervention of higher cognitive functions. Authentic emotions and emotional masks can be distinguished and if we are sufficiently attuned to our environment we can detect the subtle signals concerning what the face reveals

(Eckman and Rosenberg 2005). In processing these and other signals from around the age of four onwards, we are able to attribute mental states to other people in a process known as 'Theory of Mind' (Povinelli and Preuss 1995). We learn to sense what others may be thinking. Developing our ability to construct a theory about what is going on in another person's mind is essential to our ability to read social situations and make appropriate judgements about how we should act. We start developing this process of tuning in to the mental state of another person by the time of our birth, interacting with our mother or other carer, learning from them how we may develop and regulate our own mental state. Thereafter, the mental states of others impact upon our own. We gain experience and shape our mental complexity through our interactions externally and internally (different hierarchical brain levels and the body), shaping and reshaping our minds throughout our lives (Karmiloff-Smith 2008; Diamond 2009).

Before we go any further it may be useful to define what we mean when we say 'mind'. The working model of the mind suggested in this book is that the *mind is an emergent process of self-regulation and self-organisation resulting from the interplay of energy and information between the hierarchical levels of complexity of the brain, the body and the environment.* Recent scientific thinking suggests that the mind sculpts the brain through experience-dependent neuroplasticity, rather than the brain sculpting the mind.

Until recently the scientific understanding of how the brain works in real-time was far from clear. The technology did not exist to observe what happens as it happens. Neuroscience was based largely upon the observation of those with accidental or disease-damaged brains, or on simple neuronal-circuit models in the laboratory. Functional magnetic resonance imaging (fMRI) studies, electroencephalogram (EEG) studies and positron emission tomography (PET) imaging has changed all that. Healthy volunteers performing tasks can be scanned to see which parts of their brains become active and in which circumstances. Such studies have revolutionised our understanding of how the brain functions and how these functions can be modified. Together with advances in the fields of psychology, interpersonal and social neuroscience and the contemplative traditions, we now have unparalleled opportunities to optimise our performance. We can use the functional specialisations of our brain in a more timely and intelligent way and use them in sequence to gain multiple perspectives on challenges we need to solve. We can modify much of the wiring in the cerebral cortex that no longer serves the purpose for which it was originally configured and now tends to hold us back, unconsciously getting in our way. We can enhance the connections between the functional 'silos' of our mind, applying our full range of skills to the challenges we take on. By understanding the new insights from cognitive neuroscience and basing mind-management on a systematic understanding of the dynamically interactive nature of the mind, we can engage in metacognition, thinking about thinking, so that rather than automatically defaulting to our habitual patterns, we can actively consider whether changes are required.

Awareness of the different functions provided in our various brain regions enables us to decide whether we would like to use more of one function and less of another; for example, use less of the alarm circuitry which raises stress levels and more of our sensory circuitry to tune into what our body is telling us. We can select different modes of reasoning (linear, logical quantitative reasoning or multimodal, complex qualitative reasoning) from different parts of our brain to enrich our decision-making process. Making the changes to the wiring in our brains needed to optimise performance does not require us to visit a neurosurgeon. We have built-in neurosurgical capability. We all rewire ourselves routinely, particularly during the first two decades of life, with major overhauls of our networks taking place during those difficult teenage years and again later during the mid-life crisis. It also seems possible to consciously direct the rewiring process in what has been called self-directed neuroplasticity remodelling (Schwartz and Begley 2002). By engaging in metacognition, thinking about our mental processes, and intentionally focussing our attention on these processes, feelings for example can be modulated (Ochsner et al. 2002).

Mindfulness techniques have been shown to change the brain areas that respond to everyday circumstances (Farb et al. 2007), resulting in improved decision making, reduced stress, better creativity, improved relationships, reduced conflict, better teamwork, improved leadership skills and better job satisfaction (Chaskalson 2011). The evidence supporting the effectiveness of mindfulness techniques in these areas is growing at an impressive rate. Brain scans have shown that we can change the wiring and firing patterns of our neural networks by refocussing attention and redirecting our effort leading to long-term structural changes in the brain. Clinical studies of Mindfulness-Based Cognitive Therapy have shown health benefits in areas such as depression and anxiety control (Segal et al. 2002; Crane 2008). The evidence base for certain health benefits has withstood scrutiny by the institute charged by the British Government to evaluate the cost-effectiveness of health-care treatments, The National Institute for Health and Clinical Excellence. Professor of Management Practice at Harvard Business School, Bill George believes mindfulness helps leaders to improve. In his experience, benefits included staying calm and focussed, more self-aware and more sensitive to the impact he was having on other people. He also reported positive effects on learning and memory, emotional regulation, cognitive perspective taking and stress reduction (George 2012). Companies such as Google, Astra-Zeneca, Apple, Transport for London (and the US Marines) have studied mindfulness benefits in groups of employees (or soldiers) and reported valuable results.

Cognitive techniques enable us to look at the mental models we have in our mind for representing our take on the world as we have perceived it. Perhaps these internal models need updating to reflect how our world has evolved to today, and perhaps our perceptions are overly biased by experiences from yesterday's world. We do not need to learn technical details of the functioning of the brain in order to update our internal working models. A useful metaphor here may be to think of a television. There are the technical aspects of how a television is constructed with an array of sophisticated components to deliver high-definition pictures and quality sound. But few of us want to spend our time studying these components at a technical level. We want to switch on, select the channel broadcasting the program that best suits our needs at that moment and become engrossed in the show. Similarly we don't need to learn the technical details of the functioning of the brain in order to run programs or change channels. Our mind decides what to watch and which features to engage in order to optimise our experience. Learning to use our minds to maximal advantage requires us to gain a sense of what the various functions of the brain do without going into technical details. And unlike a TV our minds not only receive transmissions, we can send them too!

This *Mind Manual* begins by describing the functions of the most advanced region of the brain, the cerebral cortex where our higher level thinking is done. It is tempting to think of the cerebral cortex using the metaphor of a computer, particularly the part of a computer where all the computational processing occurs, the so-called central processing unit (CPU). First generation computers had only one CPU but as programs became more and more complex the single CPU format became rather slow and overloaded. Designers realised that to overcome this problem they could develop computers with more than one CPU and that the different CPUs could handle different types of tasks at the same time. We can now buy so-called quad or 4-core-processor computers that run much more sophisticated programs without getting stuck and integrate the results so that the user is only aware of one conscious output. Much processing goes on as unseen background activity. This is not a new trick; our cerebral cortex could be said to have evolved four cores (divided by a split down the middle, the longitudinal fissure, and divided between front and back, the central fissure) to enable background processing and also to facilitate some degree of specialisation within the different cores. These four cores may each use a different set of processes for evaluating sensory data. Increasingly, it seems that the right hemisphere tends to gather sensory data and synthesise it into patterns using a bottom-up approach whereas the left hemisphere tends to use frameworks created by the right hemisphere to interpret sensory data using a top-down approach. This imposes frameworks onto sensory data for rapidly drawing conclusions concerning its likely meaning.

The evidence for regional specialisation, although not universally accepted, has gained much ground recently (McGilchrist 2009; Ward 2010; Damasio 2012; Gazzaniga 2012). It is now understood that the reason for the power of the human brain is not down to its size but the way it is organised. If all the folds were smoothed out the cortex would more readily be appreciated as a highly laminated structure with columnar connectivity forming a complex mesh-like pattern. This structure is ideal for the formation of highly efficient local areas of functional specialisation and is the key to the brain's scalability. This laminar and modular structure distributes consciousness across the brain and it is the function of the association cortex to link things together to make meaning. We can perform multiple complex parallel processing tasks in the background but we cannot follow these multiple lines of reasoning at the same time with our conscious attention. We know from our own experience that processing in our brain runs in the background when, for example, we try to recall a fact such as someone's name, but can't, until the answer pops up when we are focussed on something else.

It is important to keep in mind that the brain does not function like a classical digital computer. The human brain is an immensely complex structure and it has been estimated that 'the complexity of our brain greatly increases as we interact with the world (by a factor of about one billion over the genome)' (Kurzveil 2005: 147). The brain combines both digital and analogue (continuous processing) methods, predominantly using the analogue approach; it is relatively slow compared to digital computers but processes massively in parallel, rewires itself, and uses stochastic processing (random patterns within carefully controlled constraints): 'The chaotic (random and unpredictable) aspects of neural function can be modelled using the mathematical techniques of complexity theory and chaos theory ... Intelligent behaviour is an emergent property of the brain's chaotic and complex activity' (Kurzweil 2005: 151). 'It uses its probabilistic fractal-type of organization to create processes that are chaotic – that is, not fully predictable' (Kurzweil 2005: 449). This suggests that the probability of a particular action being generated is influenced by a huge number of factors in the environment, past and present.

Dynamic interactions influence our various functions in the same way that in a well-functioning organisation, people from different departments interact and influence each other's thinking. So, rather than imagining the brain and the mind in terms of a conventional computer, to reflect quintessentially human dynamic modulating effects, the metaphors used in this book draw upon the technique of personification (Rowan 2010) in which we try to *embody* clusters of associated functions *as if* they possess a personality. This idea is consistent with the view that 'the self is constituted in some fashion out of a multitude of voices, each with its own quasi-independent perspective, and that these voices are in a dialogical relationship with each other' (Baressi 2002: 238). Using this approach we are able to embody our sense of the nature of the functions contributing to a particular mindset and we also will see why it might be useful to hold multiple perspectives concurrently about the same issue. By personifying these sets of functions and embodying our internal dialogue in role play we may be able to clarify some of our internal confusions, helping us to move forward from an impasse.

Part 2 of the *Mind Manual* discusses how the limbic system integrates information from our cerebral cortices with our embodied emotions, bodily needs and the demands from the environment. This will help to understand our motivations and what impedes progress.

Part 3 reviews how events shape the nature of our minds over time. By understanding how events have been responded to in the past we can discover where our clients have got to on their developmental journey and co-create a way to unfold authentic potential. Various psychological theories provide probes enabling us to explore the way we have adapted to experiences. Some of these theories are briefly introduced to provide coaches with an overview

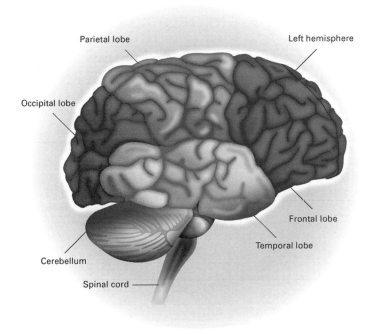

Figure 1.1 Layout of the lobes of the cerebral cortex sitting above the spinal cord, cerebellum and brain stem.

of the tools most suitable for exploring a particular facet of personality. It is important to gain a sense of this developing complexity before proceeding to Part 4 which considers how our minds interact with each other and how we can improve collaboration to maximise collective performance.

Finally, Part 5 attempts to bring together the threads from the previous parts extrapolating into the future to reveal how it may unfold should we become more skilful in managing our minds.

As coaching and leadership development professionals become more familiar with the functioning of the mind, a comprehensive framework and knowledge-base for managerial transformation may evolve. Familiarisation with the amazingly sophisticated capabilities that we all possess is an essential first step. *The Coach's Mind Manual*'s working model will need updating as new knowledge is gained but I hope that for many readers it will deliver performance enhancing insights.

Part I

Our mind's management committee

Part 1 considers our 'executive' thinking functions, capable of generating contrasting perspectives, and how we make decisions.

Chapter 2

Meta-functions of the cerebral cortex

Anyone familiar with the site plan for a large complex organisation will know that departments that need to work closely together are more effective if they are physically located in close proximity or at least very well connected. Departments are often grouped together according to functional relationships and may even have offices together in a single building or the floor of a building. This principle is followed in the brain too whose site plan has evolved over thousands of years with ineffective layouts going out of business. The result of this selection process is a personally customised yet anatomically similar structuring of our cerebrum, the most evolved part of our brain, into separate lobes in the cerebral cortex (see Figure 1.1), our limbic system (see Figure 9.1), and our basal ganglia (see Figure 10.1). Each of these major structures contains clusters of functions that interact to form meta-functions, analogous to a division within an organisation. Anyone familiar with a large business knows that this arrangement into functionally specialised zones carries the danger of a silo mentality developing so that inter-departmental and inter-functional communication mechanisms are needed if the organisation is to pull in the same direction towards shared goals. In the brain such cross-functional communication is the role of white matter organised as association tracts within a hemisphere, commissures between hemispheres and projection tracts between the different levels. A matrix concept is a useful metaphor for the functioning of the brain. The more our brains evolved the more of a matrix structure has developed, moving beyond the inflexible limitations of a top-down hierarchical functional silo approach. There is also evidence for role flexibility so that variations in the functional layout may be anticipated from individual to individual and over time.

The Swiss psychologist Carl Gustav Jung (1875–1961) developed theories about the structural organisation of personality drawing on the ideas of several German philosophers. The philosopher Arthur Schopenhauer (1788–1860) proposed that personality has four functions, with the thinking function and reflective (feeling) function in polarised opposition (Douglas 2008). Jung believed that personality is organised into fundamental polarities that oppose each other. Within each polarity the essence of the opposing polarity is represented. Jung characterised these polarised functions in 1921 in his book entitled *Psychological Types*. These theories were evolved during and after the Second World War by Katherine Cook Briggs and her daughter Isabel Briggs Myers. According to these theories, some of us prefer to perceive the world by sensing the factual circumstances of the moment (called a *Sensing* type preference); others use their intuition drawing on past experience to gain insights about what the sensory data might mean (according to their previously constructed internal models of the world, called an *Intuition* type preference). Some like to come to decisions based on an analysis of the abstracted facts (called a *Thinking* type preference), whereas others make up their minds based on a multi-factorial synthesis (called the *Feeling* type preference by which Jung meant a *reflective* evaluation). Questionnaires have been developed to help identify the preferred mode an individual has for perceiving the world (sensory awareness or by intuition) and making decisions (by linear verbal reasoning and analytic calculation or reflecting on a multimodal synthesis of possible outcomes) established according to what was most helpful in our early life experiences. Each function, Jung believed, was expressed in either an introverted or extraverted form, giving the four functional modes eight patterns of expression. This forms the basis of personality type preference classification instruments such as the Myers-Briggs Type Indicator™ among others (Car *et al.* 2008).

In the 1970s Ned Herrmann, while leading management education at the US Company General Electric based at Crotonville, New York, correlated the type indicator model with what was then considered to be the state of the art Triune model of brain functioning proposed by Paul MacLean. Herrmann associated the four thinking types to the left and right cerebral hemispheres and the left and right limbic system. A 'four quadrant' model evolved and a questionnaire was developed to assess 'quadrant' dominance (Herrmann 1996). Herrmann's model was revised as the role of the limbic system became better understood. Katherine Benziger in discussion with the neuroscientist Dr Karl Pribram, Head of Stanford University's Behavioural Research Laboratory, clarified that the functions that had been assigned to the left limbic system are more properly assigned to the rear left cerebral quadrant, while the functions that had been assigned to the right limbic system are more properly assigned to the rear right cerebral quadrant.

From the updated quadrant model it appears that contrasting perspectives are anatomically configured into our cerebral hemispheres. Another aspect of the general organisation of the cerebral cortex is that the degree of filtering (or abstracting) of information is much greater at the front than at the back. The cerebral cortex potentially receives vast amounts of information from stored memories and new sensory information according to what seems to be most relevant to decision making. Using a camera metaphor: the rear right quadrant of the cerebral cortex uses a panoramic lens surveying the landscape; the rear left frames the panoramic view in ways providing useful maps; the right frontal quadrant selects a few interesting scenes and the left frontal quadrant tends to zoom in, using a telephoto or macro lens to examine a particular scene in greater detail. Although this is a gross generalisation, it seems to be a useful way of envisaging the functional specialities (Figure 2.1).

As individuals, we tend to develop and use one side of each polarity to a greater extent than the other. We may also prefer to operate with a wide perspective or a more abstracted narrow perspective. Decision making involves the functions of the frontal areas which compare highly selected options. Exploring how we individually make our selections based on past experience can be very insightful. For optimal decision making each side of both polarities should contribute a perspective and our process for determining what to zoom-in on needs to be understood.

The main anatomical connections between quadrants are left–right corridors (especially the corpus callosum) or front–back conduits which connect the quadrants in a square configuration rather than diagonally. This helps to explain the idea of auxiliary areas adjacent to the dominant quadrant and the observation that the diametrically opposed quadrant is the inferior or weaker function. Both Ned Herrmann's organisation (Whole Brain Technology and The Ned Herrmann Group) and Katherine Benziger's organisation (KBA, The Human Resource Technology Company) have

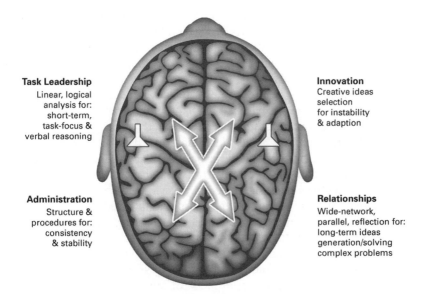

Figure 2.1 The four quadrants of the cerebral cortex filtering information forwards and in functional diametric opposition.

developed questionnaires to identify quadrant preference and have developed large databases of results from many organisations around the world. Using positron emission tomography (PET), Dr Richard Haier of the University of California found that, surprisingly, people with the highest scores on a problem solving test used *less* brain energy to solve the problem, suggesting that intelligence was associated with a more efficient brain (Haier and Jung 2008). A thinking type preference therefore may be an area of high efficiency reflecting well-developed neural configurations gained through experience.

Recent scientific brain imaging and EEG studies provide more information about sub-functions that contribute to the different thinking type preferences. These studies indicate that personality may be influenced by a mosaic of much finer functional preferences than suggested by whole quadrant models (Nardi 2011). We are in the early stages of understanding how brain functions connect together (explored in the new science dubbed 'connectonomics'). For example Dietrich and Kanso reviewed the literature for studies looking at the neuroscience of creativity and insight and found considerable variation in results from different studies (Dietrich and Kanso 2010). They also noted that the idea that creativity originates in one quadrant such as the right frontal quadrant is not supported by the research and that a more complex interaction of a wide variety of functions is most likely involved. Different types of creativity need to be delineated for progress to be made.

Simplifications and metaphors based on current knowledge will need to be updated as new knowledge comes to light, but in science this is business as normal. By considering current knowledge of the different functions within a particular quadrant instead of generalised whole quadrant models, more precise development strategies can be constructed to bolster weaker links in an otherwise strong array of well-functioning processes. As we tend to gravitate towards using our dominant function, even when it is not ideally suited to the nature of the work we are engaged with, knowing which processes we favour will help us play to our strengths and enable us to support our weaker areas, to avoid fatigue and stress.

Our fifth more elusive meta-functional role has been overlooked in assessments of specific cognitive skills because it acts to integrate functions. Jung described this using the term *transcendent function* which acts to integrate perspectives from the different polarities to create a higher level understanding. The advent of recent neuroimaging studies that reveal the cross-functional activities of networks, particularly when engaged in mindfulness-based practices, provides strong support for such a role which we will call the Chairman function. Stewart Shapiro in 1976 created an I-position of Chairman of the Board that integrates the activities of other I-positions when personifying aspects of personality (Rowan 2010). Daniel Siegel, a thought leader in the field of mind and brain research, has proposed that the middle of the foremost part of the prefrontal cortex and parts of the limbic system are involved with resonance circuits and mirror neurons that integrate the activities of widely spread brain areas (Siegel 2007). The role of the Chairman in integrating and attuning diverse internal functions and external influences may be the most vital role for synthesising an overall perception of 'self'.

This synthesising role is likely to be important in bringing together the output of two distinctly different types of information processing/thinking: *explicit* fact or rule based cognitions in conscious awareness that can be verbalised, and *implicitly* driven thinking from deep experiential learning stored in sub-cortical brain structures such as the basal ganglia. The synthesised and filtered output from these two forms of thinking is considered in the working memories of the frontal cortex for executive decision making.

This fifth transcendent function is also a polarity between integration and differentiation (or fragmentation). By fragmenting our perceptions into ever smaller and more refined pieces and then reintegrating them we achieve a more unified better connected fit. Recurrent cycles of differentiation and integration facilitate personal growth and individuation.

Within a coaching setting, in order to familiarise clients with the different meta-functions and clusters of component functions, a personification approach is proposed using the metaphor of a corporate management committee to represent the meta-functions of the cerebral cortex. At the top of a matrix organisation the different functions are overseen by what is often called a management committee or Executive Board. In a similar way the cerebral cortex of the brain, where the highest level of thinking is performed, has different functional representatives whose roles in some ways resemble the ones seen in management committees of large corporations. As in all large complex organisations much of what goes on does not directly involve the Chief Executive Officer (CEO); similarly, in the brain much happens outside of conscious awareness. It has been estimated that our conscious actions represent only 1–5 per cent of total activity (McGilchrist 2009: 187). We are all blissfully unaware of what most of our brain is doing most of the time. By improving our awareness of what our different brain functions are specialised to do and how they are connected into a matrix, we begin to see how we can more effectively use the capabilities that we have and where gaps in any set of capabilities, if addressed, will enable the set to function together at a much improved level.

Our mind's management committee has five members representing five meta-functions and their clusters of functional capabilities (Figure 2.2). Imagine these five committee members sitting around a boardroom table representing different parts of our cerebral cortex.

Our CEO provides analytical task leadership and strategic goals for marshalling commitment towards new initiatives. These functions may have evolved from task-focussed activities such as leading hunting parties during the hunter-gatherer period of human evolution. The CEO, when leading a

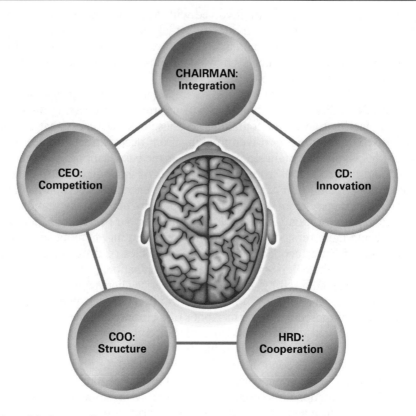

Figure 2.2 Our mind's management committee reflecting the meta-functional specialisations in the cerebral cortex.

hunting party, would propose the type of animal to be targeted (the goal) and suggest a plan of action of logical steps necessary to find and reach the goal using persuasive communication skills while emulating charismatic leadership behaviour.

Our Chief Operating Officer (COO) has the remit to build and oversee frameworks for controlling operational activities providing an orderly set of processes to give a stable and predictable foundation for what we do.

At the rear right-hand side we find our Human Relationships Director (HRD) whose concern is with nurturing and developing relationships both internally and externally, envisioning the impact of change by generating images of future possible states, achieving synergy by fostering a shared vision and harmonising the optimal interactive tones to resonate well with the prevailing culture. In certain cultures (e.g. Eastern/oriental) these functions are valued as the major leadership functions, rather than task-focussed logical–analytical functions, guiding communities using deep intuitive wisdom and long-term relationship management skills.

In the front right position is our Creative Director (CD), responsible for innovation and entrepreneurial development adapting our capabilities for the changing landscape in which we live.

The CD and the COO are oriented towards very different views and have little direct anatomical connection. Perhaps this lack of connection frees the CD to be more creative, less encumbered by how things have been done in the past. These two contrasting modes of thinking may have a tendency to view each other with a degree of cynicism ('head in the clouds' versus 'stuck in a rut' attitudes). Likewise, our CEO and HRD have little direct anatomical connection and may see the world with very differing perspectives. Perhaps this also frees the CEO to take difficult logic-based strategic decisions unencumbered by close personal relationships at the risk of appearing rather emotionally cold.

Completing the team and sitting in pole position is the Chairman with a panoramic view of both outside and within. Well-connected internally and with significant connections to stakeholders outside, this role senses the pulse and soul of our internal world and the environment's emerging demands. The Chairman has the capability to synthesise visions of how the two emerging worlds, inner and outer, may be better attuned drawing upon deep insights and visualisations that reveal realities as they are, rather than how our mental frameworks believe them to be. Unlike the other four management committee members, the Chairman does not have a separate anatomical lobe (or lobes). This cross-functional role is in charge of the interconnecting matrix rather than specialised functions. Part of this infrastructure is located behind the middle of the forehead, the rostral pole of the pre-frontal cortex, which lights up during neuroimaging studies of mindfulness practitioners behind a spot where mystics have always imagined there to be a third eye. In addition, many areas deep in the middle of the cortex and deeper sub-cortical structures are part of the Chairman's territorial network. The network of mirror neurons are also part of the Chairman's domain, helping to reconstruct internally what seems to be going on in someone else's mind. Internal and external awareness of the psychological milieu is crucial for excellent Chairmanship. As sub-cortical structures are exposed to much more information than the filtered information considered by the cerebral cortex, a feeling about what new information might mean exists before the management committee consciously consider the information and make decisions.

Now the members of our management team have been introduced, it is time to visit the functional areas within each of their remits. The basis for the locations and clusters of these functions is drawn from a synthesis of information from clinical observations of patients with accidental and pathological cerebral damage, brain imaging information, EEG studies and other observations (Siegel 1999; Cozolino 2006; McGilchrist 2009; Ward 2010; Nardi 2011). Inter-individual variation is likely.

The style of writing changes in different sections of the book, reflecting the type of thinking processes being used. The Coaching Practice sections, for example, contain specific tangible questions and details that may be appreciated by the operational thinking functions but not by the conceptually oriented thinking functions. Noticing which style you prefer or avoid may provide useful information if it is consistent with an established pattern. Switching between styles regularly helps to develop the flexibility to appreciate where different people are coming from. Similarly, noting which sub-functions your clients identify with more strongly than any of the others will be very useful information to keep in mind. We'll look at each of them and try to see what it takes to enable them to perform really well.

Chapter 3

Leadership and our Chief Executive Officer

The notion of the heroic leader has passed down from generation to generation through stories such as the epic tales from the battlefields of the Ancient Greeks or from the Hindu Mahabharata. Every culture has its own myths and legends shaping our idea of leadership over millennia. Further back in history at a time when humans formed hunter-gatherer communities we can imagine the skills that a leader of a hunting party needed for success: task focus, communication skills, analysis skills and stature learned by emulating elders. Such a cultural heritage informs our ideas about leadership today and summarised below is a concept of what leadership within a Western organisation often entails.

Sitting on the left-hand side at the front of the top floor of our mind our CEO surveys the changing landscape from his perspective, abstracting information from sensory data to gather precise details for assessing any potential opportunity. Understanding the nature of the organisation's past and sensing the opportunities that his analysis reveals, he expresses the mission that the organisation aspires to achieve. His sense of purpose can be profound and once it is clear that a useful opportunity is in sight he can be unwavering in the face of challenges. He knows when to draw up detailed strategic plans and when the time for analysis is over shifts gear to become dynamic and decisive. Being the leader he needs to inspire others to follow the path he believes has to be taken and neutralise threats that may thwart his mission.

He is highly focussed, not wanting to be deflected from the path towards his goals. He is assertive and appears self-confident, striding along the path without showing any hesitation lest others start to question his decisions or resolve. He relies upon himself and exudes unfettered confidence; whatever the scale of the task to be achieved the message 'yes we can' prevails. He has mastered his own fears and inner doubts and, having faced them himself, he is able to empathise with his followers as they struggle with theirs. He appeals to their emotions linked to their sense of personal and collective pride and engages their visceral level of motivation. By putting these feelings into words and conveying them with passion he connects with his staff to help them move beyond their self-imposed conceptual boundaries.

Apart from skilful persuasive use of language and a clear focus on the task at hand, a CEO needs to analyse situations, calculate the odds for and against success and decide which path should be taken. He leads the way and drives the deals needed to remove potential obstacles from his path. If he is wise he'll try to listen and empathise so that he knows where the people he is negotiating with are coming from by mirroring their gestures to gauge their intentions. By mirroring the behaviour of others he will be able to perceive their strengths and weaknesses, those of his own team and those of his competitors. Most of all he needs to know himself and master the art of self-control. He also needs to be proactive in intervening to stop the wrong sort of negative behaviour or discussions going on.

Our CEO's skills cluster into four key functions needed to lead effectively (Figure 3.1). First, he needs a platform or stage on which he can perform and command attention. Let's call it the Boardroom in which selected information and proposals are presented to members of the management team and discussed. In brain terms this is the verbal working memory or the

Figure 3.1 Functions of the front left cortical quadrant (the CEO).

whiteboard of the mind. His second key functional area is the ability to perform strategy analysis on incoming data. The CEO needs a strategy analysis function to select and filter information to guide his decision making. Third, he needs the capability to lead strategic initiatives, getting people behind him to follow through on Board decisions. To help with these three functions personal charisma is a very valuable fourth asset.

Board

The Boardroom of our mind is where proposed strategies and tactics are considered and decisions taken regarding courses of action, investment decisions and decisions to act. Years of experience have shown that to do this well requires that certain conditions are fulfilled which we'll call the Boardroom protocol:

- The Boardroom of our mind needs to be free from distractions and interruptions. It requires a calm atmosphere if all functions of our mind are to understand the full implications of the gathered intelligence and options being presented.
- It requires the active participation of other parts of the mind responsible for the array of different functions. These work better with low levels of stress as high stress levels close off higher cognitive thinking functions in favour of more automated limbic functions. Our CEO needs to ensure all voices are fully heard by actively seeking out and exploring other perspectives. The question 'What's in it for me?' as well as the risks need to be explicitly examined from each function's perspective if a clear commitment to act is to be achieved. To assume that there is internal consensus and shared commitment without adequately probing the other functional perspectives can be a costly mistake to make. Some functions are not so adept at using language to convey their views and their reflective evaluations take more time. Personifying one's other functions through role play helps clarify perspectives.
- One's history and culture needs to be kept in mind. If you don't have a good appreciation of where you have come from and the nature of the legacy you've inherited, your efforts may not stand securely on firm foundations.
- The verbal working memory of the brain has limited capacity and does not assimilate huge quantities of new information. Presentations need to be kept focussed with a maximum of five key ideas. Information overload will fall on deaf ears. Selective filters need to be used.
- The atmosphere should encourage optimism fostering the 'can do' spirit so that challenges are faced with a sense of adventure. You cannot reach for the stars with a spirit of pessimism; man has walked on the moon and glimpsed galaxies in the furthest reaches of the Universe. Whatever

was once thought impossible is more likely achieved with a positive frame of mind.

There is some evidence that healthy people may have a bias towards attributing positive experiences to themselves and negative experiences to other people or external circumstances. This has been called a self-serving bias which puts a positive spin on perceptions, that is, many people see the world and their contribution to it through rose-tinted spectacles. If a document goes missing in their office it must be down to somebody else; self-blame is not self-serving. This is not the case for everyone and more realistic individuals may be prone to depression. Brain imaging indicates that this may be related to how different parts of the cerebral cortex are coupled with parts of the limbic system (Seidel *et al.* 2012). Balancing 'healthy optimism' with 'depressive realism' is an important consideration in the decision-making process. A 'can do' spirit may to some extent be unrealistic but adopting this spirit, to a degree, is a healthier position to take and is more likely to enhance performance. The realistic view is also of importance and such individuals may make excellent risk-mitigation specialists.

Coaching practice

Coaches may wish to explore the 'Boardroom' metaphor with their clients to help clarify factors involved in their thinking processes. This can be achieved with a five chair cognitive perspective taking exercise. After explaining the metaphor and the process to clients, with their agreement, ask them to imagine that they are focussed on that part of their mind where they are thinking things through and trying to come to a decision. You may ask them to consider the following:

•   Imagine yourself to be in the Boardroom of your mind. It may help to bring to mind a recent difficult decision you had to make. Describe the atmosphere as you relive the experience:

    Is it calm and stress-free enough to fully appreciate perspectives from the different parts of your mind? Do you feel time-pressure or other pressures causing you to rush to a decision or do you generally feel relaxed? Is there an internal fight going on between different pulls within your mind; which perspective prevails and why?

•   Do you explicitly address the perspective of each member of your own management committee? If you can find a round table with five chairs, or make a circle with five chairs, one for each member of your internal management team, try sitting in each seat and sensing the role that each member plays in your inner Boardroom. For example, are you swayed by the cold calculated facts from a logical analysis or do you sense an underlying discomfort from the back of your brain saying 'it's not as simple as that, other factors need to be considered; we need more time'. Is there a voice telling you to stay with the familiar tried and trusted ways of doing things or is there a creative urge within you encouraging you to try something new? Sit in each chair and express your embodied opinions to the other empty chairs imagined as being occupied by other members of your management team. How does this feel? What feels most familiar? Make especially strong efforts to give voice to the less familiar team members. What feelings arise as you adopt their perspectives? If there is some discomfort, stay with this a while and make a mental note. Finally, act as a Chairman to summarise each member's position and come to a conclusion.

- Consider whether you are clear about your own history, culture, vision, mission and values and your own personal narrative, the story that informs you of the nature of the person that you are and what you want to achieve in life. Discuss these with your coach considering how these impact upon your decision-making process.
- Do you overload yourself with too much information so that you cannot see the wood for the trees? Executive Summaries for any Boardroom need to be short, crisp and pithy.

These are the key questions you may like to ask your clients to consider in order to begin the process of optimising the functioning of their internal Boardroom, enhancing their understanding of the tendencies they adopt in reaching decisions. The process of *personifying* the five management team members is suggested to raise awareness of alternative perspectives (e.g. viewing situations with both a telescopic lens and a panoramic lens). It is useful to see how easily these contrasting perspectives are embodied or avoided in such role play.

Allowing the different parts of our mind to be heard and influence our decisions is critical if we are to think with our full potential. But we may not know what these parts are and how to hear them. There are parts of the thinking brain that don't use numbers or indeed words, in fact their best thinking is not necessarily conscious linear lines of reasoning at all (particularly right brain functions and the Chairman's integration functions which engage in multiple parallel lines of reasoning). We need to be able to tune in to the feelings, mood and emotions generated by any proposal by observing facial expressions, body language, bodily sensations and the vocal tones of ourselves and others including our own gut feel. Tuning in to these sensations is essential for maximising our learning from past experience. Our memories are most powerful when bodily sensations and emotions are evoked and consciously acknowledged.

Strategy analysis

The CEO's strategy analysis function plays a vital role in providing assessments of different solutions, using logical, linear thinking processes, verbal reasoning and, where data is unavailable, inferring it according to context. In our technological world today we are highly influenced by apparently 'hard' facts, data and calculations and an inexperienced strategy analysis function may be swayed more by these rather than output from complex non-linear evaluations characteristic of the right brain. Our strategy analysis function advises us on the balance of benefits versus the risks in any proposal being considered. It receives input from our working memory about such propositions and may get very enthusiastic about the potential for new rewards (healthy optimism), but with experience we learn not to take proposals at face value and to consult other parts of the brain to get a more rounded assessment (Figure 3.2). We consult the archives (see section on the hippocampus) to see whether similar proposals have been seen in the

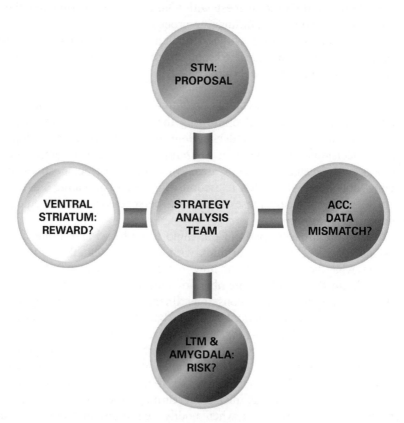

Figure 3.2 Inputs into strategy analysis by front left cortical quadrant.

past. Parts of the emotional brain within the limbic system, such as the Surveillance Services (located in the anterior cingulate cortex – ACC) are consulted as they are able to focus the activities of the senses and pick up anomalies and discrepancies in any information being evaluated. The Security Services (located in the amygdalae) are also consulted to get a whiff of any potential threat lurking in the proposal and how the organisation, the body, may react if the option is pursued. The Treasury (ventral striatum) is asked to assess the size and desirability of the potential reward. With all this input, our strategy analysis function follows linear and logical analytical processes evaluating the proposal using internal algorithms.

This may all sound very logical and calculated but this part of the left frontal cortex, in contrast to the right, tends to guess missing data according to the framework being used and can often get it wrong. Furthermore, unconscious inputs heavily influence the calculations. Long-term memories include many words of wisdom from well-meaning parents, grandparents or other role models taken on board subliminally years ago, biasing our evaluations. Some such words of wisdom may indeed be valid, valuable advice passed down over the generations providing a framework for ethically based actions and personal values, but some words of wisdom may be biased or outdated, blinding us to possible risks or rewards. Being subconscious influences from the inner recesses of our minds, we do not see these operating. It takes a trusted third party, such as a coach, to draw these to the client's attention.

The analysis performed by the strategy analysis function is based on prevailing theories and logical, linear ways of thinking. Data obtained is slotted into the pre-existing templates; it's a top-down or deductive process drawing on the frameworks of the rear-left hemisphere. Framework-free bottom-up synthesis of data into patterns to see emerging trends is the specialisation of the right brain, skilled in inductive reasoning. What is familiar is more easily processed by the left frontal area of the brain. When life is stable and predictable this process is efficient and often works well.

Coaching practice

Using this model of inputs coaches may wish to explore with their clients how decisions are reached, this time from a quantitative assessment. You may ask a client to bring to mind a decision that they have reached recently involving analysing information, and then explore the process used, asking:

- What was the goal of the analysis?
- How were the potential benefits assessed? What assumptions were made and on what basis?
- How were potential risks assessed? Were any assumptions made and if so, were any biases operating because of previous experience? Have

things changed so that prior experience is perhaps no longer a predictive guide?
- What checks were made for consistency between the different types of information used? What did your embodied 'felt sense' tell you?
- Was the analysis performed under high stress conditions? (Recognising that when stressed beyond our comfort zone any risk assessments by the amygdalae may be exaggerated and an opportunity likely to be lost.)
- What was the prevailing mood when the analysis was performed? (When feeling lonely or slightly depressed our ventral striatum (treasury) is likely to undervalue the promised rewards.)

The purpose of such an exercise is to focus on the process, not the content, to see where biases may creep in from using out-of-date cognitive frameworks, or sub-optimal processing conditions.

Some ways of enhancing the quality of analysis that may result as action items from such an exercise include:

- consultation with individuals who have a well-developed multifactorial mode of evaluation (see the HRD's Strategy Synthesis function). They may not be so enthusiastic about a particular possibility, but they may see it in a broader context. By sharing thoughts with them in an atmosphere of trust new perspectives are likely to develop;
- a full assessment of risks may require specialist advice. Left frontal area optimism can be balanced by getting the opinion of someone who uses their rear left brain mode to go step-by-step through a risk-assessment process and from frontal right oriented people who intuitively feel whether the assessment has validity after it is fully digested. Either approach may reveal new perspectives;
- a good assessment of an important strategic decision is not made under conditions of anxiety, stress or depression. Deal with these areas first and delay the decision if possible until anxiety, stress or depression are alleviated;
- if it is not possible to delay the decision, coach your clients to use mind-management techniques to imagine that circumstances are different:
  - Using visualisation techniques ask your clients to imagine that they are sitting on a restful beach under the shade of a palm tree. Say to them: 'Take a few moments to really feel as if you are there. Describe this feeling; then ask yourself what decision you would make if you felt you had all the time in the world.' Changing the sense of the timeframe you have in which to make a decision (time horizon modulation) is a useful technique. Consider how the decision changes with a different sense of time pressure to pin down the part anxiety plays.

- Mindfulness techniques such as focussing on the breath so that your mind gets a break from the internal dialogue with its concerns about the future, focussing instead on sensory input in the present moment, is proven as being effective in relieving stress, anxiety and depression.
- The outcome of an evaluation will depend on the framework used to view the facts. A vitally important skill is to *reframe* a situation so that it is viewed in an entirely different light. The same set of facts can fit different interpretational frameworks. Take time to discuss your client's thinking frameworks and suggest ways to reframe their thinking to broaden their perspectives.

Leadership charisma

Inspiring words, animated body language and impassioned commitment help to convey the impression of the sincerity of our mission to others and indeed ourselves. Words need to be chosen carefully and delivered with an optimistic air and engaging style. Charisma is not simply about selecting the right words or messages or hiring the right speech writer. Mirroring the behaviour of inspiring leadership role models to emulate their timing, body language and facial expressions and engaging in rehearsals with unbiased feedback helps leaders to connect with their audience.

Connections across the brain enable us to communicate drawing upon aspects of our whole being. We need to be able to connect hearts and minds; ours with the listener but also our own heart with our own mind. It is here where CEOs adept at strategy analysis, leading strategic initiatives and managing the politics of the Boardroom may come adrift. They need to connect with and reveal the true nature of their authentic passion for the message that they are trying to deliver. If it is not authentic errors of speech such as Freudian slips, spoonerisms or malapropisms may reveal to others what is really going on in their mind. Coaching managers to deliver effective presentations involves helping them to connect authentically with other parts of their personality, encouraging speech to flow from an embodied feeling about the subject matter. It is important to get their *mirror neurons* activated while watching recordings of great leaders delivering charismatic speeches. Mirror neurons enable us to emulate the actions of someone else in our mind's eye so that we can predict their intentions. With experience this circuitry links together our volition with our passions so that we are able to *feel* the speech of great leaders, not merely understand what they are saying. Thus, developing charisma involves watching others and then engaging in role play. Ask your client who the inspiring leaders are that they respond to. See if you can find video clips on YouTube or copies of their speeches on the internet. Using such tools ask the client to *emulate and embody* the spirit of the leader who inspires them using role play.

Coaching practice

Consider suggesting the following exercises to your client:

- To develop charismatic speaking skills try delivering a well-chosen script of a speech by a charismatic leader on your own private stage, in front of the mirror in your bathroom or better still, off-site with your coach in front of a video camera. Use your analytical skills when watching the playback noting any feelings that arise.
- After practising this with a variety of scripts from different scenes devise a script containing one or more of *your* real issues. How will you talk about these issues including answering any questions that might arise? Embody different emotional levels of connection each time you deliver your script. How does each level feel? Practise these with a coach or other supportive third party.
- If you are likely to have to talk in front of TV cameras the more practice you have in front of the camera answering difficult questions, the more you train the circuits of your brain to remain calm (parasympathetic control) and answer with your intended degree of composure. Put yourself in the mind of the viewer or listener and empathise with their heart and their mind. What tough questions would they ask? How would you answer?

A two chairs exercise enables your client to sit in both the receiver's and the sender's seat if you prefer not to use video recording and playback. They may deliver their speech sitting in the sender's seat and then move to the responder's seat so that they develop self-monitoring skills. Speaking from only a left frontal perspective risks a PR disaster. For example, think of the oil company CEO Tony Hayward who said on TV 'I want my life back' shortly after the Deepwater Horizon oil rig disaster in which 11 workers lost their lives and millions of gallons of oil emptied into the Mexican Gulf. The logic of what he was saying was clear but was the audience really likely to empathise with his position in such circumstances? He later admitted he would have done better with an acting degree than one in geology (BBC2 TV: 'BP: the $30 Billion Blow-Out' 9th November 2010). Leading effectively as CEO may benefit from acting skills but more important is a genuine empathetic feeling for others. CEOs spending much of their time using left brain logical circuitry tend to neglect their empathetic human relationship circuitry. This needs to be developed by mirroring others and embodying their feelings. So when your client sits in the sender chair, get them to deliver the message from their CEO mode and then their HRD mode and compare the results.

Strategic initiatives

A strategic initiatives function goes into action when strategic offensive and defensive manoeuvres have been decided upon. They aim to ensure that the organisation does not slip down the food chain by converting the ideas and strategies adopted in the Boardroom into action. Armed with sufficient information they work out their plan of attack, considering what-if scenarios. There is a pervading spirit of adventure; a sense of wanting to get things done. When the time for action arrives, a switch in mental mode is required, filtering out distractions to focus attention. They focus in on the task at hand, with a specific clear and measurable target, avoiding more complex issues and philosophical concerns. The thinking time-horizon needs to be changed from the long-term broader perspective to a much narrower focus. No wavering, no on-going reanalysis, no rethinking alternatives will be helpful, except at predetermined progress reviews or emergencies. This is a dynamic adrenaline-seeking bunch looking for the thrill that facing risks will bring. As they go into action they need to have high spirits. The frontal left brain instructs the ACC to focus resources on the selected goal. Using dynamic and inspiring music will help focus on the immediate task by shortening the time-horizon and promoting a unity of purpose that visual metaphors cannot achieve. Inspiring music optimises your here and now task focus minimising long-term visualisations. Ask your client to imagine what victory sounds like (Puccini's 'Nessun Dorma', Queen's 'We are the Champions' or their own choice?). Suggest they use this music as a theme whenever they need inspiration for the initiative being pursued. They need to be convinced that they will succeed, censoring any doubts and generating a unity of purpose. Only the can-do spirit prevails. Being convinced of the correctness of their own position is essential once they are committed to a course of action.

Coaching practice

Ask your client how well they identify with this type of function. Can they connect with their inner warrior or thrill seeker, their freedom fighter or James Bond? How and when do they do this? Can they give examples or role-model it now? Is this so well-developed that it dominates other subtler voices? Some suggestions for possible questions to ask your client about this function are as follows:

- If you want to increase your sense of adventure can you identify what is holding you back? Are there early experiences in life when risk taking back-fired and caused a lot of pain or humiliation for you? Can you design a program of stimulating activities that gradually move you beyond your comfort zone so that you can experience that thrill incrementally without being overcome with dread?
- Is there a part of you that sabotages your own plans? Do you know what causes you to back off? Perhaps listening to the quieter voices on your inner management team will reveal the part of you that is not committed to the initiative and the reasons why you remain unconvinced by the

intended goal (see the limbic system and the insula). Who can you work with to build your confidence so that you can re-experience the thrill of winning?

- How well do you manage your mind's focus on the present task by time-horizon modulation, resolving nagging doubts and motivating yourself with the right sort of music?

To be or not to be . . . a leader or his counsel

Boardroom skills, strategy analysis skills, leading strategic initiatives and mirroring others' behaviours are basic skills a leader requires, supported by functions usually centred in the frontal left cerebral cortex. These skills, if strong, are likely to have been learned from role models early on in life. If the connections to other parts of the brain are poorly developed these skills alone are likely to shape a very opportunistic, self-serving leader, who sees the world in categories (black or white, 'you are either with us or against us') and despite the ability to conjure up charm behaves according to cold calculations. Irrespective of gender, these basic qualities are often viewed as masculine aggressive ones but this is culturally conditioned and these functions are accessible to all. To be a successful leader requires integration with skills developed in other parts of the brain; a better balance with the right side functions, the limbic system and the body.

To really perform we need many functions to be sufficiently developed and interconnected. Our left frontal cerebral region is connected to the right frontal cerebral region via a corridor known as the corpus callosum. When the left mode is strongly dominant it tends to use this corridor to suppress input from the right frontal region. This is useful to shut out distractions when focussing on a particular task, but if over-utilised our boardroom and strategy team will become very poorly informed about the wider world, the context of situations being considered and future possibilities. When the frontal left mode is dominant people skills tend to be forgotten. Our creative potential will not be maximised and relationships with others including friends and family may suffer. According to Hebb's Law 'neurons that fire together, wire together', so that if we overuse one function and underuse others, over time this pattern becomes more and more entrenched and difficult to change. But the dominance of the left, blocking out the creations of the right can be reduced by switching away from task focus and letting ourselves go with the flow of music, art or flowing social interaction. If cut off from an empathetic connection with others, a leader can lose the trust of their followers, eventually being deposed mercilessly if followers feel betrayed. Ask your client to name famous leaders who were eventually deposed. What do they believe went wrong? Are they at risk of similar problems developing? How will they mitigate this risk? Perhaps it is time to see how to develop other brain areas too!

Chapter 4

Innovation and development by our Creative Director

Whereas the left frontal zone likes to think about things extracted from the flow of life using words, categories and quantitative analysis, the right frontal zone takes a more holistic view of life's currents over time. What is perceived here defies precise analytic or verbal description. Language and precision are best handled by the CEO's team on the left. The Creative Director prefers to keep many of his thoughts implicit lest too direct an approach destroys their very essence. He prefers visual images to words. The left brain comprehends photons as particles but the right brain sees them as waves, learns to ride them and goes with the flow! Watching the world go by is not passive; the right cerebral cortex watches with vigilance (a wide rather than narrow focus) for pattern changes and the appearance of something uniquely new. In order to convey what is seen to the other brain functions some attention to detail, categorisation and definition is necessary, although it is considered to be a provisional pragmatic approach to handling continuous and changing data rather than recording something as if cast in stone.

Our Creative Director is supported by four key functions (Figure 4.1). Instead of the strategic analysis function which supports the CEO by assessing options for *doing*, the Creative Director has a Centre for Self-Development creating the options for *being*, that is, the sort of person you want to be in tomorrow's world. By drawing upon a sense of how the future may unfold, possible options for future ways of being are selected. These designs are then compared in the design lab, which is like the *visual working memory* of the mind in which options for the future 'self' (or indeed any visual options) are visualised as holograms and assessed to see how well they will suit emerging needs. They are also assessed for how well they fit our personal values by interacting with the Centre for Ethics and Personal Values. This ensures that all innovations and the means for their realisation will be socially acceptable to those who are important to us. Portfolio Managers ensure that capabilities for our envisaged future 'self' are being actively developed.

Figure 4.1 Functions of the front right cortical quadrant (the CD).

Self-development

The centre for self-development is a well-connected area in tune with the ebb and flow of the social environment, seeing trends and predicting what is likely to change. It is constantly brainstorming for possibilities that will enable us to adapt and respond to the emerging world in which we live. Several different possibilities are concurrently explored. Who we are, our 'self', is constantly under reconstruction, shaped by experiences from the time of conception. Our established sense of self involves other areas of the brain, particularly an island in the limbic system known as the insula. The insula keeps tabs on all of the role models you've identified with during your life time of experiences. The insula is like an access point to these role models that have been assimilated to play parts in our developing repertoire. Whereas the insula gives access to working models from the past, the centre for self-development senses emerging possibilities for the 'you' of the future.

As data from experiences enter this part of the brain it tries to discern trends to help predict where attractive opportunities are likely to emerge. If any of these strike a chord, the limbic system's surveillance and discrepancy detection mechanism (see ACC) starts to raise awareness of the discrepancy between the current 'you' and the 'you' that you may need to become in order to enjoy a more fulfilling sense of purpose. Knowing which skills are already on board, the centre of self-development assesses the gap between our current way of being and a future way to be and begins to consider how to fill the gap.

Coaching practice

As a coach, exploring this part of the brain is a major area for attention. It is not so much about leadership and decision making in the present, but about considering optimum scenarios for the future and then working towards them. You probably know the sort of questions that are appropriate for exploring this area, but adding to these you may consider asking your client the following:

- Do you feel that you are performing at your optimal level? Are you satisfied with the person that you are or do you feel that a gap is growing between your sense of who you want to be in the future and the expectations placed on you by your environment today?
- Are you well-connected to your embodied sense of self? This is a 'felt sense' or gut feel rather than an intellectual idea. What is your gut feel about the person that you believe yourself to be? Is this a comfortable feeling of achievement and optimism for the future or tinged with some dissatisfaction and a bit of regret?
- Are you aware of wishing to be someone else, aspiring to be some other type of person? What is attractive about this alternative and can such a wish be fulfilled?
- If you have a clear development plan, which aspects of yourself were involved in its construction? Does the plan reflect your true aspirations, or aspirations shaped by someone else? What was the process you used to arrive at your conclusion?

Portfolio Management

Portfolio Managers oversee the evolution of portfolios of skills and abilities from a very early age, shaping the growth of personality according to the envisaged future 'self' model. They enable all members of the management committee to adapt to changes in the environment to ensure survival. Each portfolio focusses on certain types of abilities. The portfolios of skills and abilities for the CEO mode include processes for logical analytical skills, competitive tactical manoeuvring skills, charismatic leadership emulation skills and linguistic rhetoric skills. The portfolios for the CD mode include the ability to hold multiple scenarios of the future in mind concurrently, ability to hold multiple solutions for anticipated needs in mind concurrently, forecasting the consequences of ethical choices, and vigilant attention processes to recognise patterns within a mass of data. The COO's portfolios include sequential processing skills for establishing routine procedures, navigating using internal grids, applying mental frameworks to organise data, an awareness of boundaries (self and other), comprehending verbal language and the impact of social feedback, storing and recalling facts, performing routine mathematics and building internal models. The HRD's portfolios include attention to vocal harmony or discord, bodily kinaesthetic awareness, simultaneous processing skills for comparing diverse multimodal data, skills for nurturing interpersonal relationships, and synthesising visions of the future. The Chairman's portfolios include ability to listen deeply, internally and externally, to the processes that are in operation, seeing intentions well beyond the obvious, and providing insights unconstrained by our own accumulated baggage, and refining the fine art of skilful contemplative meditation, intrapersonal reflection and existential wisdom.

As abilities in each of these portfolios grow in variety and depth, development of our multifaceted, multi-skilled capability proceeds like a spiral encircling our widening repertoire of personae. Our Portfolio Managers are constantly monitoring and evaluating whether what is being done is leading towards or away from the capabilities required for the future, deciding when to invest by moving towards an opportunity or when to move away from an opportunity; or simply hold and watch. They ensure that resources are invested in the highest priority activities by redirecting the attention of the surveillance services of the ACC. As the limbic level operates using rapid-reaction default behaviours geared towards personal survival and protecting our personal strategic assets, Portfolio Management has to be quick if it wants to intervene, applying the parasympathetic brakes; the amygdala is set up for rapid defence responses with hair trigger sensitivity. With practice one can learn what sort of evolving circumstances are likely to set off the trigger and intervene more rapidly. Social circumstances can thereby be much better cognitively controlled.

Coaching practice

Using the metaphor of Portfolio Management can be a useful way to explore the development strategies that your clients have in place. You may consider suggesting to them the following:

- To see the forest instead of the trees take a bird's-eye view to map out the landscape of your developmental portfolios on a flip chart and indicate where you are going; what your priorities are; and what the opportunities are that you would like to explore? What experiences do you need to add to your portfolios in order to develop the capabilities required for your envisaged future?

- Do you have a vibrant development portfolio for each part of your mind? What new knowledge are you acquiring from your regular reading? What activities do you perform to keep your body fit? How are you developing your emotional intelligence? How much do you invest in productive interpersonal relationship building?
- Do you have a clear goal for each of your portfolios?
- How often do you review your portfolios and assess whether you are on track?
- Is your thinking brain in charge, enabling adventurous toward responses to be taken or do you default to your limbic brain-exercising prudent caution?
- Recognise the signs of your emotions trying to keep you safe while your portfolio team urge you out of your comfort zone towards your portfolio goals. Anxiety levels need to be low if advancement out of your comfort zone is to be achieved.
- Insights about development decisions (e.g. career transitions) may arise when making no conscious effort at all. It is likely that they will be difficult to initially comprehend with words. Nurture and develop your gut feelings but for big decisions sleep on it and get a reality check from another source. When logical analysis and intuitive gut feel concur, go for it! If they don't, re-evaluate your assessments to see which part of your brain perceives discomfort and why. A multi-chair approach embodying different functions may help to disentangle the different views.

Ethics and our moral compass

The nature of morality has been debated by philosophers and theologians over many centuries. Many approaches to this subject have been developed, including virtue-based approaches emanating from Aristotle, rights-based approaches as with Kant's golden rule 'do as you would be done by', Utilitarian approaches popular in the Anglo-American world in which actions are right or wrong to the extent that they maximise general happiness, and contract-based approaches such as John Rawl's Theory of Justice. In this latter approach contemporary philosophers consider morality to have an interactive relational nature, so that we need to find '*Morals by Agreement*' (Gaulthier 1986) and determine '*What we owe to each other*' (Scanlon 2000) with justice based on fairness through consensus (Rawls 1996). Ultimately it will always be down to an individual to learn to navigate through often difficult terrain and take responsibility for moral decisions and ethical actions.

Possibly it's because the right brain has the ability to run complex scenarios into the future, considering the impact of various different factors on potential outcomes, that we find that this part of the brain is concerned with moral judgements and ethical actions. This part of the brain is capable of being in tune with the interconnected nature of actions and their consequences. It is also here that a sense of what is socially acceptable is maintained. This includes ideological beliefs and matters of principle. In addition to holding cerebral concepts of ethical behaviour this function needs to interact in a bidirectional manner with the limbic system which protects our core values and the body providing a felt sense about what is right. This right-frontal cerebral function can override impulsive responses such as defensive fight or flight behaviour triggered by the amygdalae in order to enable you to act in a more principled or socially acceptable way. In the other direction another limbic area, the insula, registers disgust when it perceives behaviour that it senses as being unfair. Treating people fairly triggers delivery of chemical rewards such as dopamine, enhancing our sense of well-being, oxytocin, fostering trust, and serotonin, enhancing our interest in people and new experiences. Unfair treatment triggers a negative limbic response irrespective of whether the unfairness is to you or someone else. If you see someone else being treated unfairly, the left amygdala may urge you towards fight or flight but the expediency of a diplomatic solution is promoted by the frontal right zone which applies the parasympathetic brakes to the impulsive response. This enables us to handle unfair situations without overflowing passion, taking a reasoned and measured well thought-out response. If these right frontal functions are poorly developed, self-control will be diminished and fight or flight behaviour will prevail. Thus we seem to possess an intuitive gut feel for appropriate ethical behaviour in addition to cerebral ideas about it. Blending these perspectives is important for developing embodied morality.

Coaching practice

To develop your client's embodied moral compass, the following may be helpful:

- Considering the appropriate ethical course of action in a specific situation requires developing multiple perspectives using your different mental modes and trying to empathise with other stakeholders involved, embodying what it feels like to be in each of their shoes. The Harvard philosopher John Rawls suggested that moral judgements should be made as if behind a 'veil of ignorance' in which you step out from the world and make decisions not knowing who you will be when stepping back into it. Morality today goes well beyond following laws, religious commandments, precepts and higher authorities. Individual responsibility requires familiarisation with the different concepts of ethics and adequate interactive consultation. Select an ethical dilemma relevant for your client and then review it from multiple perspectives.

- Rather than an analysis of whether the ends justify the means in utilitarian terms, in many cultures morality is more of a synthesis of the contours of motives, intentions, actions and consequences over the moral landscape. One should consider the various motives and intentions that each stakeholder has, as well as the proposed means for achieving a particular result, and other likely consequences of using one means compared with another.
- The results of such a synthesis should be discussed with others who have experience in considering ethical questions and also considered in terms of existing moral guidelines and prevailing laws.
- Managers regularly facing issues of ethics and morality should have access to an appropriately constituted committee of advisors. Morality is socially constructed, changing over time, and cannot be judged from only an individual perspective.

Design lab

As you walk into the design lab you see a very different scene to the verbally driven set-up of the boardroom. The working memory here is not set up for presentations of words or numbers and its ambience is not so formal or restrained. You notice two or three holographic prototype models rotating in a large open floor space, dynamic and colourful with form, curves and inner structure. These models defy easy description using the medium of words. These models may be projected in from the back of the cerebral cortex (right posterior temporal lobe) where the design team reside. Their prototypes are designed for a world that is yet to arrive.

Ideas often form during REM sleep (rapid-eye-movement or dream sleep) as your mind conjures with possibilities. Sometimes they are prototypes of future versions of our potential selves based on our self-development function's assessment of future needs. But we can use this capability for generating possibilities for many creative ideas. Which of these designs will be optimal for the perceived needs cannot yet be deduced. A number of scenarios will need to be developed together and reviewed as time unfolds, to assess how they compare. The design lab assessors are excellent at pattern recognition and out-of-the-box thinking. Being close to the region for ethics and also the centre for self-development, the visual working memory of the design lab is a good place to see whether designs accord with one's values and developmental goals.

Coaching practice

When discussing with your clients how to optimise the functioning of their visual working memory it may be useful to ask them to consider the following:

- The frontal right is a visual/spatial processing facility and is easily disturbed by verbal distractions and the mind's internal chatter. These distractions need to be reduced for the mind to see patterns and flow. Quiet reflective space is needed. How do they make space for this in their busy schedules?
- The inhibitory influence of the CEO mode needs to be avoided. Getting away from the restraints of the corporate or social culture and getting out into the natural world can help. Alternatively, relax and spend time appreciating the dynamic visual arts such as modern dance, sports, creative installations or animals at play. Task focus, emails and text messages are not helpful for this.
- Consider the influence your personal values have on your attitude towards ways of being for the future. Are your long-held personal values and your aspirations in accord or discord? Were your personal values inculcated into your mind at an early stage and do they need to be revised? And what about your self-image? Do you *discount* your true abilities constraining your aspirations?
- Describe the feelings that arise as you imagine your future options with metaphors rather than in precise literal terms. If they make you feel as if you are wading through treacle draw an image of this on a pad; or perhaps a knight in shining armour rescuing a damsel in distress. Whatever image seems to suit your feelings capture it in multicolour. Whereas in the Boardroom reasoning proceeds by using verbal lines of argumentation, in the Design Lab *reasoning by metaphor* can be more productive and it is unlikely to be linear.
- Explore your dreams and visual images with the aid of another agenda-free mind such as your coach. Describe what you are seeing and feeling and see how they react. Have a flowing interactive exchange and see what this unstructured process throws up. *Mind-mapping* techniques may help capture your thoughts using an emerging structure.

Innovation and corporate culture

Innovation by definition requires thinking in new ways. Large organizations often introduce rules, regulations, procedures and processes in order to control predictability and stability which are an anathema to Creative Director types. Innovation is stifled by the imposition of routines, rules and regulations, performance targets and time-pressure. Individuals keen on new designs, novelty and things a little unconventional will probably feel more at home in smaller, informal organisations. They may communicate with metaphors and gestures in preference to a battalion of words. They may connect well to their auxiliary adjacent neighbours: CEO types using logic and verbal persuasion, and the HRD types concerned with harmonious human relations, aesthetic appreciation and cultural pursuits.

Many large corporate cultures favour vocal competitive types who excel in logical-linear thinking resonating with the CEO's style of preferring predictability and a regular stream of action-based results. Such organisations are likely to lose the type of people they need to promote the growth and adaptation necessary for survival. Once creativity declines corporations may resort to mergers and acquisitions to create something new, but after stabilisation and the imposition of the new corporate rules, the stagnant corporate mill pond may remain, it's just bigger! An alternative strategy of large corporations buying small creative enterprises can also fail if mismanaged as the creative talent begins to feel stifled and departs. Understanding the creative mindset is still a challenge for many large organisations. Over-regulation of an industry can have the same effect; for example, the output of new chemical entities (new medicines) from the pharmaceutical industry has declined significantly as regulation has increased and innovative individuals have either left the industry or struggled with the mass of regulation. Understanding and developing the capabilities of the frontal right quadrant for adaptation may be essential for survival.

Chapter 5

Operational management by our Chief Operating Officer

There is no direct route from the offices of the Creative Director to those of the Chief Operating Officer. When you get there it is a bit like coming down to earth. This is not the world of the future but concerned with the realities of today. It's all about getting tasks performed in an efficient and predictable way with four key areas for operations management (Figure 5.1). Spread across three cerebral zones, the temporal, parietal and occipital lobes and well connected to the basal ganglia storing behavioural routines below, the offices here are concerned with sequential information about tangible things and efficient reliable processing routines, rather than generating ideas.

Whenever you go onto automatic pilot, such as driving yourself to work each day or doing the weekly shopping, the sequence of activities that once required cortically driven conscious thought will have been quickly turned into a procedure stored at sub-cortical levels (basal ganglia) so that less thinking power is required to get the task done. Large numbers of our daily activities are set down in this way with self-constructed mental models providing 3-D plans and sequences that will be used regularly. Riding a bike, putting on clothes or brushing your teeth all have predictable sequences that need to be initially learned and then repeatedly followed. It is here that a vast array of our skill sets, capabilities and knowledge base is stored.

Frameworks, knowledge and procedures

Over many years we collect and refine a vast number of mental models of the world in order to rapidly draw meaning from what life throws in our direction. It is likely that we were born with limited generalised tendencies for structuring our experience. During our earliest interactions with our mother or intimate carer basic frameworks started developing according to our experiences enabling us to make sense of the world. We also will have built an internal model of our physical self, a so-called homunculus representing all the parts of our body and their neural connections. This is particularly useful for coordinating movement.

Figure 5.1 Functions of the rear left cortical quadrant (the COO).

We will have developed mental models about how to interact with others according to legal and social conventions. Without these internal mental models each time we want to do something we would have to continually relearn how to live in the world.

As sensory data arrives in the mind from the sense organs of the body (sounds, sights, tastes, smells and touch sensations) it is quickly scanned to identify whether such a combination of sensations has previously been noticed. The sensations are labelled and the search engine in the hippocampus of the limbic system checks all the previous records to see if it can find a match to a previous memory.

There are vast stores of memories from our life-time of experiences that we use to interpret the world. There are *explicit memories* that have been indexed and key-worded so that they are easily recalled, and there are *implicit memories* that were stored and exert an influence on behaviour but remain unconscious, not being indexed or stored with associated keywords.

Our explicitly conscious memory includes:

- a vast knowledge base of many facts and figures that we use to inform our daily lives with facts and knowledge of the world, and language. This is our *semantic memory*;
- a vast repository of events that we can remember, our so-called *episodic memory* which is related to context and this may be susceptible to amnesia.

Our implicit unconscious memory includes:

- the internal models we have built to represent the outer world and prime our perceptions;
- the manuals of how to perform all the skills we have ever learned, our *procedural memory*;
- things we have been conditioned to do in response to a stimulus;
- things that we do as a result of habitual patterns;
- experiences in our early lives (subject to infantile amnesia) and any experience of traumatic events (subject to traumatic amnesia) (Ward 2010).

Unlike paper books in libraries, many of these memories are regularly updated as the frameworks we use for interpreting data change regularly. It's similar to opening an old text file with the latest version of Microsoft Word except that, not only may the contents have been reformatted, the frameworks used to interpret the meaning of the contents may have been updated too. Therefore the meaning we derive from our stored memories may completely change over time. We 'see things in a different light' with the passage of time.

If a reasonable match for the observed combination of sensations can be found, the most appropriate mental model for interpreting the sensory data is quickly brought to mind. Incoming sensory information is always assessed for hints of any danger in case the amygdala's defence system needs to react. If it passes that hurdle the model is used to make assumptions about what the sensory information is likely to mean without assessing every piece of the raw data. We interpolate missing data (fill in the gaps) to see whole patterns. This saves time and valuable resources, but the downside is that the whole context may have changed substantially so that the assumptions made may no longer hold true. Another possible downside is that our unconscious gap-filling exercise may create the wrong pattern. Our COO risks responding using an invalid model, which may have worked well in the past. Middle-management in the anterior cingulate cortex will then need to alert the mind that a discrepancy is occurring; the model is no longer predicting what these sensations normally portend. The world must have changed and it is time to reconstruct the mental model for interpreting this particular pattern of sensations. For example, imagine that whenever your boss asks his secretary to call you to invite you to his office for an immediate meeting it is always because the sales in a region have not met their target and he wants answers. You immediately feel anxious and quickly pick up all the summarised regional sales reports and scan them on the way to his office. Then you get a new boss. His secretary calls and invites you to his office for an immediate meeting. You reach for the regional sales reports, preparing as usual on the way to his office. When you arrive you find he is not interested in the regional sales results at all but wants your opinion on a new proposal for reorganisation from the Board. The context for the sensory data will have changed but the old framework will have come to mind. If it fails to prepare you adequately on more than one occasion it may be time to change it. The whole purpose of frameworks in this part of the mind is to provide stability and predictability. However, we live in a changing world so that we will often need new frameworks. Then numerous connections will need to be rewired so that instead of automatically reaching for the sales reports, you now think to enquire about the topic for discussion. A different set of motor neurons need to swing into action. The period of reconstruction may be disorienting and confusing.

Linking sensory data with past emotional feelings causes biases and prejudices about how we deal with that data in the present. Correcting our responses may not involve rewiring the sets of motor neurons involved in driving an action; sometimes we may need to rewire the link between an emotion and a memory. For example, suppose that each day you drive past a football ground where a tragedy occurred. This may evoke sad feelings of loss colouring the rest of your demeanour for the day. But if instead you train yourself to think of the great victories and skills that you witnessed there over the years, driving past that place each day might inspire you to embrace those qualities in yourself. The sensory data and your physical actions will not change but the way one deals with the data, the emotional associations linked to the memory, may be radically different in terms of the behavioural mood produced. Cognitive restructuring or reframing like this can alleviate self-limiting beliefs and promote a positive outlook.

Unfortunately, the world in which we live is changing at an ever increasing pace, meaning that the mental models we have of the world need to be updated regularly. The advent of the internet, for example, has totally changed our mental models for shopping, banking, sending mail etc. More mental effort is being invested in updating our mental models than ever before which can be disorienting, exhausting and stressful. To keep stress and confusion under control we need to be aware of the earliest hints that our model no longer fits the circumstances we are dealing with. The mismatch detector in the anterior cingulate cortex in the limbic system will be sensitive to discrepancies and create discomfort as any mismatch grows.

Noticing this discomfort as soon as possible and realising that it means that an update of our mental framework is required saves a lot of stress.

Coaching practice

Consider exploring the following areas with your clients:

- Are they aware of any mental frameworks they use for understanding the meaning of experiences which seem to resemble ways of thinking used by their early role models (e.g. parents or first boss)? Which of these frameworks still work well and which have been updated?
- Do other people seem to draw completely different interpretations from seemingly similar experiences? Can they compare and contrast the differing ways of making meaning and identify whether the other frameworks would serve them better?
- What are the mental model(s) they have of themselves? Can they guess from whom they acquired them?

If the COO mode is your client's preferred way of operating, they may be more likely to hang onto old mental frameworks and stick closely to the processes and ways of dealing with the world that these suggest. Consistency and predictability come from this conservative approach but if the environment changes in a significant way, the mismatch may lead to errors. Your clients may suddenly realise that they no longer understand their world and can no longer manage situations successfully. Investment in new model construction and re-routing of pathways can no longer be avoided.

Charting progress

The parietal lobes of the cerebral cortex sit like a saddle in the middle of the cortex. Behind the stores of frameworks, facts and memories is a part of the left parietal lobe concerned with capturing and tracking information concerning progress regarding a particular plan. The information may be spatial or kinaesthetic if we are dealing with movement-based activities such as sport. Then our homunculus may come into action to provide a sense of our physical boundary. This sub-function can then visualise on a 3-D grid where we are compared to other people or relevant objects. Our graphical representation is mapped and tracked using grid type coordinates.

Part of the left parietal lobe seems to be concerned with the exact meaning of numbers, calculations and arithmetical tables with other areas, contributing to how some types of calculation are performed and understood. In contrast, the corresponding part of the parietal lobe on the right-hand side is less concerned with precision than with approximating magnitude.

Coaching practice

To review aspects of this function with your clients, consider suggesting the following:

- If the 'COO' mode is your preferred mental mode you may have a tendency to value precision and numerical data in contrast to those operating in right-brain biased modes. If your boss has a preference for the right brain mode of thinking it is likely that he'll appreciate broad approximations delivered quickly rather than precise details that take time to produce. Which would you prefer?
- If you have a left brain preference you may be uncomfortable using approximations because you want to follow the process and calculate with precision rather than coming up with an educated guess. Does this fit for you?
- Conversely, if you operate with a right brain preference and your boss operates with a left brain preference then calculations you've guesstimated may be assumed to be precise. To avoid misunderstandings it may be wise to clarify expectations regarding the level of precision required.
- Movement-based sports such as fencing and gymnastics are good ways to develop the spatial orientation skills involved with this function, while dance and Tai Chi also link this area to the aesthetically harmonious spatial flow function in the right parietal lobe.

Public relations and communications

Among the frameworks and facts in the rear left part of the brain are procedures to convert internal thoughts and neuronal activity into speech to help communicate our ideas to other people. Similarly, the reverse operation of converting their language into our mental impulses and thoughts is performed.

The idea that there is a specialist language centre in the brain for speech production is attributed to Paul Broca in 1861 and it is associated to left frontal areas known as Brodman areas 44 and 45. Soon after, in 1874, Carl Wernicke ascribed difficulties in speech comprehension to an area further back in the brain in the left temporal lobe with conduits in between. This early model of an area for speech output and another for speech input is somewhat simplified, with these areas being involved in other functions in addition to language, and other areas of the brain also contributing to speech production and comprehension. Nonetheless this area of the left temporal lobe is involved in hearing and speech.

Perhaps not surprisingly this region of the brain not only decides how to convey our words to others but using similar processes deconstructs the impact of what other people say to us. Closest to the left ear is the speaking sub-function handling everything necessary for sentence precision and listening to others. Further back in the temporal lobe is an area responsible for attending to the meaning of feedback we receive. We listen attentively to how we have come across to others and how they judge us. If we have done something embarrassing then it is in this area that the embarrassment cascade tends to arise. Having the output (speaking) and input (listening) functions close together makes obvious sense so that we can quickly modify what we are saying so as not to cause further embarrassment, assuming we have developed this function well. Whereas speech meaning and its delivery are a specialisation on the left side, the tone and aesthetic quality of speech are handled by the right side temporal lobe and this impacts our feelings more generally.

Coaching practice

Coaching your clients regarding speech delivery and active listening is a specialised area of its own. But you could consider using the following exercises to assess your client's preference for technical precision versus pitch and tonal qualities. How sensitive are they to harmonic qualities of sound? How easily are they embarrassed?

*   To develop the functions of the left side practice speaking with precision using all the technical elements of language correctly. Find someone with a pedantic streak to assess your use of semantics, grammar, syntax and articulation. This may also test your PR skills as you listen to their feedback!
*   The listening function of the left is more concerned with precision and technical meaning which contrasts with the listening function on the right which assesses the quality of tone and its more emotional meaning. Do you tend to listen technically and miss the vocal overtones? Or do you hear the emotional tones and miss the detail? Both modes of listening have their place in the spectrum of our capabilities. It is useful to know when to switch from one to the other. Who do you know who speaks with technical precision and who do you know whose vocal tones are more important? Try emulating them on video and observe the difference on feedback.

Project management

The left occipital lobe, at the rear of our head, is concerned with visualising an object such as a house, or car or diagram. Like a holographic image it may be rotated and viewed from many angles so that the relationship between the component parts can be seen. In your mind's eye, you can then work out how to construct something in a logical step-by-step manner arranged to maximise efficiency and predictability so as to reduce the chance of unwelcome surprises. Understanding the relationships between component parts and being able to visualise how they fit together means you will be able to optimise the sequence of tasks in any activity. Suppose for example you have a project to build a garden shed. There will be a number of tasks involved but they cannot be performed in random sequence; you cannot prepare the foundations as a base for the shed after it has been constructed. Some tasks cannot start until others have finished; some can start concurrently and some can start with a short delay after another. The optimal sequencing and timing of tasks will contribute to costs and overall speed to completion. For those who have developed this sub-function, use of spread-sheets, Gantt charts etc. for sequential planning activity with awareness of time, quality and costs and the use of computer assisted design tools (CAD images) is likely to come more naturally. Such individuals may prefer to see visual representations of information rather than textual details. Map reading should be easy.

Coaching practice

- To develop this functional area, get lost! And make sure you have a map and compass (and probably a mobile phone) with you!
- If you wish to develop the skills of this sub-function create a Gantt chart for a project you would really like to do and a budgetary plan. Motivate yourself by building rewards into the plan so that if you achieve the milestones according to your criteria for success, you get a reward.
- From your Gantt chart see how well your predictions turned out by comparing planned and actual milestones. How accurate were your planning skills?

Developing the COO mode

Operating in any of the mental modes that have not been well developed uses a lot more energy than operating in the preferred mental mode and clients should give themselves plenty of breaks to avoid mental exhaustion. Working with someone who finds the COO role fairly natural helps to activate mirror neurone-mediated learning.

The COO mode is about utilising processes for maintaining stability and predictability. With this in mind any of the following may help your clients to develop an appreciation of the abilities of the rear left area of their cortex:

- Study classification hierarchies for a subject that interests you or design a new hierarchical system for storing your electronic files on your computer.

- Create files for your five portfolios of developmental areas: Competencies; Knowledge areas; Activities; Exploration and Relationships, and
  track progress against goals.
- Create your own electronic spread-sheets to track your personal finances
  and calculate rolling monthly average spend and the return on investment
  of savings. This will encourage an awareness of precision.
- Form a close working relationship with a dominant rear left mode
  individual and step into their world by activating mirror neurons and
  writing down what you sense.

Chapter 6

Our Human Relationships Director

Sitting at the rear of our brain on the right side our Human Relationships Director is concerned with evaluating the significance of complex interactions within relationships between ourselves, others, and our environment now and how these are likely to be in the future. Acute awareness of others' body language and vocal tones helps us to understand the intentions and motivations of others and recognise the feelings generated, such as trust or mistrust. Visual and auditory sensory inputs are used to evaluate the health of current relationships and by extrapolation, the likely health of relationships in the future. Four key functional areas support this meta-function (Figure 6.1).

Concord and discord

Sensory data continuously represents the flow of changing environmental circumstances. The ACC scans all incoming visual information to see if it can detect information that, for example, indicates a threat or impending sexual advance signalled by the detection of the gaze of someone else's eyes. The temporal lobes are very well connected to the underlying limbic structures of the emotional brain. The junction between the temporal and parietal lobes is involved in eye-gaze detection and an area called the right fusiform gyrus is involved in unconsciously reading facial expressions and facilitating our capacity to empathise. Sensory data that passes that hurdle without triggering fight, flight or a sexual encounter is then passed up to the right temporal lobe, above the ear, where the HRD's Concord or Discord assessment centre decides on more subtle behavioural significance. The tone of voice and the fluidity of body movement of those with whom we interact are evaluated for likely meaning. With this information decisions to move closer to someone or away from them are assessed. Tones of doubt, hesitation, tremor in the voice coupled with stiff hesitant body language will swing the pendulum in the move away direction. Softer caring tones coupled with aesthetic flowing gestures swing the pendulum towards moving towards your interlocutor. Other parts of our management committee will not be as well attuned to processing such sensory data.

Figure 6.1 Functions of the rear right cortical quadrant (the HRD).

Image processing

Both eyes capture information from the left and right visual fields and much of this information travels along the optic nerve to the first processing station of the lateral geniculate nucleus, part of the thalamus in the middle of our head. From there the information from our left visual field proceeds to the back of the right hemisphere (occipital lobe). Information from our right visual field heads towards a similar area on the left side of the occipital lobe. These areas are the primary visual processing areas where basic perception of the edges/boundaries of objects, contrasts and orientations are perceived. Further information is added to this data in the secondary visual areas in the temporal lobes and we then become consciously aware of seeing an image. The image is seen as a figure surrounded by background which together form a perceptual whole organised according to Gestalt psychology grouping principles (Ward 2010). Then perceptual information travels to the visual association area of the temporal lobe where additional visual elements are added in order to interpret a meaning from the image information by drawing upon memories and their emotional or symbolic significance. This stage is highly susceptible to past experience influencing what we see today. We can interpret identical visual data in different ways according to the nature of the additional information we add to it from our memories and therefore we can, and usually do, cognitively alter our perception!

Image information sent to the parietal lobe's orientation association area helps to create a sense of what is bounded within the idea I have of myself and what is bounded within a separate other.

In contrast to the left brain which tends to track movement within a grid-based tracking system, the right brain equivalent in the parietal's somatosensory region is more concerned with flow and graceful aesthetics. When learning Tai Chi or dance, the left brain specialises in learning the positions or choreographed step sequences as if in a grid, whereas the right brain modulates the flow to achieve something of beauty. Recognition of beauty and artistic flair seems to be a strength of the rear-right cerebral cortex, and beauty generates a 'towards' response!

Sound processing

In a similar way to image processing our ears send sound information along the auditory nerve to the primary auditory cortex in Heschl's gyrus in the temporal lobe via the medial geniculate nucleus within the thalamus. The primary auditory cortex is surrounded by the secondary auditory cortex. As with image processing, different aspects of sound: frequency, volume, tempo, pitch, are processed with some degree of hemispheric specialisation. Pitch and timbre seem to be processed mainly in the right temporal lobe so that aspects of the appreciation of music (as opposed to controlling the grid locations for the fingers when playing music) seem to be more right-brain processed whereas aspects of language and finger placement for playing music seem to be more left-brain mediated (Ward 2010).

Whereas the function of language is to help coordinate tasks (left-brain dominated), the function of music is more concerned with creating social cohesion. Whereas the visual system is specialised more for spatial arrangement of information and the creation of a sense of being a separate individual, the auditory system is more specialised for temporal (across time) arrangement of information and the flowing of things intermingling together. The dominant use of language for communication and vision for perception encourages the left brain's processing approach of dividing experiences up into components and classifying them into categories, e.g. as good or bad objects. This may be ideal for deciding upon strategy and tactics (your CEO's role); however, closing your eyes and listening to the changing tones and timbres being experienced from moment to moment aids interconnection, flow and the perception of resonance or dissonance within yourself or between yourself and others. The right brain-processing mode is unifying rather than dividing. Using both modes sequentially provides a fuller appreciation of situations and their opportunities or subliminal threats.

Coaching practice

Coaches may consider initiating a discussion with their clients on the topic of concord and discord and may ask clients to reflect on the following:

- Consider for a moment the situations and circumstances that draw you towards other people, wanting to engage in conversation with them and the circumstances that urge you to move away. At social events or during the coffee breaks at conferences do you look at the participant list and decide you want to meet someone for a particular purpose (left-brain task focus) and purposefully target them? Or do you first assess the face and flowing body language of individuals to see whether they seem receptive to interaction (right-brain mode) and mirror your approach to their demeanour? Perhaps you use a combination of both?
- When speaking with someone you have met for the first time, what is it about their face, body language or vocal tones that is conducive to building rapport and what tells you it is time to back off? How can you alter your style (face, body language and vocal tones) to put others at ease and more likely to engage?
- What is the nature of charm? Can you think of people you know who are really charming? What are the facial expressions they use; what is the tone of their voice? Do they seem to be listening and reflecting back what you have said empathetically or are they only interested in their own agenda? Take a video of yourself rehearsing charm. Play it back first without and then with sound. From the playback ask yourself whether seeing or hearing this would encourage you to move closer or move toward the exit. Did it feel authentic and charming or give you the creeps?
- What is the nature of flirtation? Can you think of people you know who are good at flirting? What makes them good at it? What do they do with their eyes? What is the tone of their voice? Where is the line between flirtation and getting serious and how do you know when the line has been crossed? Repeat the video exercise and feel your gut reaction.
- Where would you like to be on the spectrum for approachability? How good are you at managing your ability to create concord (or discord)? Do you self-disclose too much or too little? How does self-disclosure turn-taking usually play out?

Developing skills in this sub-function is essential for correctly understanding the intentions and motivations of others by becoming aware of clues in their body language and vocal tones. If the skills here are poorly developed, social interactions are unlikely to give you the results you strive for. You can read what needs to be done in books about the competency of approachability but skills in the rear half of the brain are more amenable to experiential learning.

Creative solutions for the future

The right posterior temporal lobe and the right occipital lobe at the back of our head process actual and imagined visual and auditory patterns in order to predict the likely outcome of perceived trends so that you have a sense of what the future may look like and imagine different scenarios. With such an idea of how the future may emerge, different possible solutions for anticipated problems can be envisaged. This specialist function we will call the design team.

Design team members resonate with trends from the past, sense how these may be extrapolated ahead and imagine what will be needed to succeed in such a world. They consider a fluid and uncertain world of possibilities and probabilities. Creative problem solving relies on this ability. It's like looking into the flow of a river, seeing what images are floating by underneath the glistening surface and trying to grab something of their essence before they slip away. Little can be caught from the array of passing possibilities but with well-honed design-team skills you may become adept at capturing the essence of a passing idea before its ghost-like form melts away as you emerge from dreaming. This is no game of logic. It does not require linear reasoning or deductive thought. It requires broad vigilance and sustained attention, not narrowly focussed attention on one specific task. Ideas emerge from unexpected quarters, popping up like dolphins in the sea. Like dolphins, ideas may 'school' together or travel as a solitary insightful thought. Focus your telephoto lens on a particular stretch of water and they are sure to emerge elsewhere. They are not to be caught, but the essence of them merely perceived. By noting these fleeting ideas, seeing any arising patterns and becoming aware of the meaning of symbols, new designs can be created as possible solutions for the turbulent times envisioned ahead.

This complex multimodal problem solving function does not rely on words or left-brain linguistic constructs. Creative thinking of this type is often inhibited by words: 'thoughts die the moment they are embodied by words', according to the philosopher Arthur Schopenhauer (Hadamard 1945). Albert Einstein observed 'words or language, as written or spoken, do not seem to play any role in my mechanism of thought' (Hadamard 1945, in Penrose 1990: 548).

The French mathematician Jacques Hadamard studied other instances of inspiration including that of Henri Poincaré:

> [A] complicated and profound idea apparently came to Poincaré in a
> flash, while his conscious thoughts seemed to be quite elsewhere, and
> they were accompanied by this feeling of certainty that they were correct
> – as, indeed later calculation proved them to be.
>
> (Penrose 1990: 542)

Poincaré had been working on the problem of finding Fuchsian functions
(related to non-Euclidean geometry) for some time, using his conscious mind,
but without success. 'At the moment when I put my foot on the step [of an
omnibus] the idea came to me, without anything in my former thoughts
seeming to have paved the way for it' (Penrose 1990: 541). Penrose recounts
a similar process described by Mozart when composing music:

> Once I have my theme, another melody comes, linking itself with the
> first one, in accordance with needs of the composition as a whole . . .
> Then my soul is on fire with inspiration . . . It does not come to me
> successively, with various parts worked out in detail, as they will later
> on, but in its entirety that my imagination lets me hear it.
>
> (Penrose 1990: 547)

It seems therefore that creative problem solving involves unconscious
parallel processes that draw upon dynamic images or sounds in which
complete solutions emerge without the contribution of the frontal lobes which
judge the ideas later. The process starts with priming by immersing yourself
in the nature of the thing you are thinking about, trying to feel and embody
what it is like from many different perspectives. You will be unable to follow
the multiple complex parallel processes of your right hemisphere using your
left hemisphere's linear sequential style of verbal reasoning. Slowly over
time, patterns and relationships may come together culminating in the arrival
of the 'aha' moment. Right-brain problem solving involves the generation
of a matrix of alternative solutions that remain open while other possibilities
are considered. In contrast, the left brain concerns itself with a single best
fit solution (Schutz 2005: 13). A right brain approach is therefore more
suitable for considering multiple possibilities.

Penrose describes this as a process of 'putting-up' the solution and
then shooting it down: 'In my opinion, it is the conscious shooting-down
(judgement) process that is central to the issue of originality, rather than the
unconscious putting-up process' (Penrose 1990: 546). Recent research on
the neural correlates for creativity highlight that 'no single brain area is
necessary or sufficient for creativity or any of its component stages . . .
creativity is everywhere' (Dietrich and Kanso 2010: 838). With regard to
musical creativity Dietrich and Kanso reported that deactivation of frontal
regions may down-regulate metacognitive supervising processes which may
result in more intuitive and creative music playing. With regard to insight,
or the arrival of 'aha' moments, these reviewers noted that the visual cortices

and hippocampus seem to be important for generating insight suggesting the involvement of visual representations and memories. The temporo-parietal areas, especially the right superior temporal gyrus, seem to engage in a process of assigning rough semantic labels to these emergent thoughts so that remote associations may be made. The ACC is also important in reviewing these associations of visual images and detecting conflicts between options and the ideal solutions, triggering, if necessary, the 'breaking of the mental mindset that keeps one stuck in the wrong solution space' (Dietrich and Kanso 2010: 844). It seems that multiple areas of the brain are involved in creative problem solving and the processes involved include verbally accessible explicit thinking processes drawing on a limited number of facts, implicit thinking processes – not verbally accessible – drawing on internalised experiential knowledge (intuition), deliberately focussed thinking about the problem and then backing off from frontal processing to reduce the top-down imposition of thinking frameworks.

Creating the optimal environmental conditions in which the creative solutions may be generated and then following on with the mechanism for optimal evaluation is a key ability for managers and leaders dealing with all complex problems. Coaches need to understand the process and how to develop it in their clients.

Coaching practice

Ask your clients to reflect on this from their own experience by posing questions such as:

- Have you ever had 'aha' moments when solutions to problems you have been working on suddenly come to you? If you have:
  - What were they?
  - Under what circumstances did they arise?
  - How can you optimise the circumstances for the arrival of further 'aha' moments?
  - Do they arise during periods of concentrated effort, under pressure, or in periods of relaxation after trying to grapple with the problem for some time?
  - What are the preconditions? Did you fully explore the situation from an analytical, left brain perspective and reached an impasse?
- If you have developed this function well, do you have an uncanny knack of predicting what will occur in the future and then experience a sense of déjà vu?
- Developing this skill tends not to be based around words but seeing events in their flow, becoming aware of the true nature of what we see without our habitual interpretations and being aware of how things are interrelated. In what ways do you nurture such abilities?

Strategy synthesis

Rewards that foster well-being are necessary for motivating the conscious effort required for self-development and enterprise. In the brain the currency of reward is food or neurochemicals rather than monetary and one of the most important reward neurochemicals nurturing the feel-good factor is dopamine. A good meal or neurochemical fix (be it dopamine, adrenalin, oxytocin or endorphin) is a great motivator for driving mental effort. As we noted earlier, the CEO's strategy analysis team perform cost–benefit calculations based on logical, linear, sequential assessments characteristic of the left frontal lobe. But immediate short-term benefits are not the only aspects of reward to be considered and the rear-right cerebral cortex weighs up many short-term and long-term factors from different perspectives to see whether something is truly of interest and compatible with the envisioned future. Impact on personal relationships and envisioned future scenarios are fed into the qualitative and quantitative mix to be assessed. This part of the brain is strongly developed in economics students. Being also concerned with harmony and social concord, the size of any reward needs to resonate well with others if well-being is really to be enhanced. Disproportionate rewards provoking social disquiet can diminish well-being rather than promote it, counteracting the HRD's drive for harmony. The CEO's limited linear analysis may be positive, whereas the HRD's wide ranging multimodal assessment may be negative, or vice versa. In our Boardroom, where decisions are debated using the tool of language, the visually and auditory based scenario projections from the rear right cortex are hard to express. A good Chairman is needed to encourage images, metaphors and visualisation as complementary tools to words, and to invite participants to tune in to their gut feel (mediated via the insula) as well as their logic when considering a decision.

Coaching practice

To initiate a coaching conversation on the multimodal strategy synthesis function, the following items are suggested:

- How do you view your ability to assess multiple aspects of life at the same time? Do you take a short-term or longer-term perspective? How multimodal is your assessment?
- When making decisions concerning taking risks to reap rewards, which part of your mind dominates the driver's seat, the CEO or HRD or do these two independent assessment centres compare notes and perspectives? Model a conversation between them.
- How adept are you at taking in messages that are non-verbal? Are you good at standing in front of a work of art and assessing how it makes you feel? What comes up for you when standing in front of a Picasso,

Hockney, Dali or Hurst and can you use such images to convey aspects of your experience that you cannot put into words?
- Have you considered making a presentation to senior management using only images of paintings to convey your assessment of a situation? (Will they think you have lost your mind?). How well do you use non-verbal imagery or auditory stimulation to convey your message to deeper levels of the receiver's mind?

Change management

Managing change requires an ability to envision the future, hold potential benefits and risks of such a change in mind, and tune in to the degree of concord or discord within the system. The rear-right cerebral cortex has the set-up for developing competent functions for these three areas. However, change management involves the whole of the cerebral level and limbic system. The earliest stages involve a growing awareness by the frontal-right's monitoring and evaluating function that the organisation is no longer suited to the emerging dynamics in the outer world. The limbic system's discrepancy detector (ACC) is increasingly signalling that our internal models are no longer serving us well. Adaptation will be necessary in order to survive and thrive. Envisioning what this will look like requires iterative interactive brainstorming by all management team members. The strategy synthesis function will generate a number of options for strategic adaptations for evaluation in the Boardroom's verbal working memory and the Design Lab's visual working memory. The COO will need to prepare for the construction of new mental models to fit the envisioned new world. Pathways to the old mental models will need to be re-routed. The Chairman will feed in his assessments of the external world and integrate the various diverse internal change perspectives and activities.

When all perspectives for a proposal for change have been considered the overall benefit versus cost needs to be clear and endorsed by all functions to gain commitment. Any change is likely to produce a short-term cost which, if well-managed, should not last long before the benefits begin to outweigh costs. Costs will include reduced efficiency during the change, the cost of learning new ways of doing things and motivational measures to reinforce new behaviours. The internal and external drivers of change and the critical factors impinging on each of them need to be clearly identified. Risks, uncertainties and areas of potential risk, known to be unknown, will provide the basis for a risk management plan.

Bringing about change within an individual or an organisation requires heightened awareness and effort at multiple levels and is inhibited by high levels of stress which prevent new mental models being built as stretched resources defend the familiar tried and trusted methods. Transformational change, reinventing yourself, entails cutting yourself free from *many* of your internal working models which provide you with meaning-making capability, security and predictability. This re-routing process while new mental models are still under construction is profoundly uncomfortable and insecure. One needs to make sure that experienced support is available before launching into the unknown: no skydiving without a parachute! Ensure transformational change specialists are available to support clients when they start to wobble.

In order to encourage desire for change, proposals need to be examined from the perspectives of all stakeholders. A force field analysis, according to Kurt Lewin's change model, may help to map out likely early adopters, moderate sceptics and entrenched conservatives (Rock and Page 2009). Once identified, a support plan for each one of these three groups can be developed. At first, having the old model(s) in mind while building and implementing the new one(s) will lead to *cognitive dissonance* as the neural pathways will be in a state of reconstruction. Cognitive dissonance is uncomfortable because the part of the brain responsible for directing traffic towards our mental models (in the posterior parietal cortex) experiences the conflict between the old well-used and familiar routes and a new construction site, and it will take many months before it can accommodate all of the traffic and cope with unexpected contingencies. Initial use of the new path is palpably less efficient than the old one, generating more discomfort. Trust, support and commitment without premature critical judgement is necessary to keep stress levels in the productive zone (see amygdala). Mindfulness techniques (see next chapter) can help with easing this stress back into the productive zone if levels get too high. Mindful awareness of the brain functions involved in the change process helps to decouple habitual thinking by redirecting the attention of the executive brain to consciously re-enforcing the use of new neural pathways.

Coaching practice

To initiate a conversation on the topic of changing neural pathways and internal working models, the following suggestions to your client may be useful:

- List the things you would like to change about yourself and the reasons why. Then try to get the perspective of each member of your management committee in a round-table role play. What does such a change mean for each of them (which of their sub-functions need to change)? What will it cost and what will be the benefit from each perspective? Which items on this list have the greatest level of support considering all five perspectives?
- For the item with the highest level of support is the overall cost–benefit analysis sufficient to engage and inspire your commitment and urge for action?

- What knowledge do you need in order to construct a step-by-step implementation plan and training programme? Which functions have you considered in this programme?
- Identify where you have the skills and ability to implement the change management programme yourself and where you don't. Identify who has such abilities if there are gaps, and approach them for gaining support. Ensure you include support for the phase of cognitive dissonance, confusion and feeling of being cut adrift as you transition from the old mental model to the new one. Don't try to rush through this uncomfortable phase when the old model no longer shapes how you think; new creative possibilities may emerge to further enhance your new model. Get someone who supports your change intention to help you wrestle with your discomfort during this phase. Mindfulness techniques are likely to help.
- As the new model is followed don't expect too much too soon, but welcome any signs of positive changes by giving yourself rewards and encouragement to embed the new you.

Chapter 7

Integration and transformation by our Chairman

Our Chairman can sometimes be located in pole position right at the front of the cortex of the brain in the part most advanced and most recently evolved. But he is active in other places too. He sees beyond the boundaries of the individual mind, linking with the wider world over time. His attention oscillates between inner and outer worlds as he fulfils a dialectic spiral between differentiation and integration, between seeing the 'self' as an individual and the 'self' as part of the interplay of life. His main responsibility is for metacognition, thinking about thinking, and integrating how the members of the management committee, middle management and the body interact with outside stakeholders to coalesce our sense of 'self' in the world. There are times when he doesn't appear to be anywhere at all. We so often run on automatic pilot, following habitual routines. He is best at his job when things are quieter and conducive to subtle reflection.

Daniel Siegel, a thought leader in the field of mind and brain research, has proposed that the middle of the foremost part of the prefrontal cortex and parts of the limbic system interact with resonance circuits and mirror neurons to integrate the activities of widely spread brain areas involved in: *regulating the body*; *attuning communication with others*; *balancing emotions*; *responding flexibly to emerging circumstances*; *insight into the nature of 'self'*; *modulating fear, developing intuition and developing morality* (Siegel 2007).

Other researchers indicate that there are a number of overlapping neural networks such as the cortical midline structures (CMS), a sub-cortical midline system (SCMS), a right lateralised frontoparietal network, and the mirror neuron system (MNS). The MNS sets up the same pattern of neural activity in the observer as is being used to generate an action by the person being observed. The other networks are involved in integrating a sense of 'self' and 'other'. The CMS is also involved in the resting state default network used for rehearsing various scenarios and updating memories according to their importance (Knox 2011: 60–84).

Using our power of imagination the CMS draws on all these networks and circuits and, by linking to the higher functions of the right orbitofrontal cortex, is able to integrate an embodied, emotional and relational self-experience. Using these representations of 'self' in a social context enables our self-agency to be expressed (Knox 2011).

The role of the Chairman in integrating and attuning diverse internal functions and external influences may be the most vital role for synthesising an overall perception of 'self'. 'Integration is not a function of self, it is what self is' (Ogawa *et al.* 1997); 'the self is precisely the integrator; it is the *synthetic* unity, as Kant said' (Perls *et al.* 1951).

As with the other management committee members, let's look at the functions over which the Chairman presides (Figure 7.1).

Calmness

The Chairman is able to develop a state of calmness in the mind when the mind is free from being enmeshed in day-to-day operational activities. You might think that when the activities of performing tasks are interrupted

Figure 7.1 Functions of the integration meta-function, 'The Chairman'.

for a lunch break all would become calm inside your organisation with time for the mind to settle. But the activity downtime does not usually mean that the mind becomes calm. For just as in any staff canteen during lunch break, conversational chatter on a wide range of unfocussed topics breaks out, filling the activity void. The same happens in the brain. When you stop concentrating on specific tasks, rather than things becoming quiet, the midline areas of the cerebral cortex become filled with activity trying to make sense of the day's experiences by generating a narrative to form a story. Neuroscientists ascribe this sort of chatter in the brain to the *default network*, one of the *resting state networks* that come online during a downtime for task focussed work. Telling stories by weaving together pieces of information is a normal function of the human mind, trying to make some sense of what is going on out there. Sitting in the canteen of your mind all sorts of rumours and possibilities are given an airing, oblivious to the facts about what is happening outside at that very moment. The default network connects many areas across the brain and consists of a CMS and a SCMS. The canteen metaphor is appropriate as this network consumes 30 per cent more calories for its weight than any other brain area while speculating about future possibilities, day-dreaming about possible future actions and, via communication with the hippocampus, updating autobiographical memory (Knox 2011). But the Chairman knows that there is an alternative self-referential system to the normal default of narrative generation. He can transform the mind to become a quiet space more like a temple than a canteen. Sitting mindfully, he changes his attention from weaving stories drawn from experience to creating fantasies about the future, to awareness of what is going on internally and externally at that very moment. His practice normally starts with his thinking mind scanning his body to ask each part of it what it is sensing at that moment. How are his toes? Warm, cold, energized or rather dull and neglected? Just a quick bringing into awareness of what each part of the body is registering without interpretation or weaving a story is the gentle mental process required. Then he focusses his attention on his breath, the inhalation and expulsion of the air through his airways. No analysis, no stories, just lightly perceiving how warm or cold, dry or moist the air is and what the sensation is as it passes through his nose to and from the lungs. With regular practice over a few weeks he has found, like many others before him, another self-referential resting state network kicks in, the *direct experience network*, which decentres the mind's attention from the midline of the cortex out to the sides (lateral prefrontal cortex) particularly on the right side. In addition, an area of the limbic brain concerned with maintaining a sense of who we are, the insula, becomes active, again more so on the right, detecting what is being sensed by the body (Farb *et al.* 2007). Changing the coupling of the right insula from the inner to the outer cortex (*decentring*) avoids mixing direct sensation with narrative writing and creates a lighter, expansive feeling. This means your Chairman has more chance of experiencing the present moment as it actually is rather than shaping that experience to fit a particular story. This decentring practice is one of a large number of mindfulness practices, focussing your mind to pay attention to any specific activity you are undertaking with full awareness and heightened sensory perception in the present moment. This helps to avoid runaway narratives, catastrophic fables of impending doom or fantastic stories with the happy endings preferred in our favourite dreams.

Without words and imagined meanings filling our minds, free from gossip and intrusive chatter, the bubbling cauldron of thoughts in the centre of your mind fades into the background as your awareness literally expands beyond it. Data from the senses is acknowledged softly, without words or labels, as it floats away down a clear stream of conscious awareness. By changing attention to the here-and-now, rather than attending to narratives constructed about what may possibly be, anxieties about the future melt away. Our past stops beating us up about imagined dangers. Our narrative mode hands over to our somatosensory mode and imagined catastrophes disappear. The early warning threat detection system in our limbic brain (the ACC and amygdala) is no longer placed on a raised state of alert. Relieved of such anxieties we may even experience bliss.

By focussing on the breath, not only is there a decentring from the inner chatter towards direct experience, our sense of 'self' shifts with repeated practice from a visual self-image, a spatial metaphor for who we are, to a temporal metaphor, a time and process based self-image. This time based self-image is not fixed like a robot constructed with solid unchanging wiring connections, but rather a highly dynamic and flexible structure that can adapt and reconfigure itself in response to changing conditions. In other words, our idea of our 'self' as a solid discrete fixed immutable entity composed of fixed component parts changes to an idea of our 'self' as a flowing, developing, dynamic interplay with the environment with which we interact. Our self-metaphor becomes more like music than a picture. Rather than thinking of ourselves as entities that have things done to us, we open ourselves to the potential we have for seeing the world completely differently, empowering our desire to realise our potential. The initial stages of concentration meditation, when we are attached to the spatial 'self' metaphor, bring into focus the sense of having a boundary between each one of us and everything else. This sense of being separate from the rest of humanity and nature can foster feelings of isolation and loneliness. As our meditative practice develops, these feelings can cause disillusionment as we feel somewhat inadequate, incomplete and empty of real substance. As our mindfulness skills grow, the idea of the physical boundary in which our 'self' is encapsulated (an idea maintained in the parietal lobe so that spatial coordination of movement is possible) begins expanding further as realisation of the interconnected nature of ourselves kicks in. In our mind's eye our hard 'self' boundary begins to dissolve, opening up a feeling of vast spaciousness in which mental constraints and indeed physical sensation may become suspended (Epstein 1996). We are no longer an individual instrument among others on the stage of life, we see ourselves as part of life's symphony.

Focussing on the breath lightly without objectifying it develops the neural nests for deeper concentration and provides a platform for supporting insightful thinking. By reducing the break-through chatter from the default network our mind becomes less cluttered by noise and free from the pressure of self-generated expectations from our internal stories. Mindfulness courses that guide you through exercises encouraging 20 minutes of intentional mindfulness a day for a period of eight weeks are ideal for reducing stress and improving cognitive performance. Books on mindfulness practices with CDs included guide the participant through numerous mindfulness exercises, for example Williams and Penman (2011).

Mindfulness practices train an area of the limbic system, the ACC, to throw the spotlight of attention where you decide with clear awareness it should be. It may be into the body to detect a felt sense of embodied emotions or into the brain to facilitate metacognition. It is intended as a preconceptual and pre-symbolic awareness that does not need to be thought about. It is a mere noticing without judgement or further elaboration of what is present at that moment of time regarding thoughts, feeling or sensations in the field of attention, which is acknowledged and accepted as it is. Thus it may be likened to a mirror without distortions. Mindfulness practices do not require you to sit on a cushion and meditate necessarily. You can mindfully sweep leaves from a path or wash the dishes or eat a raisin – but not at the same time! Multitasking or being somewhere else when talking on the phone or sending emails when sitting in business meetings are not mindful! And mindfulness is not in its essence a sign of allegiance to a particular religious tradition. Coaches and their clients are likely to benefit from the neuroplastic remodelling that such exercises promote.

If we wish to deepen even further our neural nests for concentration our personal narratives may start to change substantially. This is best done under the guidance of a psychotherapeutically trained meditator who is able to draw upon the rich heritage of mindfulness knowledge (Anālayo 2003). Bringing about substantial changes to our self-narrative, which is important in transpersonal coaching for example, needs to be done mindfully, and suitable guidance is strongly recommended. Without such an experienced guide some of the deeper practices may be used by some as a means of spiritual bypassing (Welwood 2000) in which the practitioner dissociates from the spatial world of everyday experience, preferring the temporal world of interconnected flow instead of integrating the two.

Coaching practice

To explore the nature of the function for engendering calmness with your clients you may consider asking them the following questions:

- Do you spend most of your working downtime in your mind's inner 'temple' or its 'canteen'?
- Have you explored the sense of clarity of thinking that mindfulness practices can bring?
- Have you experienced that light expansive feeling as your mind opens its boundaries to experience the wider world?
- Do you need to reduce the chatter in your mind that creates the worries and anxieties that cloud your outlook? What methods have you tried to help you to do this?
- Are you scared of times of quiet solitude because uncomfortable thoughts intrude destroying your potential state of bliss? Have you considered discussing this with a psychotherapeutically trained meditator?

Unless our Chairman nurtures our inner state of calm it will be difficult to go further and engage in deeper metacognition (thinking about thinking) reflecting on the mind's inner process. Without a quiet time to allow the debris of the day to settle and demist your mind there will be no clarity in which to sense the subtle signs and signals of what is really going on inside yourself or outside. Finding time to sit in solitude and simply sense the quality of the moment is a good first step.

External awareness

In the same way that we can redirect our inner attention from the stories we generate in our default mode to our breath in the moment, we can also do this when going for a walk and become more closely aware of our outer world. Instead of filling our heads with worries from the media or other anxieties we can walk through a park or forest and really hear the birds, smell the plant life and appreciate the images and contrasting light. In this way we again escape our 'self' narrative-containing baggage from our past and imaginings about our future to really notice the beauty of each single moment in our day. This encourages perspective taking from a distance.

When we meet another person for the first time we normally revert to our narrative mind, imagining the sort of person they might be and classifying the level of threat they pose in order to decide on a strategy of approach or avoidance. He or she may have some features that resemble a previous encounter in our memories and before we know it we have superimposed someone's personality from our past onto the person we have only just met. We tend to err on the side of caution unless he or she reminds us of someone we trust or really like, and then we err on the side of confidence. We pick up many signals from what we observe; from body language and facial expressions. The human face is equipped with so many tiny muscles it is able to convey status information in a visual display language of its own. From our earliest moments cradled in the arms of our mother, gazing into eyes linked to the right cortex, we have developed a way of interpreting such non-verbal language and reconstructing in our own mind what is going on in our mother's or carer's mind when we intimately connect. We are normally able to read their intentions and activate the same wiring pattern in our brain that she or he is using to link the different parts of her or his mind. We are then able to link their reasoning, intentions, actions and emotions together by reconstructing their whole set of thought patterns in our own brains. Such ability is known as mentalisation and is linked to the Theory of Mind because our mind produces a theory about what is going on in someone else's mind (Prempack and Woodruff 1978).

The mirror neuron system was discovered first in Macaque monkeys in 1996 by researchers Gallese and Rizzolatti at the University of Parma, Italy, and later found in humans (Gallese *et al.* 1996). It is activated during observation, imagination, empathy and execution of hand movements. The mirror neurons bridge the different areas of the brain involved in these activities including the temporal, parietal and frontal lobes, the insula and amygdala, and the basal ganglia and cerebellum. This system facilitates our ability to imitate another person, create representations of their subjective mind, understand the intentions of any of their goal-focussed actions, and mediates emotional resonance with them. For emotional resonance to be really powerful, it is important to be attuned to one's own internal mental state and skilful at labelling these internal states and regulating them. Mindfulness practices develop this ability.

A competent Chairman is able to tune in to the subjective minds of other people and sense where they are coming from. He is able to recreate their emotional experience by engaging his own emotional middle management, especially the insula, which maintains the connections to mental models, creating a subjective sense of 'self', and his self-narrative. He is also able to use his upper temporal area to read the facial expressions and gestures of others performing a visual analysis, and tune into their flowing patterns of behaviour. In this way our Chairman is able to empathise with others, experiencing what they feel without being taken over by their feelings. Trust is a precondition for establishing this two-way link; it's like having a Walkie-Talkie in which transmission only works when both parties tune in.

Developing emotional intelligence is an essential skill for anyone who aims for high performance in the socially interactive world in which we live. There are two important aspects to consider: ability to connect and ability to notice what influences are transmitted along the two-way connection. Quietening your own internal narrative generation by decentring your attention helps to create space in your mind for noticing what is going on for someone else. Engaging one's mirror neurones helps develop an embodied sense of what is in the mind of another person. But beware: attuning to the mental state of others without developing an ability to step out of connection as an observer to guide the flow risks losing autonomy over your actions. Confluence of mindsets might be nice at first when falling in love, but even then long-term survival benefits come from the complementary thinking skills both parties bring. In groups, this linking of minds via mirror neuron-activated pathways without mindfulness risks collusion by *contagion* as one assertive individual's thoughts may trigger such thoughts in others. This can lead to *group think* when all ideas flow in the same direction instead of benefitting from the array of creative solutions from multiple minds at work. In times of stress and high anxiety, group think may close off the thinking ability of the cerebral cortex and drop into the more emotional limbic instinctual level, creating a visceral collective mood. This may even trigger one person in the group to fear for their survival and in the unconscious transmission of this sense of threat, like animals in a pack, the fight or flight survival response of the left amygdala is set into action. This unconscious form of mind-to-mind transmission can turn groups feral if their prefrontal cerebral functions are not skilled in applying the parasympathetic brakes. Riots can break out this way, causing widespread destruction.

This reversion to basic instincts shows up whenever groups of people are not able to notice anxious stress and manage it before it spreads by contagion. They generate so-called *basic assumptions* group mentality (Bion 1968). It also shows up when managers get overly competitive in their rivalry, reverting to viscerally inspired rather than cognitively thought-through combative behaviour.

Developing our external awareness and ability to connect with others mindfully fosters a civilised and socially constructive mindset countering self-centred visceral impulses. Reading facial expressions and listening to the tone of surrounding voices provides a sense of the cultural milieu influencing you, the figure in the ground. Although our left brain likes to think of ourselves as separate independent entities, the right brain feels more intensely the way in which our relationships and environment shape a dynamic and interactive self-view. The boundary between 'self' and 'not-self' perceived in the parietal lobes is not a hard boundary that cannot be crossed, but a useful tool for coordinating movement. We tend to reify it, particularly when adopting our visually based self-image rather than seeing it as a useful tool for a particular purpose.

Coaching practice

To explore the topic of external awareness with your clients and in particular their ability to connect with others without losing autonomy, the following questions may be helpful:

• Do you tend to avoid someone else's eye-gaze when you notice their focus on you? Do you sense this invitation may have an aggressive or sexual intention? Or do you see this as an invitation for empathetic connection? Do you smile or feel unsettled?

- When you look into the face of a close friend or colleague during personal interactions do you start to pick up feelings within yourself that were not previously there? Think of the people who provoke gut reactions. What is it that triggers such reactions?
- How able are you to empathise with the situation of other people and feel how they feel? Are you taken over by such feelings or can you stand back and recognise them with the clarity of distance? Can you then stand back and see their situation from your own perspective or have you become too enmeshed with theirs?
- Have you had experiences when your emotions seem to be caught up in a prevailing group spirit (e.g. jingoism, nationalism, collective affront) which is counter to your normal views or behaviour?
- When you go for a walk, do you notice the type of trees you pass, or the type of cars, or the type of birds singing? How well do you connect with the here-and-now experience? (Or do you take your troubles for an airing?).

From this sort of discussion coaches can form useful ideas about the sort of role play that may be helpful for developing alternative ways of reacting so that autonomous mindful awareness is maintained. The ability to switch (shuttle) from inter-subjective connectivity to our 'external witness' (objective observer) mode is an important skill for self-development.

Deep insight

Concentration practices initially foster calmness by focussing on the breath directing us away from our internal stories. Going beyond this stage of concentration meditation is best done under guidance but pays large dividends in terms of developing mindfulness. Instead of the vast spacious feeling of our expanded mind (sometimes called an *oceanic feeling* by people such as Freud), we gradually shift towards perceiving ourselves as part of the moment-to-moment flow of interacting energies. The changing sensations in our body are more clearly noticed by our mind, unencumbered by the superimposition of our learned mental frameworks for interpreting meaning. We sense nature directly enabling us to apply bare attention and creatively deframe the world, opening up new dimensions of direct awareness. Similarly we become more aware of the moment-to-moment changes in our feelings within. We become more aware that our thinking is shaped by acquired mental frameworks, concepts and ideas, none of which are fixed unchanging entities but provisional tools for trying to make sense of the world. As all of our 'self' ideas begin to loosen we are then able to contemplate the nature of consciousness itself and see that it too is constantly changing, influenced by prevailing conditions.

Insight practices encourage us to see ourselves from a third person perspective, becoming subject and object, the perceiver and the perceived, but with the important difference that we do not superimpose our self-constructed mental frameworks onto our perceptions in order to interpret them. We get them raw! (Remember that these frameworks evolved as useful tools to enable rapid interpretations to be made about the world using prior experience to make assumptions. These can change!) In other words these practices help us to see ourselves or any object from the perspective of a non-judgemental, agenda-free, framework-free someone else. Ideas concerning ourselves that we imbued with weighty significance are revealed to be transient constructions in our mind whose anxiety-creating significance fades away in the overall flow of time after we have de-framed and reframed their context.

Once we are adept at mindfulness of the present moment by redirecting our minds from internal storytelling towards sensory experience, this mental clarity can be directed towards thoughts about an idea, image or concept, not only about one's breathing. Being experienced in recognising how we perceive our everyday experiences through our own personal version of rose-tinted spectacles, bringing our clarified mind to bear on a particular idea, image or concept, we can start to see through the modifying layers that our own personal history adds. In our concentrated razor-sharp thinking state we do not need to actively dissect and analyse the idea we have about our self; simply bringing to mind the idea within this state of concentration and perceiving its presence illuminates aspects of its essential nature normally unseen. Any artificial constructs about what something is or even who we are may begin to change. With our focussed mental laser we gently strip away the layers of the projections that we have placed on our object until we see its naked essence. We disconnect the frameworks that the rear-left 'COO' function uses to create order, stability and predictability from constantly changing circumstances. The moment of realisation can be detected in frontal, parietal and temporal sites including the anterior superior temporal gyrus when a relaxed alpha pattern decreases and converts to a gamma burst on an electroencephalogram (Dietrich and Kanso 2010, Nataraja 2008). We cannot achieve this realisation by directly looking at something through our usual lens which takes our narrative and paints a visual picture. Mindfully concentrating on the breath and somatosensory sensation we see objects or ourselves at that moment of time. In another moment of time something may have happened to make things slightly different. We don't remain fixed but adapt, change and self-develop. We need a relaxed state of mind and positive mood in which the true nature of an object will begin to emerge, separated from the framework in which we have habitually put it. If we are prone to bolster our fragile ego with the trappings of material wealth and status we may become more aware of our flesh, bones and blood. Our craving for fame and fortune or to be immortalised may be recognised as a delusion that starts to fade; our motivations and actions may become more selfless as we increasingly see the importance of acting for the common good. A good Chairman will have refined his mind through regular mindfulness meditation, learned how to calm anxiety, and clarified his self-narrative so that he is clear about his personality, his values and his purpose in life. As the different layers of psychological processes conditioned by our experiences integrate more as we age, we may, through mindfulness practices, develop insights helping us to derive value without self-centred thoughts. Devoid of a 'self' agenda, the Chairman is free to see things and the relationships between them in a completely new light. Discussing these new facets with others who have deeply considered the topic without a prejudicial agenda can enrich perspectives. Realising that people are not as fixed as we tend to believe, our Chairman becomes aware of a vast array of possibilities ready to be explored. Such insights enable us to see opportunities and strategies beyond the grasp of less insightful minds.

This topic is probably best explored with your clients using arising process rather than preconceived questions. See what they make of this concept of insight, considering carefully how much de-framing and reframing may be necessary in order to achieve their higher aspirations.

Internal awareness

Mindfulness and insight skills develop our resonance circuitry, enhancing our ability to empathise with others and our circuitry for internal self-regulation. With an awareness of what our various internal mental functions do, we can act as an observer of our internal processes, noticing when functions become active and how they all interact. We begin to notice whether we habitually prefer one mode of reasoning over another, one mode of selecting sensory data over another and our preferred modes of interacting with others. We can note on a map of our cerebral cortex which functions we tend to overuse and which functions we tend to underuse as an image of our mental functions' constellation (see next chapter). We will increasingly become aware of whether our thinking is purely mental cognitive processing or whether limbic functions dominate our thoughts. We begin to question whether the intentions and motives behind the things we do are really consistent from an impartial observer's impression or whether these are convenient self-deceptions enabling us to avoid difficult questions. We can act as if we are our own internal coach, challenging our long-term vision and goals, our plans for how we intend to realise them and whether we really have the skills on board to make them happen. We can even question whether in the end we have truly achieved what we wanted and understood all the knock-on consequences of our actions.

With practice, this internal coach will ask incisive Socratic type questions in real time, rather than as a post hoc reflection, so that you can evaluate your thoughts as you think them. A well-developed internal coach will challenge whether the frameworks that you are using to shape your vision and plan your actions are the only frameworks worth consideration. Internal jousting within the management team inside your head may be very energy consuming particularly for a novice, but with practice the enlarged perspectives generated will foster advantageous long-term adaptation.

Developing both internal and external awareness is the key to what has been called emotional intelligence. Such intelligence evolved to provide a sense of when social adaptation becomes necessary to survive. Emotional intelligence is about self-knowledge and self-management. It's about feeling good in your own skin, knowing how you feel on a moment to moment basis and the causes of such feelings. It's about concord between the various mental and physical functions in your body so that you can express yourself and move towards being the person you want to be. But it is also about realising that we are part of a social whole and we need empathy to understand others, a sense of social responsibility and the ability to manage relationships well.

Coaching practice

Consider asking your clients the following:

- Reflect on the functioning of your own Chairman for a while. Many of us try to avoid this role. Its internal awareness alerts us to our inner fears. Its insight sees through the masks we wear to disguise our insecurities even from ourselves. How well and how often do you do this?
- External awareness brings us into contact with the pain and emotions of other people. What arises for you when this happens to you? Does emotion take over or do you move into observer mode?
- Can you access your calming function to relieve anxieties and excessive stress, moving to a state where you can just be yourself, rather than feeling under pressure to perform? Have you developed such a place?
- Do you believe that any of the 'Chairman' functions are likely to help you? If so, which ones and in what ways? How will you develop them?

Chapter 8

Constellations

The mind mosaic

In reading about the different members of the management team and their attributes we tend to identify ourselves more closely with one role or another, or at least some of the functions of a particular management team member. In contrast, we may feel little connection with some other management team member(s) or their functions. Our preference about which role(s) or functions we like to adopt depends on the functions we have found to be most useful to us in our past experiences and therefore differs from person to person. If we live in a culture that constantly values logical linear verbal reasoning above creative imagination it will be the left frontal functions that we are encouraged to develop. This sets up a dynamic in which these functions become the easiest for us to use because they are more developed and the more we use them the further they develop. Added to that, the environment in which we operate may call for more task focus than creative focus. For example, if you are a business leader answering to shareholders with a short-term profit-taking strategy, long-term creative projects will be less of a priority. The way our culture works today encourages short-term task-focussed activities using lines of verbal reasoning. One could say that the functions we develop most strongly exert a gravitational pull on our thinking so that we then habitually try to address the problems that we encounter with the same limited set of thinking processes.

To tackle some of the more challenging issues managers face today effectively requires that we have all of our bases covered, i.e. have a full set of management committee modes and functions available and the ability to switch from one to the other at appropriate times, generating multiple perspectives. Mindfulness enables us to develop a sense of knowing which functions we are using at a particular time and enables us to actively switch to another complementary set more easily. By developing mindfulness, we are more able to enlarge the scope of our thinking from the confines of our favoured thinking quadrant with its strong gravitational pull (generating so-called point-attractor thinking dynamics) by actively supporting thinking in the other three quadrants. If we find this too demanding to do alone, working with other people who provide gravitational pull from the other quadrants provides a way of generating creative thinking (see Chapter 23 on teamwork and creativity). The composition of teams working on complex challenging problems requires that all of the thinking functions are covered to levels of development as deep as possible to match the scale of the problem to be solved in terms of breath and depth of thinking capability. As individuals, we are essentially wired to be incomplete and we only can thrive by connecting with and collaborating with other minds.

Very few people are able to perform well in every role and every function. Rather than *all* functions in a quadrant being strongly developed, it seems that some functions within each quadrant are very efficient and some are relatively inefficient, tiring easily. In each zone of our cerebral hemispheres we have a pattern of stronger or weaker functions; for example, someone who has strong leadership skills in the boardroom and in strategy analysis may lack charisma and the ability to connect with others through mirroring. If the weak links in a particular quadrant could be targeted for attention, the synergies between the functions in a quadrant working together at comparable levels of capability are likely to exceed the sum of their parts. Furthermore, if all of the functions in all of the zones are harmonised and integrated well by the Chairman working in synchrony on a particular task, then what you may achieve has been described by the psychologist Mihály Csíkszentmihályi as a state of 'flow'. Flow occurs when the challenge of what we are doing requires high levels of skill, good motivation towards the goal, a good balance between the level of skills required and the level of challenge, and good feedback so that we are reassured that we are on the right track. Flow occurs when our mind is absorbed into what we are doing, a fusion of multiple skills with outstanding performance. Flow is different from insight as described previously in that flow involves accessing and integrating deeply ingrained learned routines of activity so that behaviour becomes effectively automatic and self-consciousness disappears, whereas insight requires prefrontal areas to make novelty fully conscious, evaluate its appropriateness and realise its creative expression (Dietrich 2004). As Dietrich mentioned with regard to playing tennis, functions need to flow together implicitly to work well and if you make parts of the process explicit, flow tends to get disrupted. Thus, to achieve flow, functions that have been well developed through regular practice come together when the spotlight of attention on what you are doing is switched off!

Figure 8.1 represents a composite picture of the five management meta-functions and their component functions, based on a synthesis of data from various studies of the functioning of the cerebral cortex. It forms the upper level representation of our mind mosaic.

It may be useful for your clients to rate their perception of their capabilities for each of these functions (on a scale of 1 for weak to 5 for strong) in this mosaic and total the score to give a meta-function score. Discuss these scores

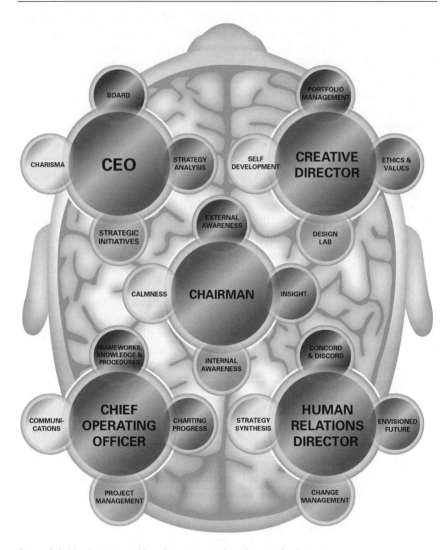

Figure 8.1 Mind mosaic of key functions within the cerebral cortex.

with them to help refine their self-assessment. For each function, review the experiences that your clients have had to lead them to the level of capability they believe they have achieved. Then identify a development plan for strengthening functions that would help them to perform better.

As more research results become available, refinements to the mosaic are inevitable, but for the moment the mind mosaic may provide a useful way to conceptualise cerebral functions in order to discuss and enhance personal development.

Getting all of our functions to synchronise at a similar level of high performance is a rather ambitious development goal to set. For most of us it may help to accept that we cannot cover all bases alone and should form alliances, working in a team. Man is a social creature and achieves most when partnered with others who complement his skill set. The mind-mosaic map may assist putting teams together to ensure all cerebral bases needed for the problem to be addressed are covered.

Competency models with a large number of business competencies (such as the Leadership Architect Suite: Lombardo and Eichinger 2004) may be mapped to the brain functional area to which they relate (Table 8.1). Coaches may wish to review the particular competency model with which they are familiar, to see how it relates to cerebral functions of the mind mosaic of their clients. Competencies that relate to brain functions that are not part of our preferred style are likely to be harder to develop and we may have to accept that our early life experience did not strengthen the neural connections sufficiently to provide a firm foundation for a particular competency. To develop these will be a bigger investment. Lombardo and Eichinger suggest substitute competencies for those competencies that may not be easily developed. They also provide ways to assess whether each competency is under-developed or overutilised (Lombardo and Eichinger 2004).

Coaching practice

You may use Table 8.1 with your clients and ask them the following:

*   Review these competency areas, identifying which ones you think you use regularly and which ones you don't. Does this match with your mind mosaic preference perceptions?

Table 8.1 Competency areas that are likely to be 'hosted' in each of the four cerebral cortex quadrants

Left frontal competency areas	Right frontal competency areas
• Decision making	• Innovation
• Goal focus	• Flexibility
• Commitment and courage	• Honour and integrity
• Inspiring communication	• Self-development
• Politically astute	• Process oversight
Left rear competency areas	*Right rear competency areas*
• Methodically organised	• Relationship assessment
• Attention to detail and rules	• Managing relationships
• Technical skills and knowledge	• Care and compassion
• Driving processes	• Empathetic understanding
• Measuring and informing	• Work–life balance

- Which ones do you think you overutilise? Are there any obvious consequences of this, particularly considering your diametrically opposite
  functional competencies (i.e. do you underutilise complementary
  functions?).
- What is your action plan concerning developing functions in your mind
  mosaic and associated competencies?

What is clearly missing from the above list is a set of competencies for 'The
Chairman'. This is not too surprising as the Chairman's function is to
integrate and harmonise the various functional areas in order that synergistic
advantage is achieved. Many managers will be able to achieve their goals
without achieving such synergies.

Transformational management

Drawing on the work of adult development experts Susann Cook-Greuter,
Robert Kegan, Lawrence Kohlberg and Jane Loevinger among others,
Fisher *et al.* (2003) proposed a hierarchy of increasingly complex meaning-
making frameworks in their Leadership Development Frames and Stages
model (Table 8.2). Developing the meaning-making frameworks associated
with the Opportunist, Diplomat, Expert and Achiever leadership frames
are probably covered by available competency models. In order to become
a transformational manager, additional Chairman competencies are likely to

Table 8.2 Increasing complexity of managerial meaning-making frames

Ironist	Broadens awareness of incongruities between mission, strategy and operations and uses intersystem processes to resolve them including satire and irony
Alchemist	Radically transformative, unites opposites, creates + sum games, time non-linear, interplay of awareness, thought, action and effect
Strategist	Creative conflict resolution, principled decisions, paradox OK, systems and process oriented, double-loop learning
Individualist	Independent, self-curious, aware of mindset limitations, finds creative solutions, maverick?
Achiever	Long-term goals, welcomes feedback, results oriented, initiator, blind to own shadow/subjectivity, self-chosen ethics
Expert	Problem solving technical logic, efficiency valued over effectiveness, dogmatic, decisions merit based
Diplomat	Conforms to group standards, seeks membership and status, loyal, face-saving important, needs acceptance
Opportunist	Short-term focus, concrete, manipulative, uses power politics, stereotypes, self-interest/denial
Impulsive	Childlike self-survival behaviour

Source: Adapted from *Personal and Organisational Transformations through Action Inquiry*, Fisher *et al.*
2003: 44 and published with permission.

be needed. Increasingly in our dynamically changing world today, trans-formational management is needed in order to realign organisations to rapidly changing business environments. The frameworks and assumptions taken for granted by managers framed Achievers are unlikely to be sufficient for adapting to the complexities of the emerging world. The Strategist stage of management evolution involves broadening the range of perspectives and reappraising the frameworks and strategies usually taken for granted. Paradox, ambiguity and the ability to hold multiple contradictory models as valid are skills that less well-developed managers may find hard to accept. A process termed Action Inquiry has been recommended for developing the more complex meaning-making frameworks and involves developing an on-going in-process awareness and evaluation of the mental processes and frameworks used for determining and carrying out actions (Fisher, Rooke and Torbert 2003). This process is similar to some of the mindfulness practices described in the previous chapter. Coaches supporting clients through a process of transformational change need to have developed themselves to at least the level of sophistication of meaning-making frameworks that their client is aiming for, or beyond.

Five categories of additional competencies have been proposed as necessary for performing at these transformative levels, including: navigating with sophisticated theoretical frameworks (e.g. understanding complexity theory and systems theory); cultivating transformation (e.g. self-transformation by developing deep self-knowledge, creating change leading communities); managing adaptively (e.g. experimenting with different interventions, flowing around obstacles); knowing oneself (e.g. mindfully seeing one's own mental processes in action, inhabiting multiple perspectives); and deeply connecting with all aspects of the mind (e.g. harvesting profound insights, exploring intuitions and being able to sit with discomfort and uncertainty while patterns emerge, rather than rushing towards rapid 'solutions') (Brown 2011).

In order to become a highly effective transformative leader we need to become familiar with our mind's capabilities, develop an ability to watch our own internal mental processes in action and make in-process adjustments, using repetitive iterative evaluation cycles in which we reframe our think-ing paradigms (so-called double loop learning). In order to be useful an insightful awareness of external dynamics is also required. Familiarisation with the functions of the mind as outlined in this book, coupled with mindfulness practices and the development of the additional competencies mentioned above is likely to facilitate powerful levels of transformational leadership by developing more complex and sophisticated meaning-making frameworks for guiding action. As we shall see in subsequent chapters, developing effective mental models and meaning-making frameworks involves functions and processes beyond the cerebral cortex.

Part 2

Emotions

Managing conflicting demands

Part 2 considers *socially conditioned emotions* shaping our behaviour for social engagement, and *biologically determined emotions* enabling us to survive and thrive. Such emotions help us to learn from our experiences and protect our fundamental *core values* as we strive towards our aspirations.

Chapter 9

The limbic system for balancing demands

The limbic system, sitting like a fist under the cushion of the cerebral cortex, has often been referred to as the emotional brain. The term 'limbic' comes from the Latin word *limbus* which means border or edge. As in the phrase 'being in limbo' the limbic system is somewhere 'in-between'; it is essentially in-between our outer world of sensory input and our inner world of thinking. We could say that the limbic system is a centre of integration where the top-down demands of the higher cognitive functions of the cerebral cortex and the bottom-up demands of the visceral body and senses coalesce with services prioritising the protection and defence of the things that we most value. In terms of our organisation metaphor, the limbic system forms the middle-management level of our organisation. Middle-management tries to find a way of ensuring that both the strategic demands of upper management and the operational needs of the body and the environment are met as far as possible without compromising our core values. This can be a delicate juggling act. In order to achieve this, the limbic system has several specialised areas. One such area monitors the sensory information coming in along various neural pathways integrated via the thalamus. These monitoring or surveillance services reside in an area called the anterior cingulate cortex (ACC). The questions considered by such services are: 'Have we seen such sensory information before?'; 'Is the sensory information suggestive of danger?'; 'How should we respond to this situation?' Other parts of the limbic system help to answer such questions: the hippocampus accesses memories, the amygdalae recognise danger signals, the periaqueductal grey area (of the midbrain rather than limbic system) monitors our neurochemical balance-sheet, signalling to the limbic system our bodily needs in order to optimally perform. The insula provides access to many possible behavioural response frameworks together with cognitive priorities to help select an action plan.

Consider the following scenario: you are feeling a bit deflated as things are not going as well as you wish at work so that neurochemicals and hormone levels such as dopamine, oxytocin or endorphins which normally make you feel good (generated by subcortical motivating networks) are at relatively low levels. You sense that you need a top-up but your close personal relationship is not going well either and is unlikely to help you fulfil your chemical needs. Awareness that your needs are not being met is beginning to feel urgent. Subconsciously, part of your limbic system recalls that activating your attraction/seeking/lust motivational systems in the past (elevating levels of dopamine and noradrenaline in central brain areas and decreasing levels of serotonin) resulted in a wonderful feeling of well-being (Ammaniti *et al.* 2007). You begin to feel that you want to go 'hunting' for a mate. This *seeking motivational system* encourages you to explore with a particular 'reward' in mind to fuel your dopamine and noradrenaline levels in central brain areas. The *attraction/lust motivational system* is a hard-wired biological system designed to motivate you to find a potential mating partner. When activated, it increases levels of testosterone and vasopressin in males, and oxytocin in females, and elevates levels of amphetamine-like substances, especially phenylethylanine, heightening sensual arousal in both (Eagle 2007). It is also remembered that as one's romantic partner becomes one's *attachment figure*, oxytocin, which regulates attachment relationships, replaces dopamine that seems to mediate the experience of falling in love. Skin-to-skin contact promotes release of more oxytocin and endorphins (internally generated opioids), promoting bonding, calming the mind and easing the pain of social exclusion (Eagle 2007). Touch and sensual bodily contact contribute to the feeling of a *secure base* (Holmes 2007) and may offer the promise of sustained access to mood and motivation-enhancing chemicals which your mother may have originally introduced to you as an infant.

If you were a rabbit then you would probably respond to the urge to top-up your feel-good motivational chemical fuel without a second thought and engage in gene-spreading activities immediately. But as a human being our 'bottom-up' biologically based motivational systems need to be tempered with a 'top-down' socially based value system. Socially constructed value systems also influence our neurochemical balance sheet. If we act in accordance with our own societally instilled values we will get some chemical rewards associated with the pride of acting virtuously. On the other hand, if we act counter to these values, the socially constructed emotion of *guilt* may lower levels of such chemical rewards after the initial chemical boost from physical interaction wears off. The limbic system mediates between the *social values system* and the *biological motivational systems* in order to select the most appropriate behaviour required to optimally meet our overall needs. Understanding this trade-off helps us to prepare, when necessary, to weather the chorus of societal disapproval which so often emerges in response to one's attempts at transformational change.

Feelings generated by neurochemicals and hormones are associated with particular emotions and are essential for imbuing our behaviour with *values*. By conferring such values, human emotions condition the way in which we regulate our own behaviour. Emotions are 'the primary *mediators of social life*' (Trevarthen 2009). Values and appropriately congruent behaviours are learned in cultures and families and passed down from generation to generation. When we get it right we are rewarded by positive socially constructed emotional experiences such as happiness: receiving positive facial and tonal encouragement from others. If we get it wrong we may receive looks of mild disapproval, making us feel uncomfortable until we adjust our behaviour. If we get it seriously wrong we may feel the socially constructed emotions of guilt or shame and the threat of social exclusion. As a result, we may learn to modify our behaviour. Our limbic system converts facial expressions and social feedback into chemicals impacting upon our mood and motivations.

Sigmund Freud (1856–1939) originally proposed a three-part mental apparatus for balancing our basic instincts with socially conditioned values. The bodily instincts form what he called the *id* (or it): 'The id, filled with energy from the instincts, strives to bring about the satisfaction of instinctual needs' (Nelson-Jones 2000: 27). Freud viewed the *id* as 'a cauldron of seething emotions' with no morality. This equates to the more chemically driven and primitive part of the brain. The second structure, which he called the *ich* (German for I; *ego* in Latin), he considered to be a portion of the *id* that has undergone development through influence of the external world and that brings reason and common sense to bear on our impulses. This broadly approximates to the limbic system. The third structure in Freud's model is the *super-I* (or super-ego), which was considered to be a part of one's self in which stored parental influence is exerted. This broadly equates to the cognitively driven behavioural models instilled into the cerebral cortex. For Freud, satisfying sexual libido was the most dominant biological motivation system which needed to be controlled by influences from the super-ego and ego to sublimate the urges into more socially acceptable behaviour.

The British psychologist John Bowlby (1907–1990) replaced Freud's instinctual drive theory centred on satisfying sexual libido with multiple interacting behavioural systems, including systems for: attachment, sexuality, exploration, care-giving, affiliation, subordination and dominance, and aggression (Lichtenberg 1989; Diamond and Blatt 2007). Bowlby's model was conceptualised as being analogous to the activation and deactivation of independent yet interrelated cybernetic systems. Each of these systems was thought to enhance survival and, as development progresses, these systems become more complex and integrated with other systems.

Jaap Panksepp (b. 1943), an Estonian-born American neurobiologist and psychologists recently proposed another replacement for Freud's sexually motivated drive theory. He proposed a neurologically based set of seven hard-wired motivational systems (seeking/desire; fear/anxiety; rage/anger; lust/sex; care/nurturance; panic/grief/distress; and play) (Panksepp 2009). Each of these behavioural systems has goals and processes oriented towards promoting the actions necessary to achieve those goals. This operates like a balanced scorecard for managing basic emotional needs providing chemical rewards to specific parts of the body using a variety of hormones and neurochemicals; for example, dopamine promotes a feeling of well-being when released into the nucleus accumbens and medial cortical region and is generated by the PLAY system and the SEEKING/desire system; oxytocin and endogenous opioids are involved in the CARE system, creating feelings of calmness and unity. Life-threatening dangers release a mixture of adrenalin and many neuropeptides such as cholecystokinin and substance P are associated with the emotion of fear. All of these basic emotion-mediating neurochemical systems converge in the periaqueductal grey (PAG) area of the central midbrain that surrounds the cerebral aqueducts between the third and fourth ventricle (Figure 14.1). The PAG is very well connected to the amygdala and autonomic nervous system for modulating defensive behaviours (Panksepp 2009; Porges 2009; Trevarthen 2009). Some researchers believe that it is around the PAG that a coherent self-representation forms (Panksepp 2005; Trevarthen 2009). The PAG acts as controller of our biochemical fuel-mix scorecard.

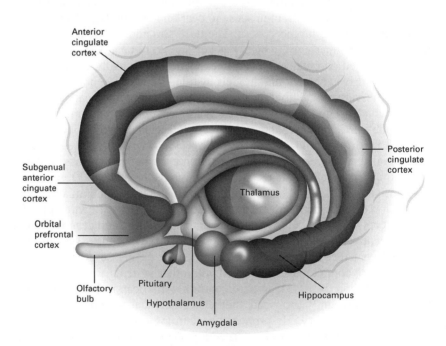

Figure 9.1 Key limbic functions involved in linking the cerebral cortex to the systems of the body and input from the environment.

To understand how the limbic system mediates between the top-down demands of the cerebral cortex, bodily needs and environmental influences via the senses, we need to go a bit deeper into the key structures and functions involved in limbic processes (Figure 9.1).

Chapter 10

Our insula and 'self' repertoire

Our insula looks similar to parts of our cerebral cortex and indeed it has been called the fifth cortical lobe although it is generally considered to be part of the limbic system. In early life it was on the surface of the brain but became covered over by the expanding frontal and temporal lobes (Figure 10.1). The insula is an integration centre that acts as a major conduit linking cortical areas to the inner limbic areas (Cozolino 2006; Siegel 2007). It is like a router that re-routes the set of behaviours we use in one role from our repertoire to another set, according to what our surveillance services detect so that our behaviour becomes more congruent with the environment.

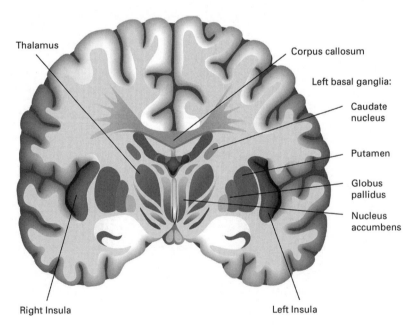

Figure 10.1 Location of the insula and basal ganglia in cross-section.

This links together our sense of the roles we have taken on as an individual and the repertoire of roles we are able to convincingly and passionately adopt. The insula also plays an important role in self-reflection and self-referential processing (Knox 2011) and the posterior insula is a primary area for receiving projections from visceral areas (Lane *et al.* 2009) providing us with our felt sense or gut feel about a situation. This is particularly apparent when something or somebody disgusts us and we get a visceral reaction, such as when we feel someone's behaviour is grossly unfair. Inequality causes the insula to light up, irrespective of whether we are the victim of inequality or someone else (Pillay 2011).

The anterior insula connects to the cerebral cortex for translating sensory input into conscious bodily feeling (Lane *et al.* 2009). Distinguishing between our own touch and the touch of another person is an example of the insula's ability to bridge bodily sensations with mental perception. The insula and ACC are involved in linking hearts and minds, both our own and to those of another person (Cozolino 2006). Using input from our mirror-neuron firing patterns, the insula activates in us the same neural networks that are being used by the person we are observing and thereby we can work out what their intentions might be (Siegel 2007). We essentially emulate somebody else's routing and network connection patterns. This emulation of another person's internal mental processes is central to our ability to read social situations, making the insula central to the development of our social brain (Cozolino 2006) so that we can resonate with what is going on around us. The insula seems to link our mirror-neuron system to our sub-cortical mid-line network so that when we observe someone else's actions we call up our own emotional networks including our 'self' representations (Knox 2011). We have built up many internal 'self' representations for different contexts and stages of our life and by matching the appropriate 'self' representation to the action we are observing we can empathise with what is going on in another person's mind; for example, if we are watching a child playing with a model train set we call up our own inner child model for the same age and context and can empathise with their feelings.

Being able to relate to the mental state of others is a process known as *mentalisation* (linked with Theory of Mind) which may be explicit (conscious, verbal and reflective interpretation), requiring effort, or implicit (perceived, non-conscious, non-verbal and unreflective), which is associated with mirroring and needs little effort (Fonagy and Luyten 2009). The insula and its links to the prefrontal cortex are essential in order to mentalise and evaluate whether what is happening in our environment is likely to impact on our own goals (Knox 2011).

The linking together by the insula of areas of the right cortex and other areas of the limbic system enables *intuitive reasoning* to take place. Intuition is when our mind is made up, using subtle information acquired through past experience, and contrasts with linear step-by-step data-driven reasoning (Pillay 2011). It is important to use both forms of reasoning when coming to any major decision. An intuition verification process or *post-hoc rationalisation* (called 'insula mapping' by Pillay) in which you analyse your intuitions using the rational linear logic processes of your frontal-left cerebral cortex is important to provide a contrasting contemporary perspective. Many people may come to decisions in this way: deciding a course of action based on subtle gut feel but engaging in post-hoc rationalisation in order to justify and communicate their reasoning in a linear analytical fashion.

Our insula mediates extremes of emotion (e.g. pain, disgust, passionate love), enabling us to resonate with people in our environment and modulate our thinking style according to where we are. It is involved in self-reflection, self-control and the embodying sensations forming part of our 'self' representations. How the connections between the neural networks mediating these processes are linked is likely to differ from person to person and may be connected to how well the person was originally encouraged to self-reflect and 'write' their internal self-narrative: 'Perhaps for some people, a childhood without help in developing a self-narrative that includes their own experiences, results in a disconnection of the insula and adjacent structures' (Cozolino 2006).

Many early life experiences influence how the insula links networks together. Bowlby proposed that we develop multiple internal working models (IWMs) containing memories of our prior relationship experiences and how these helped us to meet our goals and needs. These models are linked together with our beliefs about ourself, others and the relations between the two, and the plans and behavioural strategies by which we may achieve our goals (Cobb and Davila 2009).

Those of us not encouraged to tune into our bodily needs may spend a lot of time engrossed in cognitive thoughts (taking refuge in our heads). On the other hand, some of us may have early life experiences focussed on our own bodily sensations but not so focussed on influences from the environment or the needs of others. Some of us may set ourselves up with a preference for logical-linear reasoning while others may set up a preference for intuitive reasoning. Early life experiences that encouraged some connections in the insula and discouraged others are likely to lead to a diversity of perspectives about life in any group of people. This provides a fascinating set of contrasting perspectives for problem solving. Just as the structures of the cortex provide a range of perspectives for evaluating the world, so the insula, by making many experience-related connections, contributes to our overall unique personality. For anyone interested in self-development, it is important to become aware of the preferential pathways that our insula uses to make these connections.

Coaching practice

Coaches often focus on the preferential pathways contributing to their clients' type preferences using psychometric instruments. But these do not really capture the preference pathways of the insula. Rather than imposing preconceived frameworks onto your clients, you may prefer to explore their repertoire of roles and how they use them in different circumstances in a less structured, more creative discussion with questions to your client along the following lines:

- Are you sensitive to group moods and feelings so that you modify the 'self' model that you use according to prevailing circumstances, or are you relatively fixed in the 'self' model that you use in a particular role, e.g. chairing a meeting? How broad is your repertoire of roles and how easily do you switch? Are you a CEO to your children or a joker at work? How do people respond to the role you tend to adopt?
- Are you sensitive to injustices or inequalities that emerge or are you surprised or indifferent when other people mention such things in connection with you?
- Do you have a preference for intuitive reasoning or logical-linear reasoning? If the former, do you engage in post hoc rationalisation to verify your intuitive thoughts objectively and get your message across to other types of thinker? If the latter, reflect on how you feel about any decision you make by discussing this with an intuitive thinking type. How do these perspectives differ? (Perhaps you believe yourself to be logical, but without realising it you are actually intuitively driven?)
- Are you always well in tune with your bodily needs, stopping for coffee breaks and rests when you sense these are needed? What other bodily needs are you aware of and how do you handle these? Are you in tune with the needs of others? Are your needs or their needs more apparent to you? What might this suggest about the activity of your mirror-neuron system?

Many such questions can be formulated to explore these areas according to context and what emerges in discussion, so consider the above suggestions as purely illustrative. To promote creativity and innovation, any frameworks and assessment tools used need to be used lightly in a non-prescriptive way. The questions and discussion aim to raise awareness rather than aiming towards a 'diagnosis and prescription'.

Changing our internal routing configurations

Many of us believe that our preferences are fixed early on in life and cannot be changed. However, recent research reveals connections in our limbic system can be changed even in adult life. In a study in Toronto, adults whose average age was over 40 years were studied in a mindfulness-based stress reduction programme. One group of 20 men and women were trained over a period of eight weeks in mindfulness-based stress reduction techniques and the other group of 16 men and women were wait-listed for the training to take place after the study. Both groups were asked to engage in either a *narrative-focussed activity* by considering, for example, what a personality trait adjective meant to them, or an *experientially focussed activity* sensing their body state without purpose or goal, noticing any changes from moment to moment. Subjects were scanned in a fMRI scanner to see which areas of the brain were most active during various exercises. In brief, the narrative-focussed activity was associated with a lot of brain activity in central midline brain areas whereas the experientially focussed activity was associated with a lot of activity in more lateral (outer, side areas) of the cortex, particularly on the left side in those not yet mindfulness trained, where task-focussed activities are normally performed. Mindfulness training shifted these patterns so that experientially focussed activity in mindfulness trained subjects was associated with more activity in the right lateral cortical areas, the insula and somatosensory areas. This indicates that mindfulness training seems to change the linkages in the brain so that narrative story telling ascribing preconceived meaning to sensations is reduced, enabling us to appreciate sensations directly (Farb *et al.* 2007). These result, together with supportive findings in other studies, indicate that mindfulness training results in structural changes in the insula so that the connection pathways change within the eight-week training period and the change is long lasting. The anterior cingulate cortex is also crucial to these changes. Mindfulness training helps switch the ACC spotlight from the inner 'canteen' culture to the outer sensory world. Each time your mind wanders, re-engaging in narrative generation during a mindfulness practice, your Chairman is encouraged to notice this and redirect the spotlight back to the sensory world. Repeatedly doing this builds up the neural pathways, strengthening connections to sensory brain areas rather than self-referential storytelling brain areas so that anxieties and stress associated with such stories are alleviated. Relief from stress and anxieties promotes an improved mood and sense of well-being (affect). Studies have shown that positive affect is one of the most significant factors associated with optimal functioning, growth and resilience (collectively called flourishing as opposed to languishing) in individuals (Fredrickson and Losada 2005) and is also essential for high performance business teams (Losada and Heaphy 2004) (see Part 4).

In summary, a picture is emerging in which the insula plays a vital role in linking different systems together and how it does this is conditioned by experience and can be altered. By responding to information about the outside world via the ACC and being resonant with the mood and feelings of others, the insula draws upon behaviours from different mental models of 'self' appropriate for the circumstances. It is like finding the right costume for the part in a play from an enormous range of costumes we collect during our lifetime for our expanding repertoire. Connecting up with the right 'self' model appropriately for the circumstances is vitally important to gain social acceptance and influence others effectively. Coaches are ideally positioned to help clients broaden their repertoires through reflective enquiry and role play.

Chapter 11

Our cingulate cortex and surveillance services

The cingulate cortex provides our capability for vigilance and sustained attention to incoming information either through broad scanning and surveillance or by throwing a spotlight on what is going on internally or externally. It is able to detect emotional signals from other people and from within one's self. It is also activated when we or someone we love are in pain or when we are isolated or socially excluded, such that exclusion from social circles is often perceived as truly painful (Cozolino 2006).

The posterior portion of the cingulate cortex specialises in emotional processing and autobiographical memory. It is part of a system that attributes meaning to facial expressions that is particularly important for assessing trustworthiness or fear in others. Attributing meaning to facial expressions is also of major importance for learning to regulate our behaviour so that we receive social approval rather than exclusion. By understanding the likely meaning of a smile or a frown the posterior cingulate cortex works with the ACC and insula to modulate behaviour. In our early years much information is transported across from our parents through facial expressions including approval, disapproval and even their own experiences of fear (Cozolino 2006). It may be that when we have unconscious fears about something or certain circumstances these may originate from our parents' experiences before we were born. For example, evidence is growing that the children of survivors of trauma (e.g. from the Holocaust, WWII, or Partition of India) have indications of trans-generational post-traumatic stress disorder. The trigger for fear is often an unconscious subtle reminder of something feared in the past, such as a parent's look of disapproval if it portended punishment. The amygdala's defence processes then activate. Fear of the unknown such as organisational change also activates these processes and, while the body is in a state of alert, new learning is not prioritised. Fear needs to be managed first before new learning can occur.

The insula and the ACC often act together as the insula requires environmental input to guide how it links different networks together to call up appropriate internal working models and the ACC needs a sense of the internal working model being used to guide what is relevant for preferential monitoring. Using a theatrical metaphor, if the insula is the manager of the costume department for our repertoire of roles, the ACC is the lighting manager throwing a spotlight on what should receive attention. This role of the ACC as a *values-driven attention priority system* continues throughout life. Control of the spotlight can be developed by the mindfulness techniques outlined previously so that you may focus on what your mind wants to concentrate on rather than flitting from one thing to the next. The ACC works in close association with the hippocampus for memory recall, checking whether something it detects on the horizon is familiar, relevant for the current behavioural model being used or completely new. For obvious survival reasons, if something is new the ACC surveillance services need to check it out, putting it in the spotlight to evaluate whether it is a threat or new opportunity. Marketing executives make much use of this ACC characteristic, knowing that novel items capture the spotlight of attention. The old and familiar just doesn't attract the attention it once deserved!

Because the ACC is a values-driven attention priority system, there are times when there are conflicts between priorities. In such circumstances the ACC, in conjunction with midline pre-frontal cortical areas and the right dorsolateral PFC (the 'Portfolio Management' function), act to resolve the conflict by consciously re-evaluating priorities. This system, which also includes the superior parietal cortex, has been called the *Executive Attention* system (Siegel 2007). It comes into play to oversee planning activities, decision making, error detection, and handling novel situations and difficult or dangerous circumstances.

The ACC plays a major role in detecting discrepancies between behaviours observed and our internal working models/value system of how thing are normally done according to our personal past experiences. If the ACC detects a discrepancy between our behaviour and our internal working model of how to behave in a particular environment, an assessment is made as to whether the behaviour is inappropriate and needs to be adjusted, in which case the feeling of guilt may be experienced until the discrepancy is resolved by re-routing connections via the insula. Alternatively the assessment may conclude in a judgement that the internal working model is out of date and needs to be rebuilt. A feeling of pain associated with *cognitive dissidence* and activation of the amygdala's conflict centre is felt until a new model is built and commissioned, resolving the mismatch. Similarly, if someone else's behaviour does not conform to our own internal working model of how something should be done, an assessment is made that may result in the conclusion that their behaviour is wrong, in which case we may condemn them, or that our own model is wrong, in which case cognitive dissonance encourages us to build a new one. Between the ages of 15 and 25 approximately, remodelling of one's acquired internal working models is a necessary part of intergenerational adaptation to new environmental circumstances. New models are then shaped more by the peer group (e.g.

students at university) than by the parental home. The brain is particularly open to neuroplastic remodelling at this time. One way or another, the ACC is involved in detecting mismatches, generating neurochemical discrepancy reports that make us feel uncomfortable until we do something to resolve the mismatch (change our behaviour, change our model or project condemnation onto someone else). If feelings of guilt are generated through social disapproval or exclusion and not resolved, there is a danger of depression. An area of the ACC called the subgenual cingulate cortex has been found to be involved in feelings of guilt and major depressive illness (Zahn *et al.* 2009).

Soothing caresses or massage activates the release of oxytocin and endorphins in the ACC and medial orbito-frontal cortex (Cozolino 2006). This reduces stress, develops calmness and promotes a feeling of well-being. The ACC, orbito-frontal cortex and medial prefrontal cortical areas are activated during mindful-awareness practices (Siegel 2007) and reduce negative moods by moving attention away from the default network *canteen chatter*, promoting positive in-the-moment awareness of bodily states and feelings.

The ACC also detects discrepancies between what our value system rates highly and what we are actually doing. If we spend too much time in roles we really do not like to play, this discrepancy is apparent in the limbic system as a conflict. The mismatch between our value system and what we are doing with our time (e.g. because we are working for a company with different values to ourselves) can cause tension as the attempts by our system to resolve the mismatch are made. Fulfilling our own potential according to our personal value system has been termed self-actualisation by humanistic psychologists (such as Abraham Maslow and Carl Rogers). Self-actualisation is considered as the single basic motivating drive in the person-centred approach to therapy, and psychological difficulties are caused by blockages to this drive (Nelson-Jones 2000). Values that are not innately our own but come from persons or organisations we interact with are termed 'conditions of worth' in person-centred therapy and if these are not congruent with our own values, cognitive dissonance may result with associated amygdala activation generating stress. Similarly, if we attempt to work in roles that require us to rely on cerebral functions that are not our preferred functions, the incongruence between what is demanded and what is efficiently delivered may lead to prolonged adaptive stress syndrome (PASS) (Benziger 2009) and stress hormones may prevent proper memory storage and cognitive performance. Dr Katherine Benziger and Dr Arlene Taylor have studied this form of mismatch and its consequences which they believe activates a parasympathetically mediated conserve/withdraw reaction rather than a sympathetically mediated fight–flight reaction (see section on amygdalae). This is associated with low self-esteem, fatigue, boredom or hyper-vigilance, poor memory, poor frontal lobe function and depression (Benziger 2009).

You cannot learn and perform well if what you are doing is poorly aligned with your value system or efficient cognitive functions. You begin to fail as your body's systems sabotage your attempts to operate according to values incompatible with your personal needs and values. Cognitively you may have the top-down intentions in place, but your infrastructural set-up can thwart these with its own subconscious processes.

Coaching practice

When coaching, you may wish to ask your clients to reflect on the functioning of their 'spotlight' and discrepancy detection system by asking them to consider the following:

- How easily are you distracted by novelty or sexual imagery or new emails arriving to keep you from your plan of action? When you sense this happening, do you say to yourself: 'Hey, a distraction! Please refocus on the job at hand!' If you are truly interested in the job at hand, gently practising this refocussing often strengthens pathways in the brain, maintaining concentration so it becomes progressively easier to avoid distractions taking over. If you are not interested in the job at hand, can you analyse the mismatch in terms of your preferred internal working models and values?
- What experiences have you had with organisational change? Was it easy to shift into a new role? What facilitated acceptance of the change and what impeded it? What was your assessment of the positives and negatives of the proposed change before, during and after implementation?
- When you notice a discrepancy between what you expect and what is happening, do you react very quickly to relieve any discomfort by grasping at short-term relief measures or do you work through the issue, staying with the discomfort, in a well thought-out process to remodel and reframe the issue for a satisfactory long-term solution?
- What do other people's faces tell you about their emotional state? Do you spend time noticing these things or dismiss them as too personal and move on? Or do you adjust your behavioural style to tune in to another human being and allow your own mental structures to emulate theirs? How do you handle what comes up?
- How do you guide your focus of attention in times of a crisis? Are you able to narrow the spotlight and focus on short-term step-by-step actions? Or are you overwhelmed, caught frozen in the floodlights? Do you focus on the process and cultivate a positive approach or get bogged down in depressing details?

Change processes

Mismatch reports (cognitive dissonance) triggered by the ACC whenever we cannot match up what we are supposed to be doing with any of the models our insula has at our disposal is often seen during organisational change processes. To resolve the conflict that change creates it is important to imagine what the required new behaviour looks like in sufficient detail to build a comprehensive personal new internal working model for that new way of being, and tune in to the feelings evoked when trying to adopt this model. Role-modelling the new model with a coach or within a peer group is an important way of supporting the change process. The risks and benefits of the changes can then be more accurately assessed and addressed. In any change process, the feeling of pain, linked to cognitive dissonance, indicates that the process of trying to build a new working model for the required behaviour has started. No pain, no gain!

Change cannot be hurried if people are genuinely working towards it, as neural models have to be constructed and neural pathways re-routed. The process of building the new working model for the required behaviour is helped by repeated visualisations and embodied exercises. Applying pressure to attempt to hasten change may raise stress levels via the amygdala, which is likely to shut down new model construction as part of a general defensive manoeuvre. If people are not genuinely working towards the change management request, then it is likely that management has not addressed their concerns adequately, leaving them with unresolved fears. Although this is often viewed by managers as *resistance* to change, it is a perfectly rational defensive reaction if people's fears are not adequately addressed.

A better way of encouraging change is to openly raise *awareness* of the reasons for change and address concerns about '*what is in it for me?*', providing clarity of how things are expected to be better, individually and collectively, as a result of the change. A spirit of moderate optimism is required, together with a compelling vision of the future if *desire* for change is to be engendered (Pillay 2011) and an ACC attention priority for the change project is to be achieved. Promoting an awareness of the reasons for change and then addressing the factors involved in encouraging a desire for change are the first two stages of a five-stage change management process (Hiatt 2006). The third stage involves imparting the *knowledge* necessary for the new behaviour, then establishing a process to foster the *ability* to behave according to the new model. The final stage considers motivational incentives and *reinforcement* techniques. The model, known as ADKAR®, an acronym for the five stages, is useful as a sequential series of stages for change at a personal or organisational level. Management are responsible for persuading staff of the reasons that the changes proposed are necessary and for exploring with staff the factors that would encourage or discourage them to change. Coaches may well be brought in to support staff as they break away from their existing mental models and start to construct new ones by assimilating new knowledge. Coaches can also facilitate role play of the new behaviours in the *ability* phase. This may alleviate the stress often associated with change, which impedes new learning.

Chapter 12

Our hippocampal search engine and library services

Our hippocampi function as an internal search engine and preferred-term indexing system able to retrieve explicit memories of past experiences, particularly those with emotionally important content, and hold these memories in readiness for rapid reference. They are essential for encoding, storing and indexing memories, including semantic memories (about people, places and the meaning of words or objects) and spatial memories (including large-scale maps of the environment and the location of such things as food sources). The right hippocampus is more specialised for spatial memory storage and the left for semantic memory. Both left and right hippocampi are involved in learning and act as an expandable processing area for new information during the process of memory consolidation, which may take years, during which time memories are transferred to the neocortex. When we want to put a name to a familiar face, the left hippocampus is activated and draws upon information stored in other parts of the brain in order to make the match. Thus, you could think of the hippocampi as a key-word based search engine on the left and rather like Google Maps on the right, providing 3-D street views and mapping information.

The hippocampi develop relatively late in life, which may explain infantile amnesia (Cozolino 2006). Their development is aided by quality maternal care and soothing touch, which reduces the sensitivity to stress caused by hormones such as cortisol. Long-term exposure to cortisol can lead to the death of hippocampal neurons. The hippocampi are important for the consolidation and contextualisation of new memories, autobiographical learning and learning social rules/norms. In conjunction with the orbito-medial PFC, the hippocampi generate an expectation of the reaction of others to our intended behaviour so that we can make timely modifications so as not to offend. If these areas are not well linked during early life experience, emotional control, sustained goal orientation, humour and adherence to social norms may fail (Cozolino 2006). Coaches may encounter such clients and work with them to develop the awareness of the weak linkages, and then strengthen them through stress-free role play.

The ACC surveillance services rely on the hippocampi and amygdalae to evaluate whether or not anything on the horizon constitutes a known threat. If there is a resemblance to a past threat, then the amygdala defence systems go into a state of alert. Unconscious threats from the past, perhaps experienced in early childhood or during trauma, trigger this alarm but often without the contextual knowledge of the event being available as the narrative around traumatic events is stored implicitly to protect from re-traumatisation. Memories of events normally consist of an event narrative (the storyline) and the embodied feelings and emotions associated with that event. Normally the hippocampi associate the two explicitly so that the memory is easily recalled. In the case of overwhelming traumatic events, this association is not made explicit until sufficient resources are available to cope with the overwhelming circumstances. Therefore, fear reactions may be triggered with no conscious understanding of the reason why. Coaches may occasionally encounter clients in whom such reactions occur. Psychotherapists are trained to develop the resources of the client so that, gradually, conscious awareness of the embodied feelings becomes possible and eventually the event narrative.

From a coaching and development point of view, the two most important aspects of hippocampal function are whether it is stress free and whether retrieved memories are creating a context that is no longer relevant to current issues. Some of these memories, created when circumstances were very different, contribute to *self-limiting beliefs*. These are ideas that you hold about yourself and your abilities that limit your potential, based on a context that is no longer valid. *Fixed Gestalts* is a similar concept, meaning the idea that the normally fluid process of gestalt formation has become frozen as one interprets the world with an out-of-date framework.

It has been found that London taxi drivers gain expanded right hippocampal volumes as they learn more spatial mapping information about the London environment (Ward 2010). The hippocampi recall 'archived' explicit memories from other parts of the brain and hold them in readiness when these facts and details may be needed, such as for an impending exam or complex problem-solving exercise when we need to gather together relevant information and keep it available for rapid access. In the same way, when preparing to solve a complex problem creatively, a phase of immersion in all of the relevant details, namely, *hippocampal loading*, is necessary. Once this has been done, it is advisable to disassociate the information from the interpretive frameworks used in the past (e.g. during REM sleep) so that the raw information, without any structured framework for interpreting its meaning, can be re-associated in many different ways together with other information. By evaluating multiple possible interpretive scenarios, new patterns may start to appear so that a new interpretive framework yielding important new insights emerges. This is an important aspect of the functioning of the hippocampi, contributing to creativity (see Part 4, Creative process).

Coaching practice

With these functions in mind, you may wish to explore the following with your clients by asking questions along the following lines:

- What ideas do you have about the type of person you are and the capabilities you have? How long have you held these ideas? On what basis were these ideas formed? Is this basis valid?
- Do you notice that when you feel stressed you have more than usual difficulty in recalling people's names or facts? Does your behaviour when you are stressed lack the social refinement normally available to you? Does your sense of humour desert you? What anti-stress measures have you considered?
- Do you ever say: 'we tried that before and it didn't work' when a suggestion is made for a particular solution? What do you remember about the previous experience? What was the context in which the solution was tried? Can you disassociate your habitual meaning-making framework and reinterpret the raw information afresh?
- What steps do you take towards hippocampal loading prior to attempting to solve complex problems? Can you think of ways of improving this preparation phase?

Chapter 13

Our amygdalae

Diplomacy or defence

The amygdalae (Latin for almonds) exist as two almond-sized structures beneath the temporal lobes of the cortex (one on the left side and one on the right: Figure 9.1). Whereas the hippocampi are specialised for explicit memory storage and vary in size according to current requirements, the amygdalae have a much more stable memory, specialised for remembering threats, generalising these memories to other possible threats and keeping them available so that any resemblance to current situations picked up by the surveillance services is quickly identified (Cozolino 2006).

If our surveillance services identify a threat on the horizon, then within about 14 milliseconds the alarm in the amygdala goes off, placing the bodily defences on a state of alert that has three different levels (Porges 2009). The first level is known as *active alert* and is the most evolutionarily advanced process in which the right amygdala, via the nucleus ambiguus, reduces the braking effect of the myelinated vagus nerve of the parasympathetic nervous system, which normally keeps our heart rate lower than its own default setting (Porges 2009). This system evolved in mammals, encouraging the development of prosocial behaviour and is part of our *Social Engagement System*. Known as the smart vagus, this neuronal circuit is normally active when our risk appraisal system assesses things to be safe, maintaining a calming influence on the heart and blood pressure and promoting socially engaging facial expressions and vocal tones. This system is under a higher degree of control from upper management, particularly our right frontal cortex and the upper motor neurones, than the systems controlling the next two alarm levels. Onset and offset of this smart or myelinated vagal braking control system is quick, with few long-term metabolic consequences, unlike the situation when the sympathetic or older parasympathetic (controlled by the dorsal nuclei and nuclei in the solitary tract: Figure 14.1) systems activate.

The threshold for triggering our alarm is initially set early on in life and has been shown to be strongly influenced by how well our mother or carer handled our early stressful experiences. 'In one sense, a child "borrows" the prefrontal cortex of the parent while modelling the development of its own nascent brain on what is borrowed' (Cozolino 2006). It appears that early life experiences influence how and when the three different defence systems come into play. At the first jump in risk assessment our vagal brake is reduced and the heart rate jumps up towards its automatic default setting. This provides our body with increased resources for action for a limited time without activating the sympathetic division of our autonomic nervous system. Motor nerves to our facial muscles (the trigeminal nerves) also get activated to convey the heightened sense of alert to others via our facial expression.

If vagal tone is poorly developed in early life, children have difficulties in regulating their emotions, and are seen as irritable, easily distracted, hyper-reactive, impulsive and prone to withdrawal (Cozolino 2006). Most healthy adults are able to modulate their emotions and autonomic nervous systems. Some adults, whose parents may have been preoccupied in their first few years, may have developed a self-reliant mode and become rather avoidant of emotional contact with others. Their social engagement system may therefore be less well developed so that they more rapidly progress to defence level two, activating their sympathetically driven flight system.

Early life experiences not only set vagal tone – the system is linked to muscular tone and the functioning of the immune and cardiovascular systems (Ogden 2009, Porges 2009). Tone in brain systems is reflected in body systems and vice versa; mental stress causes physical tension. As the amygdalae are under reciprocal control from the orbito-medial PFC, the trigger for setting off the fight/flight response can be modulated by the cerebral cortex by increasing one's awareness of the escalation process, the stage one is at in the process, and strengthening parasympathetic braking. A coach who has a well-developed parasympathetic braking system can model this calming behaviour. Vagal tone can be improved later on in life using mindfulness practices which provide a range of health benefits (Chaskalson 2011).

Many managers will be familiar with the level one alert state when, for example, giving a presentation to the Board or any important audience, heart rate goes up, providing extra resources. This level of arousal is necessary to get the body prepared to perform well cognitively. Escalating to the next level is not ideal in such situations. The sympathetic nervous system is not so highly evolved and its activation is geared towards optimising survival. Higher cerebral thinking is not prioritised in such circumstances, so access to facts and figures for your presentation or indeed appropriate words are simply not top priority once level two kicks off. Your mind may go blank. Fast, automated survival systems are prioritised. Beta-blockers, drugs that block the effects of the sympathetic nervous system, may help you to stick to your presentation, but developing a stronger smart vagus is preferable. When encountering someone with an activated level two defence, those with well-developed circuits for parasympathetic braking are more able to engage with those less able to control level two and help talk them down from going into fight or flight mode by modelling calming facial expressions (Ogden 2009). Turning your back on the situation tends to provoke escalation.

If the social engagement system fails to diplomatically manage the threat, defence systems involving activation of the sympathetic nervous system are triggered. This is analogous to 'mobilising the army' and is very resource consuming, involving the release of adrenaline and noradrenaline into various organs of the body, and stress hormones such as cortisol, further preparing the body for sustained action. If 'mobilising the army' is prolonged or frequent, then freedom to think becomes constrained within a highly reactive defensive system in which our best thinking functions remain in a 'cognitive bunker'. The periaqueductal grey (PAG) and the amygdalae manage defensive behaviours (Porges 2009: 46–47) rather than the cortex. If escape seems possible, flight is generally the instinctive defence of choice, but if aggression seems more likely to be effective or if you feel trapped then the fight response is preferred (Ogden 2009). However, the preference towards fight or flight also depends on early-life attachment patterns to your attachment figure (e.g. mother), in that those who develop a preference for avoiding close emotional interactions will favour flight and those whose early life experiences included tense emotional entanglements may favour the fight response (Cozolino 2006). These two responses, fight or flight, are known as *mobilising defences*.

When the mobilising defences seem unlikely to succeed or have failed (the 'army' has been defeated), the third level of defensive behaviours comes into play in which the activated sympathetic system gradually gives over to the older form of the parasympathetic system to create alert immobility, floppy immobility including playing dead, or submissive behaviours (Ogden 2009). These are types of *immobility defence*. These states are associated with activation of ventro-lateral areas of the PAG in which opioid mediated analgesia and dissociative states (the cortex is disabled) may evolve, characteristic of traumatic experiences. Commonly, these 'freeze states' provoke feelings of helplessness, loss of control and feelings of inadequacy. Clients exhibiting such states during stressful situations may benefit from appropriate psychotherapy.

In the work place many managers require some degree of 'stress' in order to get their brain functions to a reasonable degree of arousal. They have a personal zone in which pressure drives performance into the coping/thriving level. But there is a point beyond which further pressure starts to reduce performance in a way described by the Yerkes-Dodson curve, named after the psychologist who studied this in 1908 (see Chaskalson 2011). Thriving may result from sufficient pressure to get all the cerebral functions to work together in a synchronous way to achieve what has been called a state of 'flow' by the psychologist Mihály Csíkszentmihályi (1991) but it is unlikely that this will be achieved once the sympathetic mobilisation or parasympathetic immobilisation defences have been activated. Clients with a well-developed social engagement system are most likely to be successful.

Coaching practice

Exploring the way in which clients respond to and manage stress is a valuable and important exercise.

- Do your clients recognise that they need a minimum level of stress to get into their zone of optimal performance? How much stress do they need and where does it come from?
- What does this feel like? Is it mediated via the vagal brake or sympathetically mediated? How can they maximise the former and minimise the latter?
- How do they notice excessive levels of stress (e.g. bumping into door frames or muscular twitches)? What do they do to manage this?
- Are they aware that much stress may come from self-generated concepts and working models? When did these models get created? Is a reframing exercise needed?
- Have your clients considered mindfulness exercises to refocus away from anxiety-promoting internal 'chatter' to in-the-moment sensory awareness? Mindfulness-based stress reduction therapy has been well researched and many guides with audio CDs are available to provide self-support (e.g. *Mindfulness: A practical guide to finding peace in a frantic world*, Williams and Penman 2011).

Chapter 14

Our periaqueductal grey

Linking motivational systems

Our periaqueductal grey matter is located in the evolutionarily most ancient part of the brain below the thalamus (Figure 14.1). Areas at the top of this structure are involved in mediating the fight response and areas at the bottom mediate a flight response. Ventro-lateral areas are involved in immobility reactions and dissociative states and there are good connections

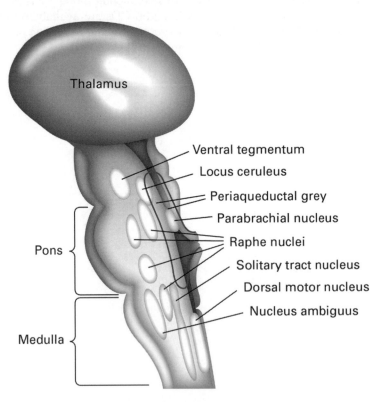

Figure 14.1 Location of key brain-stem functions including the periaqueductal grey area.

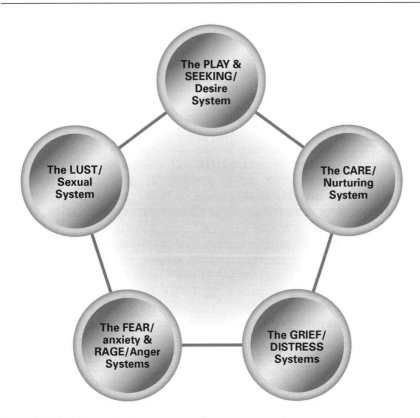

Figure 14.2 Biochemically driven emotional motivation systems.

to the amygdalae. In addition, the PAG is involved in mediating a range of biologically determined emotional motivation systems involving hormones and neurochemicals interacting with our self-representation to create our affect or emotional states. This has been described as our *primordial 'core consciousness'* which is also influenced by the emotions of others (Trevarthen 2009: 67).

Neurochemically driven emotions provide strong fundamental motivations for behaviour, serving basic bodily needs that must be accommodated in order to survive and thrive. As mentioned previously, different researchers such as John Bowlby and Jaak Panksepp have proposed such systems, but the model from Panksepp is more recent and more extensively elaborated. Panksepp's model is based on studies using deep electrical brain stimulation activating core primary processes. Bowlby's Attachment Theory describes five such systems (Lichtenberg 2007) and Panksepp describes seven systems although neither scheme claims to be complete. The independent but interrelated systems are summarised using Panksepp's terminology in Figure 14.2

and, following his convention, to denote when we are talking about the system rather than the behaviour to which it relates, the nature of the SYSTEM under discussion is CAPITALISED.

The CARE/Nurturing system

Unlike offspring in some other species, humans and other mammals require a lot of care in order to survive after birth. This care provision is so important for the survival of our species that we pass on genes to ensure the construction of a relatively hard-wired CARE motivating system. Hormone levels change towards the end of gestation in order to alter maternal behaviour, promoting skin-to-skin contact with the new baby. This includes an increased level of oestrogen, reduced levels of progesterone, increased prolactin and raised levels of oxytocin. Such hormonal changes alter the values-driven attention priority system, mediated by the ACC, such that the baby gets top priority attention and the mother role-model behavioural framework is selected in preference to other roles from the repertoire via the insula. Once the baby is born, the CARE system aims to ensure that strong bonding between mother and baby takes place so that feeding is facilitated and regular bodily contact helps the process of attunement via face-to-face contact. Gradually, the baby is able to match observed facial expressions to a particular perceived emotional state through this interplay with the mother and configure his or her own emotional systems in a similar way.

This neurobiological system seems to have many parallels to the psychologically described attachment behavioural system proposed earlier, from 1969 onwards, by John Bowlby. Although this system is very important in early life, Bowlby believed it to be important throughout the lifespan whenever proximity to others is needed for support. 'Others' include relationship partners, close friends, romantic partners, teachers, supervisors, coaches, therapists and symbolic protectors (often with spiritual meaning). Bowlby conceptualised a person's hierarchy of attachment figures to whom the person would turn in times of stress. If proximity to any of these attachment figures is not possible, the individual experiences stress and has to manage it alone, stretching their own resources. In contrast, attachment figures provide a real or potential *safe haven* with comfort, support and protection. In addition, attachment figures provide a *secure base* from which the person can engage in sustained exploration, risk taking and self-expansion (Shaver and Mikulincer 2009).

In ideal circumstances after birth, a baby should have reliable access to an attachment figure fully emotionally available to modulate the baby's emotions when necessary. If so, a state of secure attachment is established and it is more likely that in adult life secure attachments will also form with other adults. It is believed that such secure early attachment relationships play an important part in the emotional regulation of one's own multiple emotional behavioural systems and those of others (e.g. to facilitate de-escalation of anger, anxiety and sadness). Bowlby considered that secure attachment provides the foundation for personal growth and mature autonomy. If, however, after birth the baby does not have reliable access to an emotionally available attachment figure, secondary attachment strategies with hyperactivation or deactivation of emotional behavioural systems occur. This may lead to patterns in which there is an exaggerated need to be close to an attachment figure (clingy) but still feeling insecure (hyper-activated variant) or somewhat self-contained, self-reliant and detached from emotional involvement with others (deactivated variant). Although the basic CARE system is hard-wired, the adaptive variants are amenable to modification and this is discussed further in Part 3.

Coaches may wish to form a tentative hypothesis about which, if any, of these patterns may be operating in their clients to inform their coaching approach. Any hypothesis formed should be explored with the client sensitively so that the safe haven and secure base are maintained.

The GRIEF/DISTRESS Systems

Should care and emotional support not be forthcoming when needed, another hard-wired system is activated in the baby, which is the separation/distress circuitry that causes emotional pain, initiating crying to signal distress. When the attachment figure (care-giver or the person to whom the child has bonded) is present, the system releases oxytocin and endogenous opioids (endorphins) into their brain to control the emotional pain of being alone in an unfamiliar and unpredictable world. The system resembles an addiction process in which emotional bonds reflect underlying chemical addictions. Separation resembles a withdrawal reaction that, if pronounced, may result in an increased risk of panic reactions (hyperactivation of motivational system) or depression (deactivation of motivational systems), depending upon how coping mechanisms developed in the first few years of contact with the attachment figure. This system is active throughout life and these withdrawal reactions are seen whenever significant attachment figures disappear from your world. The system may be activated following redundancy or upon retirement or whenever the structure of daily life is radically changed, removing you from a 'secure base'. Secure predictable relationship patterns providing support are suddenly shaken up. Some of the circuits used to provide endorphin-induced calm and oxytocin stress-relieving support when you need it, not just as a baby but throughout life, are provided by the attachment figure (e.g. significant other). When they are no longer there, part of your emotional support circuitry is missing. Another emotional system is normally then triggered to motivate you to find a replacement attachment figure or a way to adequately self-support by readjusting your mental models of how you see yourself and your world.

Coaches may like to form a tentative hypothesis concerning how active such a system is, particularly if there has been a major change in the organisation or relationship patterns of their clients. If this biological motivational system is active its influence is likely to be considerable so that coaching approaches need to adapt to the priority of sorting out new support systems.

The PLAY and SEEKING/Desire systems

Once the baby has gained sufficient confidence to be sure that care and emotional support will be forthcoming when needed and a secure base is available, he or she learns to manage separation anxiety. Systems promoting interactive games (e.g. infant–parent turn-taking and imitation) and exploration to find and accumulate novel items or things to eat then develop. These systems are essential for developing self-agency by providing urges that influence the motor system to respond to our needs (Knox 2011: 72) and support our innate drive for exploration which is so fundamental for human beings.

The PLAY system is an essential motivational system as play promotes social interaction involving behaviours that test the boundaries of what can and cannot be done to someone else and that encourage the shared fun of social relationships. Many chemicals are involved in this motivational system but predominantly dopamine is involved in generating a sense of reward and well-being, driving an appetite for exploration, interaction and the acquisition of new things. The mechanisms behind these systems also have an addictive character and are involved in socio-sexual bonding, loving feelings, greed, gambling and mediating various drug addictions.

Coaches may wish to form an impression of how active the SEEKING and PLAY systems are in their clients. Are they hyperactivated so that the pursuit of new acquisitions dominates motivation or hypo-activated so that exploratory behaviour is not supported? Does the client wish to change the level of activation of this motivational system? In the case of hyperactivation, consider the pros and cons of weaning the client off dominating novelty seeking behaviour. In the case of hypo-activation, consider the client's access to an adequate secure base or whether fear is operating (see below). In either case a graduated step-by-step programme of behavioural change jointly developed with the client can be elaborated.

The FEAR/Anxiety system and RAGE/ Anger system

The FEAR/Anxiety system is important for responding to dangers triggered by using memorised information via the hippocampi about the context in which you are operating and from the amygdalae about specific cues such as something appearing to be a snake. Various neuropeptides are involved in the system which, if active, is associated with general anxiety disorders, neurotic disorders and specific phobias. The system is similar to the RAGE/Anger system, although the two systems use different pathways. RAGE/Anger is triggered by restraint, feeling hemmed in or being frustrated in getting what you want. These systems trigger the diplomacy/defence systems of the amygdalae. Consider the following situation: you are walking alone through the Canadian Rocky Mountains and suddenly you encounter a grizzly bear. After your initial shock, when your heart rate goes up, if you have developed sufficient 'presence of mind' through life experience, you may be able to control your response using your smart vagus, the ventral parasympathetic nervous system, which reapplies the brakes, bringing down your heart rate and blood pressure, and removing any signs of fear from your face that would otherwise say to the bear 'yes, I'm scared, I'm your dinner!'. This rapid right-brain intervention preserves your thinking functions while you assess your options. It stops you from immediately running or hiding your face which might provoke an immediate attack. Hopefully, this diplomatic intervention enables a strategic withdrawal to be planned, but this energy-consuming process is difficult to maintain. If diplomacy fails, the second level in the process, mobilisation of defences, diverts resources to muscles for running or fighting, not to the brain for thinking. Fighting a grizzly bear is probably not a good option so flight may be the best hope. Playing dead, a level 3 strategy, is riskier still and may quickly lead to 'game over!'

Unfortunately, fear is used as a motivational strategy by senior management in some organisations. Coaches need to evaluate whether this is the case for any of their clients. If the FEAR system is activated, coaching approaches need to accommodate this by considering the cause. Is it, for example, linked to implicit memories being triggered unconsciously, bringing past fears into the present because of lingering associations that are no longer valid? Or is there an evident present cause such as the 'rank-and-yank' appraisal system in which some companies routinely fire a certain number of employees? How should this be best managed? Stress management and support will be vital.

LUST/Sexual system

The LUST/Sexual system is obviously important for encouraging repro- duction for the survival of our species and provides a strong dominating motivation for sexual behaviour. Humans can restrain such urges via higher cortical areas but sexual attraction increases levels of amphetamine-like 'reward' substances such as phenylethylamine (also present in chocolate), heightening arousal and sensitivity (Eagle 2007). Self-restraint blocks access to motivational energies associated with testosterone and the neuropeptide vasopressin in the male and oestrogen and oxytocin in the female. The goal of the system is to focus attention (ACC mediated) on finding a preferred mating partner, which may well be different from the goal of finding an attachment figure: the adult goals of finding an attachment figure and finding a mating partner are 'conceptually distinct' in Attachment Theory (Diamond and Blatt 2007). Furthermore, competition is involved in finding the preferred mating partner, so that eugenic selection operates to improve the human gene pool. Competitive aggression therefore plays a key part in the expression of this motivational system, particularly in men, active in sibling rivalry, the Oedipus complex and power politics.

Coaches need to be aware that if this system is hyperactivated the focus for attention (scanning the horizon for certain types of information) will be the main preoccupation. This is a particularly strong motivational system and redirecting it is likely to be unsuccessful. Harnessing the motivational energy is more likely to be successful by developing associations ('sexing-up') achievement of business targets. This is notable on the trading floor of stock exchanges, for example, where the testosterone-fuelled risk-taking behaviour of young, usually male, market traders engages the LUST system. It needs to be used with great caution under vigilant cognitively driven supervision. If this is not in place, excessive risk-taking behaviour can become uncontrolled. This system is by its nature and primary purpose (propagating the most successful genetic material) focussed on competitive individual success.

Chapter 15

Emotional constellations in the workplace

The limbic system is essential for managing a range of biologically determined and socially conditioned emotions that drive behaviour aimed at protecting our core values. These systems influence the selection of an appropriate persona (internal working model or 'I'-position) from our repertoire of possibilities developed through life experience. Furthermore, through interpreting subtle clues regarding the internal mental processes of another person (mentalisation), the limbic system enables us to develop an awareness of the intentions of others. If we are sufficiently open to what is going on in our environment and have developed sufficient *emotional intelligence* through truly connecting with others, we will be able to refine our internal working models of the various personae in our repertoire in order to select behaviours optimally suited to the social/business circumstances we face and get the most out of productive working relationships.

Emotional Intelligence has become an area of substantial interest in coaching circles in recent years despite the fact that Charles Darwin published his book on the role of emotional expression in survival and adaptation in 1872. The American psychologist Edward Thorndike referred to 'social intelligence' in the 1920s and 1930s but it is only in the last 20 years that psychologists have really tried to develop such a concept for social and professional development and measure it using psychometric instruments (Stein and Book 2006). Daniel Goleman popularised the subject in his book *Emotional Intelligence*, published in 1995, which became a bestseller (Goleman 1995). One way to measure emotional intelligence developed by Reuven Bar-On looks at five areas or 'realms': the intra-personal realm; the interpersonal realm; the adaptability realm; the stress management realm and the general mood realm. The intrapersonal realm includes emotional self-awareness, assertiveness, autonomy, self-regard and realising one's own potential. The interpersonal realm includes empathy, social responsibility and interpersonal relationships. The adaptability realm includes problem solving, reality testing and flexibility. The stress-management realm includes stress tolerance and impulse control. Finally the general mood realm includes happiness and optimism. It is hoped that by developing an understanding of the functions of the cerebral cortex and limbic system from the preceding chapters, ability to manage the further development of emotional intelligence will be enhanced.

Before the recent increased attention towards emotional intelligence there was relatively little consideration of the role emotions played in the workplace; indeed, this was generally discouraged. Much greater focus was placed on the way in which the cerebral cortex determined behaviour through its cognitions about the nature of the wider world. The emotional arena was not considered as an appropriate area for explicit discussion. However, there can be little doubt that fear plays a substantial role in the workplace and indeed some CEOs think that fear is a good way to motivate people to perform better. How many of us have experienced an increase in heart rate when the CEO calls you into his or her office? Do we quickly apply our parasympathetic brakes to calm our system down and remove signs of fear from our face or do we suddenly freeze with our mind going blank, indicating that our higher cognitive thinking is not operating well? Perhaps we adopt a childlike submissive transactional position? Understanding the biology of the FEAR motivational system helps to make it clear that activating the FEAR system as a management strategy can never result in improved cognitive performance. It merely activates exhausting defensive systems geared to protecting the core values of the individual, not the values of someone else or an organisation. Anxiety in groups has been well studied by psychologists, with the research of the British psychoanalyst Wilfred Bion (1897–1979) being particularly relevant: 'Bion was concerned to identify those mental activities which impede, corrupt or sometimes support the rational group process. They derive from powerful emotional states which push the faculty of judgement into second place' (Bléandonu 1994: 71). Bion found that when work groups feel threatened 'anxiety causes the group to withdraw energy from dealing with the task at hand and use it to defend itself against these anxieties' (De Board 1978: 137). Such defences include each member of the group subconsciously transferring their autonomy and sense of leadership to a particular individual in the group 'whose personality renders him peculiarly susceptible to the obliteration of individuality' (Bion 1968: 177). The group in effect become dependent upon an 'idealised' leader in whom the hopes of the group are invested, often unrealistically. It is a regressive strategy reminiscent of finding an attachment figure such as a parent who will rescue and protect you as a child in situations that are too big for you to deal with. Other possible defences include group fight or flight responses. If coaches and managers are not aware of and attuned to anxiety in the workplace and do not understand how such emotions operate, major mistakes can be made regarding motivation of the desirable performance or inadvertently fulfilling the 'parental' or 'messianic' rescuing role which is unlikely to succeed and may end in humiliation. Staff may 'mobilise their armies' and exhibit underlying hyper or hypo reactive defensive behaviours.

Coaching practice

Coaches may wish to explore with their clients the topics of fear and anxiety in the workplace and their clients' experience of regression of work groups to basic assumptions:

- Have you experienced fear in your working environment? What were the circumstances? How did you respond? With the benefit of hindsight how would you respond today?
- Do you have experiences in which you felt that the leadership mantle was placed on your shoulders by a group because of their anxiety? How did you feel? How did the situation evolve? How did it end? With the benefit of hindsight how would you handle the situation today?

Motivation without FEAR

As activating the FEAR/Anxiety motivational system is inappropriate as a motivational strategy in the workplace, which of the other basic motivational systems provide the best platform upon which to build motivational strategies? Clearly the GRIEF/DISTRESS systems are not suitable options. Many marketing experts turn to the LUST/Sexual motivation system to promote their products. Historically, testosterone-fuelled aggression has been widely used to motivate highly competitive behaviour reminiscent of sibling rivalry during childhood for gaining adult attention in order to get needs met. This may be useful in military campaigns where individual autonomy is subverted under a hierarchy, and for some critical turnaround/business rescue situations, but this often coercive and competitive approach needs to be tempered at work in situations where collaboration, cooperation and creative problem-solving skills are called for. This leaves us to consider the CARE/ Nurturing system, the PLAY system and the SEEKING/Desire system.

Regarding the CARE/Nurturing system, the take-home message from knowledge about this system is that in order to optimise exploratory behaviour a dependable safe haven needs to be created. This requires a high degree of *trust* to be built over time. Given what we know about the amount of information conveyed through facial expressions and body language, genuine trust depends on authentic face-to-face interactive communication. Unless managers are open to the emotional milieu in which they operate (by developing their emotional intelligence) it is unlikely that sufficient attunement of emotional mindsets will be achieved. Empathetic understanding may not be enough. A state of sympathetic shared feeling about a situation facilitated by the mirror neuron system, achieves a deeper level of connection for problem solving. In order not to remain in this state of 'confluence' with another person, risking collusion with their agenda, coaches and managers need to step back from the emotional connection in which sympathy was achieved and engage in 'cognitive perspective taking' (Pillay 2011: 223).

This involves engaging in counter-mirroring so that you are no longer picking up signals and emulating the emotional state of another person as a subject, but moving into your abstracting PFC and evaluating the situation objectively. Such an oscillating/shuttling technique of moving between subjective contact with another and objective evaluation of the overall context is an essential skill for coaches and an increasingly important skill for senior managers.

On the basis of a well-established CARE system in an organisation, the SEEKING/Desire system may provide the best model upon which to base motivation strategies. Business-game simulation workshops for a variety of scenarios likely to be encountered in the workplace provide an analogous learning space to the PLAY system vitally important for the integration of a newcomer. Optimal motivation to achieve the goals of the organisation depends to a large degree on how the goals of the individual, operating according to their core value system, accord with the goals of the organisation, operating according to its implicit value system. Despite it being known for years that financial remuneration is only a motivator to a limited degree, many companies focus goal-setting and motivation strategies around financial outcomes. EBIT (Earnings before Interest and Taxes) targets or similar are often given primary importance in management communications regarding corporate goals and many companies spend a lot of resources on providing information to staff and investment analysts regarding the company's share price and likely influences upon it. Comparatively little effort is invested in truly understanding the core value systems of the staff within the organisation and how initiatives derived from such values could unleash a cooperative and highly motivated shared enterprise.

Four values that often emerge as major motivational drivers for staff are:

1   engaging in work that provides benefits to the wider community providing a sense of greater purpose;
2   engaging in work that permits learning, development and a sense of competence and mastery;
3   engaging with work that provides a sense of connection with others and fosters positive interpersonal relations with co-workers; and
4   the ability to live an integrated life, so that work roles and other life roles are neither inherently in conflict nor clash with personal values (Pfeffer 2010).

If organisations truly wish to capitalise on the immense potential of a motivated workforce, it would seem appropriate to spend more effort in ascertaining what the drivers of staff motivation really are in some detail and using this as a starting point for evolving a bottom-up corporate value system to integrate with the top-down perspective, rather than imposing explicitly or implicitly a purely top-down perspective.

Shifting from a competitive model based around the LUST/Sexual motivational system to a cooperation model based around the SEEKING/Desire motivational system is likely to entail a major rethink regarding the required leadership style for different contexts. Research into effective leadership indicates that the best leaders do not rely on only one leadership style but have access to several styles, selecting from a repertoire of six contrasting styles according to circumstance (Goleman 2000). The most aggressive of these styles was termed the coercive style. Such a style involves demanding immediate compliance from subordinates. This can mean bullying and demeaning executives and failing to motivate them by showing them how their role fits into a bigger picture. Goleman reported that this style works best in a crisis or to kick-start a turnaround. Such a style was found to have the most negative impact on the organisational culture. The second most negative style, also highly aggressive, was termed the pacesetting style in which the leader role-models extremely high performance standards, about which he or she is obsessive, highlighting when others fail to reach these standards and then replacing them. Such an approach did not improve results, Goleman noted. Trust, flexibility and responsibility evaporated as work became focussed on second-guessing what the leader wanted. Such a style can get quick wins for a limited time from a highly motivated, well-chosen team but over time the highly competent team members develop their own agendas. Leadership styles with higher underlying levels of emotional intelligence competencies such as empathy, relationship building, collaboration, developing others and self-awareness (styles termed coaching, democratic, affiliative or authoritative) had a positive impact on culture and these styles were associated with decidedly better financial results than the styles negatively impacting on culture. Efforts to tune into the emotional milieu of the workplace, understand the drivers of motivation within the workforce and pay appropriate attention to these is likely to be increasingly important for success.

Coaching practice

This is fruitful territory for coaches to explore with their clients.

* What is the repertoire of management styles (IWMs) available to your clients? In which situations would they deploy each style? Which emotional behavioural system do they think is impacted by such a style and in what ways? With the benefit of hindsight, how would your clients alter their use of these styles?
* Do your clients have an emotional intelligence development plan? Which of the five areas outlined (the intrapersonal realm; the interpersonal realm; the adaptability realm; the stress management realm; or the general mood realm) do they feel they should prioritise? Can you co-shape a development plan to enhance such an area?

Anachronistic social taboos and self-limiting beliefs

Although the biologically determined motivational systems have evolved over thousands of years to help human beings survive and thrive, social conventions and anachronistic taboos often act to prevent changes to the social order and prevailing power structure. As with personal internal working models, such conventions and taboos may well have had a useful purpose at the time that they developed, although sometimes their rationale is obscure and lost in the mists of time. The construction of social conventions involves a process of building internal working models of how our world operates, with parents and 'elders' instilling these into us during our upbringing. Just as adolescents have a rebellious phase in which their brain's neuroplasticity is particularly flexible in order to build updated working models to adapt to emergent environmental changes, the same updating process should be the result of an on-going and evolving discussion in which all well-informed members of society have their points of view considered. However, the older we get, the less likely we are to be open to rebuilding our internal working models. Thus, there is likely to be a biologically based tension between young adults wanting to implement new working models of the world and older adults wanting to keep it the same. When such date-expired IWMs restrict access to pools of people whose perspective is likely to enrich our ability to solve the complex problems of today, the pressure may build towards a tipping point in which the drive for change gains ground and society becomes more and more influenced by new internal working models. As we have seen, discrepancy between what is observed and one's internal working models causes mismatch detection messages in the form of neurochemicals generating feelings of guilt if internally attributed (retroflection, which if unresolved may cause depression) or judgement if externally attributed (projection of blame). In either case, marginalisation or social exclusion may result for either party. Guilt reflects the accumulation in the subgenual portion of the ACC of the chemical discrepancy records of how you are behaving, according to social conventions compared to your personal core value system. When coerced to follow social conventions that conflict with personal values, accumulation of 'discrepancy records' may prevent personal growth and societal contribution. Topical examples of such coercion include situations relating to the role of women in society, discrimination on the basis of sexual orientation, racial background or class and failing to appreciate the qualities, perspectives and attributes of those considered mentally different. The negative consequences of operating according to social conventions and attitudes related to outdated models can be considerable both for the individual concerned and for society. The adolescent mind is programmed to rebuild inherited mental models in order to adapt to the emerging world and society progresses in the same way. Confounding this process with fundamentalist and entrenched world views jeopardises our ability to cope with the complexity of the challenges we face today. Adjusting mental models is a difficult and time-consuming process necessitating cognitive dissonance. Leaders aware of the mental processes required to realise such changes may be better able to organise support initiatives including coaching.

Resolution of the conflicts between a client's socially conditioned self-concept (shaped by societal 'conditions of worth') and their innate personal value system requires leaders and coaches to adopt *unconditional positive regard* towards the client. When an environment conducive to growth is established, people accept others as unique individuals, become more open to the opportunities of the moment and encounter fewer defensive obstructions (Nelson-Jones 2000). Management coaching principles based on this philosophy developed by Carl Rogers 'provide an excellent starting point to help in the formation of a coaching partnership' (Passmore 2010: 159). The six elements necessary for establishing an environment conducive to growth are: positive self-regard (of the coach or coaching manager); unconditional positive regard (of the coach/manager towards the person being coached); empathy; a non-judgemental mind; congruence (between what is felt and what is expressed by the coach/manager); and non-possessive warmth. Coaching on this basis affirms the self-agency of the manager being coached and enables sustainable creative solution-finding capabilities to emerge and become embedded. It is analogous to the situation in early life when ideally a parent or other attachment figure provides affirmative positive support as an infant engages in early explorative activity motivated by the SEEKING/Desire system.

Coaching practice

So before leaving Part 2, let's reflect on aspects of your clients' emotional value protection and biological motivational systems. Consider discussing the following:

* Keeping the basic emotional motivating systems in mind, identify examples of when you have encountered situations in which each system is active:

    – The FEAR/Anxiety system and RAGE/Anger system
    – The LUST/Sexual system
    – The CARE/Nurturing system
    – The GRIEF/Distress system
    – The SEEKING/Desire system and PLAY system

    What were the circumstances in which the system was active and how did you experience the feelings associated with it?

Which of these play the most prominent part in your day-to-day emotional life and which play the least prominent role?

How do these systems influence your cognitive thinking processes?

- Take some time to think about your own core values, i.e. what is vitally important to you. Make a list and give each item a rating between 0 to 5, with 5 being something of high value and 0 being something of no value. (If necessary, prompt with suggestions such as: What value do you place on the qualities of loyalty, trust, integrity, honesty, humility and commitment? Do you work purely for money or is a 'higher purpose' important for motivating what you do? Is being part of a community important? Is it important that your work life and personal life are well integrated?) Extend the scale to −5 to list items with negative value such as things you dislike.

- What social value systems are operating in your place of work? What aspects of behaviour do they constrain and what aspects do they enhance? How congruent are the values operating at work with your personal values? Of course, we each need to make trade-offs such as going to work to make money to support ourselves and our family so that we can afford to do the things we value. Are the trade-offs worth it? What are the consequences of any mismatch? How can these be managed?

- Can you sense when your heart rate goes up as the smart vagus nerve backs off to heighten a state of readiness? Are you able to control it and calm the system down again? Role play and use mindfulness techniques to develop this capability.

- What are the 'costumes' your insula has access to? Which ones are your favourite and what is the range of your repertoire? Are there roles you would like to play but you don't yet have the right characteristics to give a convincing performance? What are you plans for acquiring these? Do your present circumstances prevent you from adopting the role(s) that you really feel you would like to play?

Part 3

Developing our infrastructure

Part 3 considers our mind's development through the major stages of life and explores the impact of key events in shaping our thinking patterns. By clarifying our 'self-narrative' (life story) to date, development strategies to achieve our future aspirations may be elaborated.

Part 3

Developing our
infrastructure

Chapter 16

The nature of development

Imagine you are lost in a forest on a journey to a destination you vaguely have in mind. You have no GPS satellite navigation device to help you but you do have a map which so far you have not needed to consult. Unfortunately, you have no idea where you are on the map, noticing several forests widely dispersed. You know where your journey started but you don't really know whether you left it travelling north, south, east or west. Knowing that would at least give you a 'ball-park' idea of which part of the map you are likely to be in. Then, later information remembering the more recent features of your journey may help you to refine the area of the map to be searched. Until you know where you are, plotting a course to your preferred destination is likely to be a pointless exercise. In the same way, coaches wishing to guide clients towards development goals need to establish with the client where they are and how they got there. The earliest part of the journey will have disproportionately more significant influence on this. A basic understanding of developmental psychology is therefore of considerable importance to all those interested in nurturing adult development.

In part three we will explore a number of different psychological theories that seem to relate to the developing complexity of the human mind. At first, coaches may be perplexed by the variety of seemingly competing theories; however, a model is suggested in which these different theoretical approaches provide an array of 'probes' that are useful for illuminating different aspects of complex personality. By gaining a preliminary sense of what each probe is able to illuminate, coaches may then be able to select which probes are most appropriate for their area of interest and explore this area more deeply for themselves. In the terrain of personality, knowing where we are and how we got there requires an understanding of what lies beneath the superficial masks we tend to wear to understand what subconscious influences are operating in the background.

We start at the beginning by considering where knowledge comes from and how perceptions shape our personality.

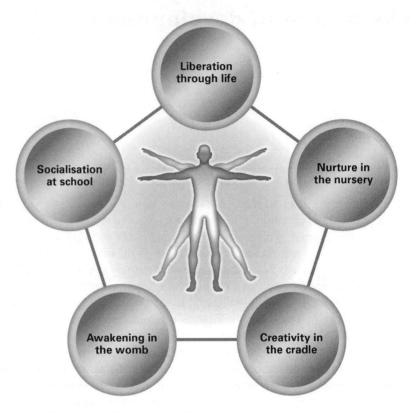

Figure 16.1 Five stages of personal development.

A philosophical perspective

Philosophers have long debated whether humans are born with inbuilt mental content or not. The Roman term *Tabula Rasa* denotes the belief that human beings are born with their 'wax covered writing tablet' erased, in other words with no innate mental content or intelligence and that all intelligence comes from sensory experience. Advocates for this position included Aristotle (384–322 BC), St Thomas Aquinas (1224–1274), John Locke (1632–1704) and Jean Piaget (1896–1980). Locke summarised his view with the statement: '*Nihil est in intellectu quod non antea fuerit in sensu*': (There is nothing in the intellect that was not previously in the senses). David Hume (1711–1776), a Scottish philosopher, argued that all knowledge comes from direct experience alone which cannot be separated from the subjective condition of the knower, therefore no objective knowledge can be known for certain. This view came to be part of what is known as *empiricism*, which opposed the rationalist position of Descartes

(1596–1650), Spinoza (1632–1677) and Leibnitz (1646–1716) among others, who viewed knowledge as coming from the mind's ability to recognise self-evident universal truths using pure reason, reminiscent of thinking originally formulated by ancient Greeks such as Pythagoras (c.582–507 BCE), Parmenides (c.480 BCE) and Plato (c. 428–347 BCE). Plato's work *Meno* introduced the idea that we are born with a priori knowledge – a collection of what we had once known in an earlier existence (Bostock 1995). He extended this line of thinking in the *Phaedo*, suggesting knowledge comes from attempts to recall transcendental 'archetypal Forms' or Ideas and that the mind perceives derivatives of the universal set of Forms. Plato's thinking was developed further by Neo-Platonist philosophers who began to conceive of a hierarchy of transcendental Forms in which the highest Form began to be called 'the One'. The soul's ascent to this divine reality required escape from the sensory body towards the divine mind, this becoming the basis for what became known much later as the Cartesian dualist split between mind and objects such as the body. In this model emotions were seen as obstructions to rational comprehension.

The Prussian philosopher Emanuel Kant (1724–1804) tried to resolve the empiricist vs rationalist positions by proposing that the mind does not passively receive sense data but structures incoming data using pre-existing frameworks. Kant believed that: 'Neither experience nor reason are alone able to provide knowledge. The first provides content without form, the second form without content. Only in their synthesis is knowledge possible' (Scruton 1982: 17). According to Kant, space, time and the concept of causality are all parts of the a priori conceptual frameworks, these being regulative ideas that the mind uses to structure experience, rather than characteristics of the world itself (Tarnas 1991). An alternative view was proposed by Georg Wilhelm Friedrich Hegel (1770–1831). Rather than accessing some form of transcendental knowledge through pure reason, the human mind develops through a dynamic 'dialectic' process of conjecture and refutation leading to ever more refined and complex versions of reality (Scruton 1982). Hegel believed that human moral purpose can only be discovered through interaction with others in community. For Hegel, community consisted of the 'interlocking web' of relationships and activities including art, religion, philosophy and government (Ebenstein and Ebenstein 2000). Peter Singer described Hegel's book *The Phenomenology of Mind* as 'a gripping account of how the finite minds of human beings progress to a point at which they can see that the world beyond them is not alien or hostile to them, but a part of themselves' (Singer 1995: 342).

Philosophical considerations of the human mind converged on the view that the human mind cannot access transcendental knowledge in order to know reality but is shaped by a multitude of overlapping factors providing it with a relative, rather than absolute, dynamic grasp of reality (Tarnas 1991: 354):

The mind is not the passive reflector of an external world and its intrinsic order, but is active and creative in the process of perception and cognition. Reality is in some sense constructed by the mind, not simply perceived by it, and many such constructions are possible, none necessarily sovereign . . . All human understanding is interpretation, and no interpretation is final.

(Tarnas 1991: 396–397)

Thus the philosophical quest to understand the mind evolved into a quest to explore how our interpretations are constrained by culture and linguistics.

A neuro-psychological perspective

A contemporary scientific perspective on the mind's development evolved through another dialectic process and one resulting 'synthesis' from the UK Medical Research Council proposes that 'the innate content of the infant mind consists mainly of initial predispositions and attention biases which activate learning' (Knox 2003: 47). Our genetic inheritance provides our initial predispositions, guiding our interaction with the environment particularly early on to facilitate neurological attunement with the mother's or primary carer's emotions through facial expressions. Rather than being born with a blank slate, our slate appears to have dimples! Each dimple may represent a particular spatial notion forming a set of primitive meanings (Mandler 1992). Once attunement with the mother or carer is established, the vast amount of information received can be organised according to the self-organising properties of complex human mind(s). It has been proposed that the first step in organising sensory input is the formation of *image schemas*, which constitute the earliest form of primitive conceptual knowledge based on internally mapping spatial structures into conceptual structures (Mandler 1992). Later in life these are refined into more complex frameworks, schemas or internal working models shaped by the prevailing environment: 'genes, brain, cognition, and environment dynamically interact, multidirectionally influencing one another in multiple ways' (Diamond 2009: 2). This on-going process is called representational re-description. Furthermore, image schemas are thought to develop to represent *embodied patterns of imagination* in which meaning emerges from bodily experience via imaginative projection (Knox 2003: 207). In this way emotions and the body's contribution to their formation play a vital role in human reasoning, contradicting the Cartesian dualist view. That means that working with the body and exploring the 'felt sense' of our experiences provides a route to greater understanding of our perceptions (Gendlin 2003) and a way of developing our conscious awareness of where we are in life and where we feel we need to go.

Image schemas are believed to lie behind Object Relations theory, an early relational theory superseding Freud's ideas about the development of the psyche. The concept of Object Relations was updated by the psychotherapist John Bowlby who modernised the idea of internal 'objects' with the idea of an internal working model (IWM), which was more compatible with cognitive science (Knox 2003: 79). Initially the working models are simple, representing polar opposite perceptions such as something being either good or bad. As more and more experience is gained, more refined perceptions emerge and more sophisticated working models of the world are constructed. In addition to these IWMs, 'schemas-of-being-with' representing models for relational experience have been proposed (Stern 1995). Such models represent complex information about how the physical world might be expected to behave and how the mother and other significant persons might behave as well as the infant. This is the *constructivist* position for knowledge acquisition because we construct our own individual models of our world as a result of our unique interactive experiences and dynamic filtering processes, rather than perceiving a shared external world directly (as in the cognitivist position which assumes a common mindset is accessible in which all people on the planet will see the world in the same way).

Commenting on the development of the human mind from infancy to adulthood, Combs stated:

> One important theme that runs throughout development is a persistent increase in internal complexity which lies inside and powers the growth of the mind. This complexity presents itself in the form of increasingly sophisticated schemas and patterns of schemas all of which constitute a person's mind.
>
> (Combs 2009: 89)

Increasingly, we understand that the tension between the opposites of differentiation and integration sets up a dialectic process creating the paradoxical dynamic of stable instability (like a heart-beat) and conforms approximately to the non-linear mathematic models of complexity theory. This dynamic tension drives a process, producing increasingly refined schemas (or internal working models). This is essentially a complex adaptive process of self-organisation which is particularly sensitive to initial conditions, meaning that events at the earliest part of life (pre and perinatal) will have major impact. This model of development has no predetermined end result as in Kantian systems thinking, but provides multiple creative possibilities as a result of the emergence of schema through multiple interactions (Stacey 2012: 12–18).

To convey this with a different metaphor, at the time of our conception a process is initiated leading to a chain of unfolding events. In these early days we are like a simple computer with no operating system, only a basic input/output system (BIOS). We need to construct our own operating system according to the conditions we encounter and to do this we need help from our mother or other attachment figure. If attunement circumstances are ideal our experience of prevailing conditions helps us to construct a well-adapted operating system. Some of this co-construction occurs before we are born but much of it takes place after birth. After birth our pre-programmed attention focus causes us to seek eye contact with a mother or attachment figure. The conditions in the cultural milieu at the time of this co-construction influence how the operating system is set up and the nature of the downloads received from the attachment figure. In times of war or conflict a negative view of human nature may form as was the case for the philosopher Thomas Hobbes. Being born suspicious and on your guard may confer a survival advantage in times of war. In more peaceful times a more positive view may be engendered. Throughout life our operating system set-up is updated so that we may engage with ever more sophisticated programmes to drive our performance and fuel our imagination.

A framework for thinking about the array of psychological theories that have attempted to delineate different parts of these complex processes is summarised in Figure 16.2. At different stages of our life a new 'layer' of neuro-psychological conditioning superimposes itself on the previous layers and the process of integration gradually proceeds to produce ever more sophisticated meaning-making frameworks. Attachment Theory aims to explain psychological processes concerning our relationship with our 'attachment figure' who helps us to construct our initial operating system by sharing 'downloads'. These processes may begin before birth and continue to play a role throughout life but are of particular importance soon after birth. Psychodynamic theory looks at the earliest shaping of our operating system to support the development of autonomy by considering how we manage the flow of our mental energy as we encounter external objects, develop interpretive frameworks, enhance competitive survival behaviours and establish psychological defences. Gestalt Therapy raises awareness of the processes we use, looking at how we experience 'figures' emerging from the field of our experience and whether we use habitual pathways to interpret our experiences. Jungian shadow work helps us to look at aspects of ourselves that we tend to disown. As our personality develops, we can use Transactional Analysis techniques to see how we tend to respond to others using our parent, adult and child role-model behaviours. As we become older our mental frameworks get more sophisticated and we build further internal working models of different personality 'archetypes' which may also be explored with Jungian psychological approaches to develop our capacity for imagination. We can look at how we use or misuse our cognitive frameworks to guide our behaviour using Cognitive Behavioural Therapy techniques. During adult life the developing complexity of our meaning-making frameworks may be envisaged as outlined in Table 8.2. Group dynamics within either the family or an organisation may be explored using what are called constellation approaches. Our 'mid-life crisis' reflects a biological process enabling reconfiguration of neural networks to facilitate the emergence of contemporaneously adapted models of a new world order. This supports adaptation to new social conditions. After our 'mid-life crisis' we may start to explore more fundamental aspects of our existence and move towards the transpersonal level of human interaction. This is an existential approach based on a high level of integration that aims to connect humans at a deeper level than via our cognitive frameworks as we contemplate our mortality and our legacy.

- Before birth four basic perinatal matrices have been described: BPM I, the 'amniotic universe'; BPM II, 'cosmic engulfment and no exit'; BPM III, 'death and rebirth struggle', and BPM IV, 'death and rebirth' (Grof and Bennett 1993).
- After birth eight psychosocial stages have been proposed (Erikson 1959). The first post-natal phase, 'Hopes', is concerned with establishing trust. Attachment Theory, providing a secure base for exploration and attunement between mother and child is particularly important at this time.
- The second post-natal phase 'Will' is concerned with establishing a sense of autonomy rather than dependency. Psychodynamic theory considering competitive-seeking behaviour including sibling rivalry and developing ego defences is particularly important at this time.
- The third post-natal phase 'Purpose' is concerned with developing initiative and managing guilt and can be addressed by integrating shadow

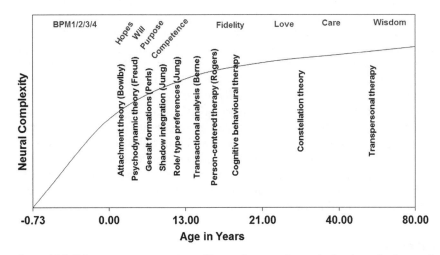

Figure 16.2 Schematic representation of increasing neural complexity through phases of development as different psychological processes embed and integrate.

aspects using Jungian theory or person-centred theory or Gestalt Therapy theory.

- The fourth and fifth phases 'Competence' and 'Fidelity' are concerned with becoming capable of being productive, establishing a self-identity and clarity of values, and may be addressed by person-centred therapy, Transactional Analysis, Jungian role preferences, and cognitive–behavioural therapy.
- The sixth and seventh phases 'Love' and 'Care' are concerned with developing intimate relationships and nurturing the younger generation. Constellation work is useful for modelling and exploring these themes incorporating any of the range of humanistic approaches.
- The last phase, 'Wisdom' is concerned with contemplation of the nature of life, our part in it and after it. Transpersonal approaches are important here such as Psychosynthesis (Assagioli), Individuation (Jung: Zurich school), Core Process Psychotherapy (Sills) and Transpersonal psychotherapy (Rowan).

At the individual level this development process evolves from the initial starting position of *unconscious unity*, through an exponential inflationary period of differentiation into multiple personae and un-owned, split-off shadow elements up to the point commonly referred to as the 'mid-life crisis' (Alschuler 2008). This is a period around the point at which the balance between differentiation and integration often shifts in favour of the latter and may not occur in the middle of life at all. In some it may occur early in life and some may never reach this point. The integration phase involves a reflective evaluation of one's life in which guilt, low self-esteem and feelings of inferiority may emerge if one's sense of purpose has not been well served. In this Jungian-based concept of development, detailed archetypal imagery is not perceptible from the start but is apprehended through the mind's growing capability for imagination. As Tarnas puts it, 'it is only when the human mind actively brings forth from within itself the full powers of a disciplined imagination and saturates its empirical observation with archetypal insight that the deeper reality of the world emerges' (Tarnas 1991: 434). As a metaphor, one may imagine one's own 'Big Bang' experience of exponentially expanding from a cellular 'singularity' into a vast universe of different personality constellations, providing differing perspectives. A point is reached at which predominant inflationary tendencies give way to mainly deflationary tendencies and the process of integration eventually brings our essential *fundamental unity* into conscious awareness, a process that Jung described as individuation.

Intelligence

Contemporary theories of intelligence contend that intelligence is comprised of 'multiple intelligences'. Howard Gardner originally proposed his theory of multiple intelligences in 1983. He considered that eight abilities met his criteria for intelligence, including: spatial, linguistic, logical-mathematical, bodily-kinaesthetic, musical, interpersonal, intrapersonal and naturalistic abilities. Moral and existential intelligences were also considered for inclusion on this list. There has been much debate over this theory with criticisms that it is too closely aligned to a modular rather than integrated cognitive model. In a more comprehensive model, Ken Wilber renamed multiple intelligences as developmental lines because he argues that these intelligences evolve progressively in multiple stages (Wilber 2006). Wilber's research brings together aspects from many other experts in the field and proposes numerous developmental lines with ten of them more clearly specified (cognitive, moral, emotional, interpersonal, needs, self-identity, aesthetics, psychosexual, spiritual, and values lines). Development is conceptualised by some as progressing in a spiral fashion with advances along multiple development lines contributing to overall progress. Importantly, it is the integration of different levels of thinking along a development line and across development lines that contributes to overall intelligence.

Wilber's development-line concept defines levels of attainment which he colour codes and maps to terms used in other development models such as those of Piaget, Graves, Kegan and Loevinger/Cook-Greuter (Wilber 2006). Although a healthy personality is governed by the highest structure that has emerged, earlier structures are still accessible, providing a rich spectrum of understanding (Combs 2009). Under stress, regression to earlier structures, namely, earlier working models of the world that have become more deeply embedded, is likely to occur, with more refined structures being less accessible.

In summary, development may be conceptualised as a process of reconstructing and refining our internal working models of the world by widening our range of perceptions within and across multiple development lines by adding relevant content incrementally from our experience. Ultimately through dialectic refinement of our self-understanding we enter an integration phase, coming to see the inherent unity of our world and its creative process.

Chapter 17

Awakening in the womb

Following the fertilisation of an egg by a sperm, a single cell structure is formed called a zygote which contains mixed maternal and paternal genetic material. After travelling down the Fallopian tube and undergoing a number of cell divisions over about eight days, a ball of cells called a blastocyte is formed; this may or may not implant into the uterus; many in fact don't. If plantation occurs, the embryonic stage of development begins from the fifteenth day after conception. The most sensitive time for the development of the central nervous system is from three to 16 weeks after conception (Moore and Persuad 1998). Rapid brain development is seen from weeks 25 to 28 such that a premature baby born at this time may possibly survive. Birth is normally at around 40 weeks. The brain is far from being ready for separate existence at this point, but remaining in the womb until all networks are ready to go would extend pregnancy to around 24 months (Gould 1977). Carrying and delivering a baby of such size would be highly problematic! Childbirth is already frequently traumatic.

You may think that life in the placenta before birth would be an idyllic existence in which the foetus gets all its needs met without effort, providing a sense of omnipotence, as if in heaven. However, evidence suggests that threats from the environment can influence our development even before conception. Animal studies indicate that stress experienced by the mother well before conception has long-lasting effects on the offspring into adulthood. Basic emotional motivation systems seem to be sufficiently developed before birth to activate in response to threats, including a self-care system for coping with traumas such as toxaemia of pregnancy and the trauma of birth (Trevarthen 2009).

Let's consider what is likely to be going on in the nascent mind of the yet to be born baby, according to different scenarios. Let us first consider what seems to be, at first glance, an ideal scenario. In this scenario the mother is not stressed before pregnancy and is perfectly happy with life. Her support system supply chain, namely, the father, her parents, her friends and colleagues are all delighted for her about her pregnancy and entirely supportive. Her SEEKING/Desire and CARE/Affiliation systems receive lots of positive strokes, releasing uplifting neurochemicals such as dopamine to parts of her midbrain, providing a wonderful feeling of well-being. The biochemical milieu influencing 'umbilical affect', that is to say the chemical messages passing along the umbilical cord supplying the unborn baby, is likely to be highly supportive too. The interactions in this entire mother–baby environment dynamic all support an optimal feeling of well-being that in the nascent mind of the baby, with no knowledge of 'self' or 'other' at this stage, feels simply omnipotent. The SEEKING/Desire neural network is encouraged to reach out into the world with optimism.

Now let's consider a different scenario. The support supply chain for the mother is not continuously delivering the needed support and there are times when morning sickness and other hormonal changes create problems leading to stress or a degree of depression. The 'umbilical affect' is not continuously good. Possibly there are times when toxaemic reactions threaten. Activation of the maternal GRIEF/Distress system or the FEAR/ Anxiety system may also influence the development of such systems in the unborn baby. According to Donald Hebb's maxim, *neurones that fire together wire together* (Siegel 1999), such an influence at such a time may predispose a baby to increased sensitivity to distress or anxiety after birth. The CARE system is also likely to activate if survival is threatened and images of helpful archetypes may be encountered. The fragile nascent mind may vaguely perceive a sense of goodness and a sense of badness but cannot associate such perceptions with any context at this time. The cultural milieu surrounding a pregnant woman may therefore have an important influence on predispositions towards optimism or pessimism as the new born baby enters the world.

Research in the area of prenatal psychology is limited partly owing to ethical considerations. However, some researchers have explored this area using a variety of techniques regressing patients to pre-birth experiences. As complexity sciences would predict, the earlier in life a tendency or pre-disposition is formed, the more it is likely to reinforce itself as development unfolds, thereby having more pronounced long-term consequences. Trauma or adverse chemical exposure, particularly during the period of rapid brain development is likely to result in significant long-term problems that will not necessarily be relevant for the practice of coaching but falls within the remit of psychiatrists or psychotherapists. A tendency towards deep depression, a sense of meaninglessness, various psychoses and sexual dysfunctions/deviations, violent or self-destructive predispositions, and hysterical reactions and neuroses have been linked to events occurring in the second and third basic perinatal matrices (Grof and Bennett 1993).

Coaches need to be aware that some of the predispositions that their clients may have may be very deep and well beyond techniques for coaching. Recognising these limits is essential and if clients seek advice in such areas, referral to qualified therapeutic practitioners is appropriate. Guidance on recognising clinical conditions may come from the Diagnostic and Statistical Manual of Mental Disorders of the American Psychiatric Association or a clinically qualified Coaching Supervisor.

Less clinically significant dispositions may also originate from early times and coaching interventions should not aim to change these but acknowledge and support such predispositions, possibly helping to provide hypotheses as to why they might have formed in order to enhance the client's self-narrative coherence. Providing a putative external cause for a particular predisposition, whether accurate or not but at least plausible, has the potential, if conveyed with unconditional positive regard, to relieve the cognitive dissonance between 'perceived' self and 'desired' self. Retroflected (internalised) 'blame' can be changed to external projection, releasing energy for more creative and interpersonally connecting possibilities.

- A predisposition to seeing the world through rose-tinted spectacles, so-called 'healthy optimism', or conversely 'depressive realism' may arise from an early age. Both of these predispositions are necessary and valuable for generating multiple perspectives when trying to solve complex problems, but these need to be balanced within a healthy range.
- Vague feelings such as being a stranger in a foreign land or an observer of life rather than a participant may relate to the prenatal milieu. Standing back as an observer of life is a valuable attribute and awareness of such a predisposition may in itself encourage a more participative interaction.
- The ability to empathise with another person's distress or anxieties and activate a calming care response may also be promoted at an early age. The foetus's CARE system may be activated in response to maternal stress in a concept called the 'foetal therapist' (Sills 2009). Some of us may be better able to tune into our own anxieties and anxieties within our environment than others. Recognising and valuing this ability provides a valuable early warning system to any organisation.

Valuing predispositions in this way and providing tentative possible 'causes' may help clients to develop self-awareness, self-acceptance and self-confidence via the generation of more coherent self-narratives. By providing possible circumstances that might have led to predispositions that the client perceives as potentially problematic, the client may then be better able to project 'blame' outwards onto circumstances rather than inwards and thereby alleviate any sense of guilt. Advice on this approach should be sought during coaching supervision.

Chapter 18

Creativity in the cradle

Birth can be a very traumatic process. For the baby the idyllic safe haven of the womb suddenly disappears. Instead of a world that we can vaguely perceive as either good or bad with our limited simplistic polarised thinking, we now encounter a much more complex world containing multiple objects. We need to start the process of making the transition from a physically entwined symbiotic relationship with our mother towards a separate physical self. When our SEEKING/Desire system gets going we become motivated to explore new surrounding objects and we may initially only sense part-objects, being unaware of what constitutes a whole object or person. We may gradually sense our separateness from such objects. We may attribute such objects with qualities such as good or bad with our fragile preliminary perceptual framework. There is likely to be a state of confusion as it is not clear how such objects relate to each other. Our biologically programmed priority for our SEEKING (and CARE) system is to find our *attachment figure* who will provide us with a secure base. Our ACC will be on the lookout for the whites of our mother's eyes within a pattern resembling a face in order to identify our likely provider of warmth, food, reassurance, skin-to-skin contact and the gentle touch that is vital for well-being in our vulnerable state.

Gradually, as our mental capabilities develop, we learn to make connections between the part objects we encounter and the qualities we associate with them. We don't simply sense these things and forget them; we construct internal representations of what we encounter and 'schemas-of-being-with' them, as the American psychiatrist Daniel N. Stern put it (Stern 1995). Such representations and schemas may include visual–spatial images possibly stored as holograms, sounds, feelings and other qualities associated together. By building up a collection of such representations, we begin the process of constructing an internal model of our external world. We gradually learn which of these representations constitute parts of our-self and which constitute parts of something or someone else. We can only start to know ourself in relation to other things. And at this early stage of life the 'other things' mainly relate to forming internal working models of our mother or attachment figure and learning to connect to her emotional management systems.

Within the first two months of life the areas in the cerebral cortex responsible for making and recognising facial and vocal expressions are detectable (Tzourio-Mazoyer *et al.* 2002) and the sense of an 'emergent self' has developed (Stern 2000). The importance of being able to emotionally attune with the mother is not with the aim of forming a dependent relationship but with the aim of encouraging the development of circuitry to support the growing self-agency of the baby, the ability of the infant to make his or her own choices. A careful path, known as 'good enough parenting' needs to be taken by the attachment figure navigating between too much and too little interaction, consistent with 'good-enough' parenting. This interaction between mother and child is a form of right cerebral hemisphere to right cerebral hemisphere interaction and it is the right hemisphere that takes the lead in structuring complex connections at a deep level in the first two years of life (Schore 2009). At this time the child learns much by activating the PLAY system, engaging in turn-taking games with the parent and developing a sense that actions can be directed towards a purpose preceded by intentions.

During these early relational experiences, the linking together of the memory of an experience, the emotional quality of the experience and to which object the experience is linked may not be straightforward. When a parental interaction that is normally good, on a particular occasion is perceived as bad, it is likely that the infant cannot understand the wider context and the possibility that an entity can sometimes be 'good' or sometimes be 'bad' or somewhere in between. Nuanced perspective formation comes much later. When constructing internal representations of the experience it has been suggested by the Scottish psychologist Donald Fairbairn that the infant mind splits the experience in order to process it more easily, making three representations: one representation of a rejecting object, one of an exciting object and one of a relatively satisfying object. It may not be clear that these are representations of the same object. In order to maintain the idea that the outside world is good, the infant mind may associate the badness with a representation of his or her self. If this recurs often, then a pronounced pattern may form of internalising bad aspects of others as if they represent bad aspects of one's self. This can lead later in life to low self-esteem and feelings of guilt (Sills 2009: 61) and subsequent depression. In order to protect against this growing burden of guilt, later on, the defence of projecting this guilt feeling onto others as blame may emerge, that is, negative events are assigned to external causes, reflecting the way the PFC and limbic system are coupled (Seidel *et al.* 2012). This may evoke a feeling of shame in the person on whom the projection lands, setting up the guilt–blame–shame dynamic of defensive strategies which manifest in later life as the victim–persecutor–rescuer dynamic described as the Karpman Drama Triangle (Karpman 1968). The guilt–shame–blame dynamic often seen in life, including working life, can therefore be seen as the operation of psychological defences set up in early life at a time when the mind is unable to handle nuanced attributions according to context. As before, if this defence is used a lot it may become habitual. Coaches need to be on the lookout for this dynamic as they may have rescuer tendencies themselves and get drawn into colluding with the client regarding a perceived persecutor. If this is not handled carefully the coach could become the victim as positions switch.

If we get all the attention and support we need reliably from our attachment figure when we need it we may attribute goodness to this relationship and form what is called a secure attachment, in which the attachment figure is fully emotionally available for our emotional needs. The mother's circuitry for handling distress or anxiety is then available to the baby, helping to model how and when such circuitry can be used and managed. The provision of a safe haven through secure attachment encourages the baby to explore and self-reflect on his or her experiences, deepening the learning process. Research originally conducted by John Bowlby and Mary Ainsworth in the 1950s has shown that those who had the benefit of secure attachment in their early life tend to have balanced perspectives, better ability to reflect on mental processes, better ability to mentalise (perceive what may be going on in someone else's mind) and have fuller, more coherent self-narratives in adult life (Siegel 1999). Secure attachment and the creation of a haven in which the child feels safe and emotionally supported is the basis on which trust is built. Trust is the perception of attuned emotional states and an essential precondition for any authentic relationship. It encourages the child to express his or her self naturally, without having to adapt behaviour in order to get approval. The same is true in a coaching relationship.

If, however, our attachment figure is regularly preoccupied with their own issues so that there is emotional distance, the linking up of emotional systems to provide support may not develop well, so that the baby has to develop more self-reliance. The baby's circuitry for connecting with another's emotional circuitry and their ability to manage their own emotional circuitry then tends to be internally focussed and relatively poorly developed and so they may avoid emotional feelings concerning themselves and others. This is termed an avoidant attachment pattern. As an adult, such individuals tend towards a dismissing state of mind regarding emotions, preferring to handle emotional crises in a quiet space on their own, often not recalling much detail about their early childhood. The lack of recall is likely to be related to lack of self-reflective practice with the parent and lack of association of memories with emotional values. Self-narratives are rather sketchy so that an integrated sense of self over time and in relation to others is not so well developed (Siegel 1999). Once trust is established coaches can support a process of strengthening self-reflection and narrative formation.

Value-laden memories are much easier to recall, so early life emotional experiences and self-reflection in connection with the mother's emotional system are likely to help hasten the emergence from childhood amnesia. Coaches are likely to encounter clients with sketchy recall of their childhood, which may reflect the lack of emotional connection to parents who, for example, may be highly academically gifted, having taken refuge in their heads, but not emotionally available, either because their own systems were not developed with their attachment figures, or as an avoidance of past trauma. Generation to generation transmission of predispositions is common.

If the behaviour of the attachment figure is not consistent, there may be times when they try to connect to the infant's state of mind but in an insensitive intrusive way. On other occasions the emotional states might attune. Because of this lack of predictability, rather than follow an emotional deactivating strategy as above, the ambivalently attached child has emotional mismatches thrust upon them with expectations sometimes met and sometimes thwarted, maximising attention on emotional distress and the relationship. As an adult, such a person tends to become preoccupied by relationships that may be described at length in a rambling fashion, reflecting the unpredictability, and are dominated by emotional concerns about the security of the safe haven. Such a pattern can also reproduce itself from one generation to the next.

A further attachment pattern has been described, termed 'disorganised' or 'disoriented', with more problematic relational patterns. Here, the child becomes disoriented because the attachment figure, who should be a source of comfort and support, experiences paradoxical sentiments summarised by the paradoxical injunction 'come here and go away' (Siegel 1999). Furthermore, the parent may be the source of the fear by adopting frightening, threatening or abusive behaviour with the child. Trauma may also be experienced, and swings in parental behaviour may be related to such issues as alcoholism. This form of insecure attachment leads to long-term difficulties with regard to developing a coherent mind and predisposes towards a controlling and aggressive adult personality style.

Object Relations and Attachment Theory have illuminated the importance that early interactions have in creating long-term behavioural tendencies. During the first year of life the child has to come to terms with the sudden loss of the sense of being unified and omnipotent, to finding his or her self as having apparent boundaries with the possibility of separation from all life-support structures creating obvious anxieties. Splitting up the world to process it, projection defences and denial defences may have their origin at this early time: 'Defences used at this stage are aimed at changing not what is happening, but rather the perception of what is happening, in a primitive attempt to bypass anxiety' (Gomez 1997). If in later life we develop more sophisticated ways of handling our anxieties, falling back on these primitive methods should not be necessary, although they are often unconsciously utilised, particularly if stressed, when one tends to regress to using earlier more deeply embedded working models.

You may be asking how relevant any of this is to the world of your clients. Perhaps you think that CEOs will all come with a history of a secure attachment pattern. This is unlikely and coaches need to take special care not to remodel pre-existing insecure attachment patterns by, for example, not being sufficiently available for their clients because of their own preoccupations. In such situations transference from the past is likely to destroy the chance of a trusting coaching safe haven. The distinguished psychotherapeutically trained leadership professor Manfred Kets de Vries, director of INSEAD Global Leadership Centre has a lot of experience with CEOs of major organisations. In his book, *The Leader on the Couch*, he provides many examples of corporate leaders whose early childhood experiences explain their later leadership styles. Their undoubted qualities often come with other predispositions such as a range of psychological defences that are remnants of early adaptations to cope with situations that no longer exist. We will explore some of these further in the next chapter.

The take-away messages are:

- Early life experiences with attachment figure(s) (parents or carers) contribute to establishing the sensitivity of the different emotional motivation systems and our ability to manage them. Circuitry set up at this stage tends to have an enduring effect in later life but, with awareness and commitment, modifications can be made.
- The creation of a safe haven in which trust can be built is an important precondition to enable authentic rather than adaptive self-expression. The development of a 'false self' is often seen among organisational leaders who may have poor connections with their emotions and 'gut feelings' by preferentially developing only their left hemisphere world.
- Ego defence strategies set up at this early stage include splitting, projecting and denial and these form the basis for victim–persecutor–rescuer roles seen as primitive defence strategies in later life, particularly when contextual and nuanced perception is compromised by anxiety or stress.
- Coaches should be aware of these processes in order to form hypotheses about the possible reasons for what they observe, how this may influence coaching intervention strategies and to provide 'place holders' in the personal narratives of their clients to strengthen narrative coherence. The possibility of transference of past relationship patterns into the coaching relationship needs to be monitored, particularly if these have potential to jeopardise trust.

Chapter 19

Nurture in the nursery

If creativity in the cradle can be summarised as the process of preparing the foundations for trust and perceptions, then nurture in the nursery is about preparing the foundations for personal power and self-agency.

Sigmund Freud derived much of his interest in the quest for self-autonomy and personal power from experiences in his own family setting. Born as Sigismund Schlomo Freud in Moravia in 1856, Freud grew up in an unusually complicated family setting. Freud had two half-brothers, Emanuel and Philipp, from his father's first marriage. Emanuel was older than Sigmund's mother, Amalia, and Philipp one year younger. One of Emanuel's sons John, that is, Sigmund's nephew, was his playmate and one year older than himself (Gay 2006). To Sigmund it seemed that Philipp had taken the place of his father in his mother's affections and later as a child he speculated that Philipp rather than his father may have been responsible for his younger sister Anna, born when he was two years old. He later revealed to his colleague and friend Wilhelm Fliess that his psychoanalysis had revealed that his libido towards his mother was awakened after seeing her naked at an early age. Psychoanalysis also revealed that he had welcomed the death of his younger brother Julius, born seventeen months after himself with 'malevolent wishes and genuine childish jealousy' (Gay 2006). It is with this background, together with Freud's interest in the work of Charles Darwin on competition for survival, that Freud later developed his theories of sibling rivalry and infant sexuality, including the Oedipus complex in which male rivalry with the father arises for the sexual attentions of the mother. Freud also is known for highlighting that many psychological processes operate below the level of conscious awareness. A recent perspective on these theories contends that, when the developing child reaches the stage of realising that his attachment figure, usually the mother, is having a sexual relationship with someone else that excludes the child, the child needs to make sense of the mother's intentions and motivations as this impacts upon the quality of the child's emotional connection with the attachment figure. This involves engaging in fantasy as a way of trying to make meaning from experiences in order to create and update internal working models of one's parents. 'The child's own emotions and imaginative narratives that he or she constructs to make sense of the world or to maintain a positive sense of identity become included in unconscious "working models" as they develop' (Knox 2003: 123). Memory can become fantasy and fantasy can become memory. Fantasy can in this situation be seen as a form of defence, activated when the special attachment bond feels threatened by others and, in order to keep the mother 'good', the father or siblings are portrayed as rivals and therefore 'bad'. This is a necessary part of the process to move away from what was called by the Scottish psychologist Ronald Fairbairn the primary narcissism of immature dependency upon the mother towards a sense of separate self-identity. Remaining in this narcissistic state enhances the infant's expectation that other people exist for the purpose of recognising his or her needs and satisfying them. If the mother or others respond to this by fulfilling these needs efficiently the progress to the mature interdependent form of narcissism characterised by increased respect for and empathy with others is not promoted:

> The early years are characterized by the tension between that grandiose self-image and the helplessness that is the true state of childhood. Inadequate resolution of that tension produces negative feelings (shame, humiliation, rage, envy, spitefulness, a desire for vengeance) and a hunger for personal power and status.
>
> (Kets de Vries 2006: 26)

Attuning emotionally with 'good enough' parents and engaging in self-reflection and emotional modulation is important as a means for resolving the tension in these early years and converting primary narcissism to constructive narcissism.

Constructive narcissists are not preoccupied with a personal quest for power; they have a vision and sense of purpose related towards creating something of value for the wider community. They take advice from others, value cooperation and do not regress to blame games as a form of defence (Kets de Vries 2006). In contrast, if this conversion is not made well, the result is a reactive narcissist who tends to feel inadequate deep down, bitter, angry, depressive, with feelings of emptiness surfacing from time to time. Their insecurities are managed by fantasies of self-importance and grandiosity; a sense of being special together with a sense of entitlement and a need for admiration. There may be arrogance, envy of others and a lack of empathetic understanding. A number of examples of business leaders who fall into this category and the consequences of such leadership on their companies has been well described (Kets de Vries 2006). Reactive narcissistic tendencies feature as part of the psychological make-up of many corporate or political leaders, often in combination with other psychological patterns linked to being controlling, paranoid or antisocial.

Other parental influences on the path to selfhood set up the conditions predisposing towards many types of behaviour seen in the corporate world. Parents who do not give their children sufficient room to explore and become over-controlling, using shame and guilt to influence behaviour, are likely to create future managers who micro-manage, are inflexible with regard to rules, impede creativity, and adopt ingratiating upward management relationships and despotic downward management relationships. A further variant of this occurs if parents are highly intrusive and constantly watching their children and also controlling them with shame and humiliation: the paranoid management style. Instead of developing well-contextualised and nuanced internal working models, such managers may tend towards earlier polarised models, splitting the world into good and evil. Blame games become a habitual pattern for defending themselves by projecting guilt onto others or going into denial. Feelings of helplessness are combatted by indulging in fantasies of grandiosity or persecution.

Where a disorganised or disoriented attachment pattern has been established, the necessary 'downloads' for empathetic connection with others, upon which trust is built, may be missing altogether as well as mental models for how to behave ethically in the world. If such individuals make it into management positions in later life, often attracted by the power associated with such positions, then they may well become charming compulsive liars who form shallow relationships and use people for their own purposes remorselessly. Kets de Vries has observed that such individuals often hide behind the smokescreen of a restructuring strategy to give the appearance of strong creative management. This style has been called the antisocial management style.

These aggressive leadership styles in which autonomy has been achieved by creative fantasies hyperactivating the LUST/Sexual power system contrast with managers with detached dispositions who similarly find relating to others difficult, and avoid emotional situations by using creative fantasy to engage in introspective thinking within their own world. These managers have made the transition from primary narcissism to selfhood by self-reliant means rather than with the support of their preoccupied attachment figure's emotional framework. Spending so much time cognitively thinking tends to produce great specialists, academics and original thinkers but not charismatic motivating leaders. Their LUST/Sexual power system tends to be hypo-activated so that instead of aggressive or sexually motivated interactions with others, they are conflict avoidant and also avoid emotional contact with others as a preference.

Where managers have grown up in family situations in which they were made to feel that they were the cause of things going wrong, a build-up of guilt, as mentioned before, is likely to lead to a depressive management disposition characterised by a self-deprecating style, activating the creation of an internal working model of a saboteur through projective fantasy and generating a pessimistic outlook.

In summary, the seeds for future management style may be sown early in life at a time when the basic emotional motivational systems are laying down connection pathways whose strength reflects the need for each system within the family of origin before the age of five. Also configured at this time are internal working models of parents and interactions with and between parents. These internal working models provide sets of behaviours linked to value systems which will be called upon to help interpret experiences as the child moves out from the home to start exploring the wider world. Although the neurological pathways configured at this stage are relatively enduring, neuroplastic remodelling in adults to modulate their early predispositions is a possibility if there is a genuine desire for change as attachment styles have been found to change over time with appropriate experiences. Psychodynamic coaching and therapeutic approaches based on Freudian theory, together with concurrent development of emotional intelligence provide methods for doing this.

Psychodynamic coaching aims to make unconscious processes conscious as an initial strategy of raising awareness. Freudian theory has uncovered many ways that the self, or ego, protects itself or significant others in order to understand the world in a meaningful way. When anxiety is provoked, a number of different types of defence mechanisms unconsciously come into play to cause behavioural changes. Adaptive defence mechanisms include: avoiding your own feelings by helping others or becoming engrossed in a diversionary task; using humour as a diversionary tactic; displacement activities that provide a sense of achieving something while ignoring the 'elephant in the room'; engaging in rituals; over-identifying with the organisation or leader giving up our own values, and spending time preferentially with others who provide a receptive ear, tea and sympathy.

An alternative set of defences include denying that there is an 'elephant in the room'; detaching our self from our feelings; post-hoc rationalisation of why an action that failed would have been a bad thing anyway (the sour grapes rationalisation); projecting our own feelings as if they originate from someone else; complaining to disguise a feeling of inadequacy; and passive aggression, that is, not doing something deliberately in order to create a problem.

Psychodynamic coaching involves identifying when and where such defences are used by a manager or organisation, examining whether there is a good basis for trust to flourish in a relationship, examining whether family dynamics are reproduced in the workplace and assessing whether the conversion to constructive narcissism has successfully been made (Peltier 2001). The psychodynamically trained coach will utilise transference and counter-transference techniques to assess what is occurring in the emotional space between coach and coachee. Transference is about the coach picking up a sense of the internal working models that the coachee is using in trying to form a view of the coach. These internal working models will originate from past experience; for example, will the coachee see the coach as paternal and therefore call up the stored model of his own father, warts and all? This saves a lot of mental effort in creating a new accurately detailed internal model of the coach, and by using a few clues for reminiscence, a whole set of assumptions can be called up and projected onto the coach. The coach for his or her part does the opposite, counter-transference, noting which internal working models are called forth by reminiscences provided by the coachee. By allowing the interaction to evolve according to the natural course preferred by the coachee, the coach notes the process in flow and the associated evoked feelings and considers whether this process has parallels to what occurs between the coachee and other people. These techniques enable a hypothesis to be formed as to the motivational systems and working models being used. By exploring this hypothesis the coach and coachee are able to develop increased awareness of behavioural patterns and customise interventional strategies for trying to modify them. This is easier said than done and both parties need to be aware that the construction of new more appropriate internal working models and re-routing motor activity pathways to these new models is a time and energy consuming project involving cognitive dissonance and its associated confusion.

When changing to a new model seems not to be taking place, some may call this 'resistance'. The coachee, however, may call it an unconvincing risk–benefit assessment and poor realisation plan. These both need to be addressed if real commitment to making the investment needed for reconstructing internal working models and re-routing behaviour is to be achieved. To support change, peer-group workshops may be considered to create a learning community and provide a supportive transition space in which change can occur (Kets de Vries 2006). This reduces cognitive dissonance and improves feelings of social acceptance.

Chapter 20

Socialisation at school

During the 'Competence' stage children acquire and develop a range of skills and talents, putting these to use to solve problems, draw pictures, write messages and make things. Sporting and creative activities broaden the range of capabilities. Talent recognition and evoked positive feedback from parents and teachers when these talents are demonstrated builds self-confidence and encourages further development. If nascent talents are not recognised and developed, low self-esteem and demotivation results. The phase called 'Fidelity' is concerned with establishing a self-identity and identifying which of the vast range of roles one is exposed to fits well with the developing self-image. Thus, this phase is concerned with resolution of one of the major identity crises that one has to deal with. It is a time of major reorganisation of neural networks in the brain with a significant reduction in grey matter through neuronal pruning and a significant increase in interconnecting white matter (Cozolino 2006: 44). Up to this time the brain has remained relatively flexible so that it may be reconfigured quickly to learn new skills and build new internal working models. Starting from the back of the brain and progressing towards the front until about 25 years of age, myelination (encasing neurons in a fatty sheath) takes place to increase the speed of impulse transmission. Frontal lobes retain flexibility for longest. The left and right hemispheres become better connected by thickening of the corpus callosum and links to the hippocampus improve the integration of memory into decision making. Risk-taking behaviour, necessary for exploring new ways of being and moving out from the security of the parental home, tends to peak at around the age of 14–17. Dopamine sensitivity, which is high during this risk-taking phase in order to provide a bigger payoff from risk taking, then reduces. The prosocial hormone oxytocin gains more influence, increasing the importance of social connections. The brain's reward circuitry is reorganised as rewards come increasingly from friends and new attachment figures and less so from parental influences as the process of becoming more independent gathers pace. Therefore, tensions may be generated within the family of origin, particularly in those turbulent teenage years as internal working models are all changing, leading to confusion and exaggerated behavioural self-expression. Significant relationships associated with these stages include those made at school, peers and role models. This represents a shift in emotional investment from relationships of the past to relationships for the future.

We enter the first of these stages with a limited number of internal working models of key characters who have played a part in our lives up to that point, such as our parents, other adults, other children and of course an internal working model of ourself. We may in fact have a number of models of each of these role types according to the variety of experiences we have had with these categories of people. In addition, associated with each model we will have 'schemas-of-being-with', which add qualities to the relationship such as the type of emotions experienced when in contact with that particular 'model', our bodily posture and gestures that are used in that relationship, and whether our body is relaxed or tense in their presence. We then use these models and schemas-of-being-with to navigate our way through our expanding world as we go to school, using clues from our experiences when interacting with new faces to help us select an appropriate set of behaviours and gestures.

A Canadian student of Erik Erikson, Eric Berne (1910–1970) was concerned with interpersonal relationships and communication. He developed the idea that a particular consistent pattern of feeling and experience directly relates to a corresponding consistent pattern of behaviour. He called such a particular consistent pattern an 'ego-state', using an idea of another Freudian psychologist, Paul Federn. Today we might instead use the idea of image schemas representing the basic framework for an ego state without specific content and internal working models (IWMs) with their associated 'schemas-of-being-with' (complexes with content). The three main types of image schema in early life are parents, adults and children. Berne was interested in how these types of 'ego states' interact with each other, or to use his terminology, transacted. Analysing such transactions has resulted in a psychological approach to looking at relationships called *Transactional Analysis*. We probably all recognise that parents speak to children in a certain way which is different from how they normally address each other or other adults. They may say things that nurture the child in a caring way, or set boundaries/constraints for controlling the child. Similarly a child will respond in a different manner to another child as compared to its parents. If a parent addresses a child from the IWM of a parent calling up its associated behavioural schemas-of-being-with-a-child, that is, from a parent ego state to the child ego state, then the response from the child would normally be expected to be from their IWM of a child and schema-of-being-with-a-parent. It would be unexpected if the response came from an IWM of an adult (or parent) and associated schema-of-being-with-an-adult (or parent). The expected situation (parent to child responding with child to parent) is known as a *complementary transaction*, whereas the unexpected example (parent to child responding with adult to adult) is of a *crossed transaction*. Berne found that so long as a transaction remains complementary, then communication can continue indefinitely, whereas when it is crossed, a break of communication occurs and one or both parties will need to shift ego-states (IWMs) in order for communication to be re-established. Conversely, to escape from an adult to adult discussion because you are not winning the argument, you may default to addressing the other person from your 'parent' IWM and schema-of-being-with a child, for example: 'I don't care what you say you are not doing it and that is final'. This approach may then activate their 'child' IWM and elicit a corresponding response!

Later in life a third type of transaction is seen in which what is said (words alone) and what is meant (words plus tones, facial expressions and gestures) have different meanings. This is called an *ulterior or duplicitous transaction*: the words used may have one cognitive meaning which conforms to an adult to adult transaction, but the vocal tones and gestures reveal a psychological intent which is often more of a parent to child transaction or child to parent. When used we are psychologically invoking a shift out of the adult ego state with the intention of inviting the responder to shift into the ego state of child (if a superior position over them is intended) or to the ego state of parent (if help from them is being elicited). The parent and child ego states are subdivided into controlling parent and nurturing parent, and free child and adapted child. Vocal tones and gestures condition the type of ego response being sought. In this way, psychological power politics can be revealed by TA which also considers whether communications are supportive (containing so-called positive strokes), negative (containing negative strokes) or contain distortions of reality such as overgeneralisations or partial omissions known as *discounts* (e.g. negative stroke: 'you made a mistake'; discount: 'you are careless').

Transactional Analysis includes evaluating how groups of people structure their time. When groups form with no plans concerning how to structure the way that they will interact, a degree of discomfort arises that can be resolved in one of six ways: withdrawal from the group; engaging in rituals such as introductions; talking about events (particularly pastimes) but not engaging in action; engaging in activities; engaging in psychological games and engaging in authentic interpersonal communication. Psychological games are played when two or more individuals in the group exchange ulterior transactions and distort or skew information exchange to discount it. Berne popularised Transactional Analysis in his book *The Games People Play*, published in 1964. In contrast to game playing, authentic communication between group members does not discount information and a psychological subtext is not implicitly included.

Recognising that the human mind has a yearning for structure and is adept at meaning making and narrative generation, Berne developed the idea that early in life we generate a life plan or 'drama' for ourselves that has a particular outcome. This is known as a *script* and the outcome is called the *payoff*. This acts as a road map, setting a subconscious default route to guide our actions in life towards a particular destination. It is a road map to help us survive by following a route we are encouraged to believe will be the safest one to take. It provides a default route and destination in the absence of a well-developed sense of self-agency. The script may have formed to some degree in the nursery years and is reinforced by parents repeatedly but is capable of being changed. The script is conditioned by many messages, implicit or explicit, from the parent telling the child how to behave or do things and delivering value judgements, and together with early life experiences impacts on our developing sense of self. Messages may come from all three ego states of either parent addressed to the different ego states of the child. Apart from script conditioning messages from parents, the expression of certain types of feelings in childhood may be met in the family setting with parental disapproval, whereas other types of feelings may be rewarded with approval, thus promoting the substitution of an authentic feeling with an inauthentic feeling, such as don't get scared by bullies, fight them. Fighting is then labelled as a positive behaviour that receives praise and the child may subconsciously set up circumstances with an increased likelihood of fighting so that praise is received. The bravado is a 'show', covering up a 'disowned' feeling of fear instead of acknowledging the fear and managing it.

Using inauthentic feelings in adult life to garner positive strokes is called 'racketeering' in TA. Racketeering reinforces the default script that you have constructed about yourself, based on parental conditioning, which encouraged false attribution of feelings of grandiosity or guilt to your own internal working model at a time when your perception could not handle the full context. This generates false self-beliefs that are likely to be self-limiting as they are based on discounted feedback and false attributions. In order to move away from the default script, Gestalt Therapy techniques encourage a coachee to re-contact the feelings he or she experienced as a child in the family unit by recreating scenes reminiscent of the childhood situation. Volunteer actors are asked to enact key roles in the family setting by using evocative phrases, gestures, vocal tones and actions. By setting up conditions in which the family dynamics are remembered, re-exposure to the feelings and thinking processes enables unconscious patterns of behaviour to become conscious. Once in this conscious state the road map route plan can be redrawn by exercising autonomy, thinking through preferred behaviours, values, processes and associations so that internal working models and schemas-of-being-with are reconfigured to meet current rather than past needs.

So far we have looked at the three main character models encountered in our early childhood. As we move out into the wider world we will encounter a diverse range of people and find that none of our models fit what we experience. Our surveillance service in the ACC will then register cognitive dissonance, triggering the construction of a new IWM or 'schema-of-being-with'. During this stage of our life we will construct an enormous number of such models and schemas to create a pageant of personalities that could be categorised for simplicity according to the range of 'archetypes' often associated with Carl Jung's psychological theories. We may have a category of 'Mother' in which to put our collection of working models linked by common features such as a schema-of-being-with containment: someone who will contain or modulate our emotions and care for us. Perhaps our nursery nurse or early school teachers may evoke these qualities. From the types of people we meet, the myths and fairy tales we hear that provoke our imagination, the characters in films and on the TV, we expand our pageant of personality IWMs and decide which of these provide us with useful role models for our behaviour.

There has been much debate as to what an 'archetype' actually is. Originally this idea seems to relate to Plato's idea concerning 'transcendental forms' that constitute reality. More recently, the Jungian psychologist James Hillman has described archetypes as metaphors that 'evoke feelings and images, and touch on themes that are universal and part of our human heritage' (Bolen 1989). A large number of such metaphors have been described, including the following archetypes: the King, the Warrior, the Innocent, the Orphan, the Seeker, the Magician, the Lover, the Caregiver, the Destroyer, the Creator, the Sage, the Fool (Rowan 2005). Other cultures seem to have similar concepts such as a range of deities embodying differing aspects of a possible human persona. It seems that individuals raised in a particular culture are not constrained to the archetypes of only that culture (Grof and Bennett 1993: 161). These abstract metaphors for common universal principles may form an imprint in our minds, captured as image schemas, IWMs and schemas-of-being-with, representing our internalisation of archetypal forms.

Another observation put forward by Carl Jung was that people seem to either be extraverts or introverts. Extraverts tend to thrive in more dynamic environments that provide them with external stimulation and they tend to be more optimistic and outgoing. Introverts tend to prefer quieter spaces in which they are able to generate internal stimulation from their own thoughts and imagination. They tend not to be as optimistic as extraverts and are less inclined to initiate approaches to people they don't know. The reason for this difference is not fully known, although early life experience may have encouraged the setting up of such behavioural preferences and it may have a genetic component. Relatively few people fall towards the extremes of the spectrum. Genetic predispositions and/or early life experiences will influence whether your brain develops neural networks that direct your conscious awareness to your outer world or towards your inner world. If as a baby you have lots of positive interactions with other people, animals or things that capture your attention, neural connections to facilitate interaction with the external environment are likely to be developed more strongly. On the other hand, if as a baby a lot of time was spent alone developing imagination, then neural pathways in this inner space would develop more strongly.

Hans Eysenck's 1967 theory was that introverts have a lower threshold for arousal in a system in their lower brain region called the reticular activating system. As their own imagination provides on-going entertainment, they seem to need little external stimulation to reach the arousal threshold necessary to perform well in cortical processing of sensory information compared to extraverts who need more arousal to operate effectively. Conversely, in noisy environments with high levels of arousal, extraverts process sensory information more effectively although if arousal levels get too high performance drops off. The phenomena may be linked to the release of dopamine or noradrenaline but no theory as yet fully explains the observations. The upshot of this is that each of the cerebral hemisphere's meta-functional polarities may develop in an introverted or extroverted guise. This is the basis for the eight 'Jungian' personality types. Practically, it is useful to know which type is yours so that you can manage your arousal level into the zone of optimal performance. In the same way that introversion or extraversion develop according to predispositions and/or early life experiences, the same seems to be true for the cortical functions. Early life experiences developing logical thinking and verbal communication, for example, will tend to develop the 'CEO' functions which over time are likely to be reinforced as the preferred evaluation mode, rather than the multimodal reflective evaluation mode of the 'HRD' functions (or of course, vice versa). Early lifetime exposure to creative play and imaginative stories or fantasies may progressively favour the CD functions as the main mode for interpreting the world as opposed to the direct sensory mode preferred by the COO functions. Whichever of these four develops most strongly is known as the dominant function, expressed in an introvert or extravert guise. For extraverts this means their dominant mode of cognitive function is always apparent to others as this is their preferred mode when interacting with other people. For introverts their dominant mode is not as obvious to others as it is used in their preferred inner world. More obvious in the case of introverts is their secondary function, so they are often viewed by others as favouring a role that in fact they do not: they may be seen as being more logical than intuitive, for example, when in fact the reverse is true.

During our school days the way in which we gather and interpret data will show increasing diversity. We will increase the range of our possible personae by engaging in a range of activities, giving us many mental models of how to behave and skill sets, so that we can see where our talents lie. It is important that we are guided internally in this process and not used as an extension of our parents, providing them with another chance to fulfil their dreams and ambitions. It is in any case likely to be a period with much role confusion as different possibilities are experimented with while social pressures to conform mount. In order to build confidence, positive feedback from others is needed.

The goal of this phase of life is to clarify self-identity as one leaves the family home to forge a life for one's self. The experimentation with different identities starts to decline as the favoured personae are put into practice in the next phase of making one's way in the world. Exactly when one reaches this position of clarity over one's self-identity in this stage is variable depending on how many opportunities for exploration are available. Further education at university for example extends this phase of experimentation, delaying the point at which self-identity needs to be clear. As mentioned previously, the connection pathways, particularly at the front of the cortex, are kept relatively flexible until clarification of one's self-identity is achieved. After this time myelination occurs, improving the speed and efficiency of cognitive operations.

Coaching practice

The goal of coaching is not to go on an archaeological dig into the past but to concentrate on the future. However, as the past and the future are parts of a continuum, it is useful to get a sense of the current set-up. Coaches may wish to form a view as to what personality preferences may have evolved during their clients' adolescent phase as a working hypothesis, or you may wish to raise the client's awareness of such preferences by asking questions along the following lines:

- Can you identify key 'archetypes' or role models that imprinted themselves in your mind during your school days? How do these manifest themselves today?
- When do you use parent–child transactions? When do you notice ulterior or duplicitous transactions?
- Do you have a sense of having a life plan?
- In what circumstances do you feel that you are engaging in authentic interpersonal communication? In what circumstances are other types of interaction apparent? How can you communicate more authentically?
- How do archetypal models influence your powers of imagination?

Chapter 21

Liberation through life

Once a reasonable sense of self-identity has been achieved in the preceding phase you are ready to make your own way in the world without dependence upon your family of origin. Your SEEKING/Desire motivational system will promote a drive towards finding rewards to enable you to live, so it is likely that you will have to be able to convince an employer that you are sufficiently clear about yourself and why you are worth employing. You will have to tread the fine line between revealing what makes you stand out from the crowd in a useful way and how well you have been 'normalised' so that you will fit into any organisation. Your SEEKING/Desire motivational system is also likely to encourage you to find a new attachment person who will complement your range of talents and be able to care for you, modulating emotional turbulence when required. Once self-identity is clear it is easier to make valid long-term commitments. At the same time the LUST/Sexual motivational system is likely to promote the quest for finding a sexual mate. For various reasons, what is required from your attachment figure and what is required from your sexual mate may or may not be found in the same person. Once in a relationship, your CARE motivational system is likely to motivate the establishment of a new home and safe haven in which you can recuperate from the stresses and strains of everyday life to manage your FEAR/Anxiety system. The GRIEF/Loss motivational system may be active, driving feelings of missing the support of the original family home and maternal care and containment.

At the cognitive level, construction of internal working models may now focus on companies and organisations, their value systems and schemas-of-being-with them. These may not be entirely congruent with your own IWMs and there will be a process of finding which IWMs in your repertoire fit best in the corporate culture, minimising cognitive dissonance by adopting roles requiring the least amount of compromise. The complexity of meaning-making frameworks will evolve as one advances from the opportunist frame, through the frames of diplomat, expert and achiever, in order to find one's self as an individualist (Fisher *et al.* 2003). Advancing to the trans-formational frames of strategist and alchemist will require an awareness of the functions of the mind, in-process action inquiry, mindfulness skills and a radical reappraisal of existing meaning-making frameworks.

On the basis of a well-established safe haven, good self-management skills and a comprehensive set of useful working models for social inter-actions, success in gaining acceptance, and feeling valued enables the CARE motivational system to promote behaviour to guide the next generation. Observing how children develop is a source of wonder, joy and insight, enabling you to see your own development in a different context and from a different level. Guiding children into their own adulthood with 'good-enough' parenting provides a full spectrum of emotional and cognitive experiences and if they are successfully guided towards finding their own authentic self-identity, pride is a great parental reward. Once they leave home and assert their own autonomy your GRIEF/Loss system may activate, as part of you goes off on its own journey.

Coaching support to help smooth the way through these life stages may involve constellation work in which neutral volunteer actors personify key figures from the family or business environment, so that subconscious aspects of personal relationships can be represented on a safe stage and rearranged so that they can be explored within conscious awareness (Horn and Brick 2005). The process of constructing and then modifying how actors are physically placed in relationship to one another, incorporating relevant gestures and phrases from past recollections is helpful for bringing into awareness hidden relationship dynamics. It is also likely that somewhere in the middle part of life the compromises made in order to be socially accepted into an organisation will become less acceptable as your sense of self and your values conflict more and more with those of your peers and organ-isation. You may hit another crisis of purpose or meaning as your internal reward system readjusts, much as it did during adolescence, so that neurochemical rewards are derived from different environmental sources. As with all such personal crises, your infrastructure tells you that there is a mismatch between what you are doing and what your value system values, inviting you to take up the challenge of doing something about it before serious adverse consequences to health and well-being are experienced. Transpersonal coaching is well suited to engaging with such circumstances to enable a creative and more congruent alignment to be achieved between an emergent purpose and life activities (Whitmore and Einzig 2010).

Connecting with clients at a deeper existential level in the latter part of this stage of life is likely to play an important part in contemplating life's purpose and reflecting on one's part in it. Transpersonal coaching aims to address this need, built on the foundation of earlier stages of development. Experiential learning is essential now rather than conceptual learning in order to cultivate 'framework-free' direct core-to-core interpersonal connections. A number of approaches to this spiritual dimension have been developed, including psychosynthesis, Core Process Psychotherapy and Jungian trans-personal individuation (Rowan 2005).

At such a time, the business, professional or family interests that have dominated your activities since leaving formal education no longer captivate you in the way they once did. As your mind integrates more and more life experiences into meaningful but possibly inexpressible patterns, an increase in contemplative reflection may emerge as larger than life questions are pondered upon, not so much academically but existentially. This represents a shift from the task-focussed activities centred on the left cerebral hemisphere towards the multimodal parallel processing activities characteristic of the right cerebral hemisphere. This transition, which follows from years of life experience and developing expertise, is hard to express, and can be misunderstood by some managers as a lack of clarity and goal orientation. Thus, the wisdom many senior managers start to access as their right hemisphere becomes once again more dominant may be side-lined and ignored by task-focussed thinkers delivering short-term results. Our ability to integrate contemplative thinkers into organisations and society appears to be diminishing with time as we focus on short-term goals more and more.

As a metaphor for contemplative development, imagine that you are on a mountain, perhaps one with a conical peak. Imagine that at the base level of the cone, where it meets the plain, there are a number of villages each with unique characteristics and traditions. An aspiring individual in a village may look up to the peak on a clear day, and he or she sees a path to the summit; let's call it a line of development. Each village has its own development perspective. Suppose, as a foreign explorer you wish to ascend to the summit very gradually, taking in all perspectives by taking a spiral route, round and round the mountain, crossing the development lines seen by the different villages again and again, each time at a higher level, providing an altered perspective from the previous crossing. There are many paths to the summit, all with different perspectives, but you resist the temptation for a quick peak experience as it would limit your exposure to the rich variety of perspectives from different parts of the mountain. You want to ascend slowly, taking all perspectives in, savouring them individually. As you witness all the scenes, encounter all the people, all the animals and plant life and soil types, rock structures, air textures and shadows and light patterns in your circumambulation of the mountain, you begin to see the interplay and harmony of all of this complexity. You see the ecosystems and support structures, kindnesses and cruelties, and seasonal patterns of life and death. Having taken all of this in you can now ascend to the summit from where you can gaze in all directions, seeing for the first time how it all fits together down each of the slopes and across the plain. You see the unity and interplay of all that you have experienced as seemingly independent events. It is a moment of realisation in which your journey makes sense in the pageant of the bigger picture. Way off in the distance, shrouded in mists, you perceive the vague image of a much bigger peak; you smile, then laugh, then cry and slowly descend with tears rolling down your cheeks. Back on the plain, you decide to herd oxen in the direction of the mist-shrouded peak.

Ploughing your own furrow may be very tempting at this later stage of life. There is less concern for garnering social approval and more concern with seeing one's life as part of the on-going flow of human enterprise. If efforts are made to harness the wisdom of the individuals who have reached this stage of development, organisations and society may have much to gain. The wisdom of elders who may be more able to see patterns, causal relationships and the inherent common ground between seemingly disparate things was once prized highly in many cultures. Materialist pressures to achieve short-term gains may have comprised this at significant cost.

Coaches with substantial life experience can be excellent guides for clients facing the turbulence of business life. Coaches who have developed an understanding of the nature of the mind and mindfulness skills will be able to recognise how their clients are using their cerebral cortex (Part 1), their felt sense of embodied emotions (Part 2) and recognise past adaptations that have become habitual patterns (Part 3). From this recognition, possibly by tuning in to the parallel processes evoked via activated mirror neurons and the processes of mentalisation, coaches will be able to use interactive techniques as outlined in this book to estimate where their clients are in their development journeys. Then, by raising their clients' awareness of where they seem to be and how they seem to have got there, a process of co-enquiry can unfold to reveal the path towards releasing the authentic potential of each client. Coaches familiar with working at this level are likely to be well placed to work with teams and organisations (Part 4) to maximise the release of collective potential too.

Part 4

Relationships with others

Part 4 considers how we interact with others. Insights into interpersonal dynamics help us to assess options for achieving optimal creativity and collective performance.

Chapter 22

Interpersonal contact and connections

The German philosopher Martin Buber observed that when we speak with others we can either adopt the attitude of viewing the other person as an object or we can adopt the attitude of viewing the other person as a far more complex being with depth and with whom we are ultimately connected in spirit (*geistigen Wesenheiten*). He used the German word pairs *Ich–Es* to denote subject to object relationships and *Ich–Du* to denote subject to subject relationships. We tend to adopt an objective (left hemisphere) attitude regarding others during our casual everyday experience, whereas we adopt a more intimate subjective attitude in close relationships, and this world can only be entered with our whole being (Buber 1923). All *real* living, he observed, is a meeting of minds without barriers. It is a relationship of considerable depth, exposing us to powerful emotional currents.

Our casual everyday interaction may be characterised as communicating from behind a 'mask' according to a role selected according to our normalising social conditioning. This enables us to match particular internal working models of particular roles to the prevailing social circumstances. This is essentially an adaptation to enable us to survive and thrive in social situations. When operating in this way, psychological processes below the level of our conscious awareness cause us to view the world through interpretive frameworks shaped by past experience. From the merest whiff of a familiar pattern, our brain can fill in the rest of the pattern using images from our memory banks before we see the complete picture. We then may project attributes onto others because of some subtle reminiscence of a person we once knew. We may even transfer the whole personality of someone from our past onto someone we have just met and adopt date-expired ways of interacting with them.

For one reason or another, how we interact with others is heavily influenced by social conditioning and subconscious processes that prevent us from really making contact with another mind.

Imagine meeting someone on a one-to-one basis for the first time during the coffee break at a conference. Our adult to adult transactions will tend to follow the rituals dictated by social convention: 'Hello, my name is Azmat, how are you?' etc. The reply normally accords with the ritual 'Fine thanks' irrespective of whether it is true or not. Barriers are respected as trust and intimacy have not been established. Following ritual we may move on to talking about the weather or pastimes, such as places we have travelled to or people we mutually know. Following such social conventions keeps things safe and superficial until sufficient common ground has been established.

If, however, we have approached the individual we have just met with an ulterior motive in mind we may bypass parts of this risk-mitigation strategy, moving on to game playing using duplicitous communication, trying to hook the other person into our game. We may flirt or use a double entendre to create suggestive overtones in our communication. Our LUST/Sexual motivation system may be viewing our interlocutor as a potential sex object. Physical intimacy may be on the cards, or we may have a habitual pattern of using flirtation or humour or projections as a defensive pattern with no real intention of following through. Whatever the reason, if we are not connecting with the person at a genuine level without games or projections we will not begin to develop the emotional space based on trust and authenticity that genuine contact requires.

Genuine personal development, growth and creativity do not come about from interactions of this type. If you or your clients adopt this form of interaction during coaching, nothing new will be created because no real meeting of minds will have occurred. In Gestalt counselling and therapy a useful model of the stages involved in making genuine contact has been developed (Clarkson 2004). The first of the seven stages is called 'sensation' in which a 'figure' emerges from the 'background' and is vaguely perceived at a subconscious level. Once this perception becomes conscious, the 'awareness' phase is said to be reached in which the figure becomes the focal point of interest. Sensory information is reviewed and meaning making starts to occur. This is followed by the 'mobilisation' phase in which excitement about the contact is generated, leading to mobilisation of one's resources in preparation for the next phase of 'action'. In the action phase perceptual, behavioural and emotional activities come together and a course of action is selected from the options available. This is followed by 'full and vibrant contact' characterised by whole-hearted and full-bodied engagement with the figure of perception: 'Contact is the source of our richest joy and our most intensely painful moments' (Clarkson 2004: 42). It is followed by a phase called 'satisfaction' or afterglow and the final phase of 'withdrawal' back into the neutral state of the 'fertile void' from which some new figure may emerge. If we leave this cycle uncompleted, this unfinished business utilises resources in the mind, creating an unsatisfactory feeling. Because of the intimate nature of the contact being made, if an atmosphere of trust has not been established, there are many ways that someone might consciously or unconsciously interrupt the cycle. We may, for example, *deflect* another person's invitation to connect by avoiding eye contact and replying in a cold matter-of-fact way which redirects the subject of the conversation. Those with an avoidant attachment style may often interrupt the contact cycle in this way, retreating into their own cognitive world and becoming desensitised to approaches from others. Another way of interrupting contact is to follow internal rules that have been instilled into you, such as 'you should not reveal your feelings to anyone you work with'. You then censor yourself, behaving in a way that is not authentic. Such instilled rules are known as '*introjects*': rules you have unconsciously taken on board without question. You may '*project*' aspects of yourself that you have never consciously accepted onto your interlocutor rather than seeing them as they actually are. You may transfer aspects of someone else's personality onto them by drawing on memories about someone who resembles the person now before you. '*Retroflection*' is another interruption to contact when instead of responding to the person before you authentically, for example, when they have done something annoying, you blame yourself and engage in self-castigation. Again, such habits may have an early origin in life from a time when you were polarising the world into good and bad and could not accept anyone you relied on (such as your mother) as being bad; you set up a dynamic in which you attribute the 'badness' to yourself. As a coach, how many clients have you seen 'beating themselves up', causing you to think 'don't be so hard on yourself'? This is what Gestalt practitioners mean by retroflection, which interrupts genuine contact. A final interruption to the cycle of contact is when, once contact has been made at a genuine level, the two persons involved remain at this intimate level of contact, behaving as if they are one person, for example, 'finishing each other's sentences' and thinking about everything in the same way. This is called a state of '*confluence*', which impedes further genuine contact as an autonomous independent being open to a new cycle of experience.

Coaches need to be on the lookout for the interruptions to contact that their clients use, often without awareness, which close down rather than open up opportunities for genuine contact with others. Genuine contact with others is essential for creativity, particularly in teamwork. If team members only engage in 'transactions' that are ritualised by custom, or psychological game playing, or use Gestalt type interruptions to contact, creativity in teams is unlikely to develop.

A true meeting of minds is unlikely to be achieved through the exchange of words alone. Communication using words has significant limitations, representing the limited scope of linguistic frameworks. Wittgenstein described language as a 'cage' that limits thinking. It is the tool of the logical, linear practical mindset for working on tasks and activities, that is, for doing something; but it is not a good tool for managing relationships. As with a new-born baby, it is necessary to see 'the whites of your interlocutor's eyes', facial expressions, body posture and gestures in order to begin the process of establishing sufficient trust so that the defences can come down, the mask be taken off and genuine human characteristics revealed.

Deciding who may be allowed to see behind the mask(s) is usually a slow incremental and reciprocal process. 'I'm not going to let you see some of what is behind my mask, until you agree to let me see some of what lies behind yours!' is often the sentiment. Often behind the current mask is an earlier mask that provided safety in former times. Building trust involves engaging the psychological processes that develop towards either end of the life cycle, namely, attachment processes or transpersonal processes. Interactions based around psychodynamic power-based processes, role types or cognitive processes may be a deflection away from the genuine contact needed to build trust.

If trust and a safe haven between a client and a coach is established the client may explore their vulnerabilities, taking masks off without fearing that what lies underneath will be judged. Unconditional positive regard by the coach is required. Constraining conceptual frameworks can then be decommissioned as new personal narratives are written and new frameworks constructed to match future aspirations.

If you really connect well, 'emotional contagion' is a possibility in which you not only resonate with your client's mind, you adopt their emotional status as if it is your own and it starts to drive your behaviour. Such emotional contagion, mediated by mirror neurone activation and connecting the emotional processing in use by two minds is like the confluence state mentioned previously. It is important that you and your client are able to tune into it each other's emotional states, resonate and are then able to dissociate from one another so that you can see each other's world view while maintaining your own. Oscillation between these two perspectives (subject to subject and subject to object) is an essential coaching skill. For this reason coaching supervision is absolutely essential for ensuring that confluence does not last.

Chapter 23

Teamwork and creativity

Beyond the sum of the parts

Imagine that you have been invited to a meeting by an organisation with which you are unfamiliar. You know the time and place but you don't know the topic or any of the other participants. Nor do you know who is responsible for the running of the meeting but you do know that it is very important and could change your life. There is no time to drink coffee and chat to others before the meeting to try to see if they know anything about the purpose of the meeting; you simply go into the meeting room and take a seat, one of 12 arranged in a circle with no table or anything else obstructing the space in between. There is nowhere to put any computer, mobile phone or writing pad except on the floor under your chair and the clear instructions that came with the invitation stated that all communication devices must be switched off for the duration of the meeting.

You exchange 'hellos' briefly by acknowledging other participants but you don't want to say too much and reveal how little you know about why you are there. You are wrestling with that question yourself and part of you is getting frustrated about this intrusion into your busy schedule. All seats have been taken and all participants have had the chance to assess the appearance of everyone else. What clothes are they wearing? What does this say to you about them? What are their facial expressions? Who exudes the air of being the leader? Your ACC may be scanning the room to identify an 'attachment figure' able to allay your concerns. Time passes and nothing seems to happen. It may only be a couple of minutes but in the silence and uncertainty it seems like hours. Then somebody cracks: 'Can anyone tell me why we are here?'

This sort of unstructured meeting process is often used in Gestalt Therapy theory classes so that group processes are explored in an undirected experiential way. This encourages non-task-focussed ways of thinking and acting to emerge, although in a therapeutic setting it has been pointed out that too much structure and too little structure are both negatively correlated with a successful outcome (Yalom and Leszcz 2005). Groups of people very often start by exhibiting the need to identify a leader or facilitator to calm anxieties by providing a structure for their time, and a framework for interaction. Right from the start it seems we need at least basic frameworks and structure, just as we did when we were born, and as then, initial starting conditions may strongly influence the likely final outcome.

Suppose, returning to our imaginary exercise, that no one in the room has been appointed to lead or facilitate; the room is being watched and listened to remotely. How then will the group decide how to structure their time, and who will take the lead in establishing a process? Will the participants engage in the ritual of introductions? Will some participants withdraw and go off angry? Will someone say 'I've experienced something like this before' and open up a conversation to share past experiences? Will a leader be nominated on the basis of what is said? What remit will such a leader have? What will be their objective(s)?

Suppose it turns out that all 12 of the people in the room had applied for a very important senior position, but they did not know that this meeting is part of the selection process. Meaning making was somewhat delayed, but if this connection is made would you expect sibling rivalry to emerge through competitively motivated behaviour? What defensive behaviours might you expect to see?

Alternatively, it could be that someone in the group emerges from this interaction that sees the potential for turning the event into a networking opportunity by identifying how each of the participants remaining in the room could cooperate in a joint venture. They might even explore together what such a joint venture might be. They might informally assign roles for such a joint venture: who will act as 'CEO'; 'COO'; Creative Director; Relationships Director; Chairman? What will be each role's remit? What will be the vision, the mission and the goals?

From a meeting with no agenda and no leader or direction a new enterprise has emerged from a cooperative attitude of mind. Those who left the meeting angry had a different attitude of mind, feeling rather affronted by this waste of their valuable time. Had they known this was a selection process their competitive spirit would have surely made them stay and assert their 'leadership' qualities over the others. Perhaps another time!

Group mindset formation

How soon in any team-building exercise should you define the initial starting conditions if you are mindful of not wanting to constrain potential outcomes? This may depend on the purpose of the team and the degree of innovation required for achieving the best results. And what then is the role you require of a leader? Language, coming from the left-frontal cerebral cortex, likes to abstract things from their context, deconstructing reality into component parts so that each component can be looked at in isolation. We are then encouraged to believe that there is such an entity as a 'leader'. But, as Martin Buber observed in 1923, you cannot consider *Ich* in isolation; you may have an *Ich–Es* relationship or an *Ich–Du* relationship. You do not exist outside of a relationship! Neither does a leader and that is something language and our archaic predilection towards grandiosity encourages us to forget. Thus, we cannot consider a leader without also considering a follower and the relationship between them; the unwritten contract and neurological 'schema-of-being-with' each other that needs to be formed for our mental models to work. We cannot consider leadership without considering followership at the same time, for neither can exist in isolation irrespective of what our language tries to say to us.

It is in the process of interactions between participants in our imaginary exercise that the person with the most robust qualities of leadership within the group may emerge to fill the vacuum. These interactions represent a form of jousting to test one another's mettle. When new teams are formed, the first stage as captured in Bruce Tuckman's group development model is called *'forming'*, characterised by *Ich–Es* interactions between participants. Participants are concerned to form impressions of each other and gather information in a relatively safe and unrevealing way. At this stage there is no group mindset, the team is, as yet, a collection of individuals coming together, exchanging introductory formalities and learning about the project, goals or on-going responsibilities. Once the team members start to address the problems or challenges to be managed, differing ideas and perceptions are almost certain to emerge and compete with one another for attention. This phase is called *'storming'* and could be somewhat turbulent if roles, responsibilities and underlying concerns are not clarified in this phase. The new team members engage in subliminal jousting to get a sense of the real nature of the other team members so that a social order and group mindset may emerge. Irrespective of whether a leader has been appointed or not, issues of power and rivalry are likely to emerge together with 'Freudian' defences. Some of us may be happy to consciously or unconsciously confer our own sense of leadership onto someone else who seems keen and able to assume this role, whereas others may not be comfortable to cede control so easily. Team members may subconsciously default to past adaptive behaviours, once necessary for their survival, so their behaviour should not be taken personally, driven more by past experiences than current circumstances necessitate. During the conscious and subconscious jousting that occurs during the storming phase of team formation we may 'project' our sense for leadership onto the person in the group who appears to have strongly developed leadership skills and a strong preference for using them. They, often subconsciously, may accept the invitation by calling forth these skills in response to the 'invitation'. In this non-verbal contract each party may sacrifice something of themselves, at least for a while. The subliminally acknowledged leader sacrifices his or her right rear quadrant preference for being one of the team. And in order to build and retain the trust of members of the group, the leader needs to ensure that a sense of stewardship for the good of the organisation as a whole is his or her main concern, not his or her more visceral drive for personal enrichment. Whoever is the real leader of the team must be capable of listening to and empathising with the emotionally driven concerns of team members if the team is to operate with their full potential. A secure haven is needed in which team members feel safe enough to reveal vulnerabilities without feeling threatened if they are to move beyond their comfort zones. Leaders need to be masters of self-control, captains of their urges and masters of their emotions. Once trust has been established and the group enters the *norming* and *performing* phases of team development, the leader's actions and thoughts no longer have to be constrained by the harmony of 'group think'. The leader needs the courage to stand alone and challenge the harmony and mindset of the group, without provoking counterproductive levels of anxiety. And, for the moment, the group members sacrifice their right to lead, ceding this function, at least temporarily, to their chosen boss. Unless this process is allowed to proceed and is well facilitated, trust between team members will not develop and the performance level will be less rather than more than the sum of the parts. A *team mindset constellation* needs to form and the thinking geometry of the group encircle all functional capabilities (see Figure 23.1).

In a study of encounter groups for personal development conducted at Stanford University four important *leadership functions* were identified that significantly influenced the success of the group:

1   Emotional activation was found to be important using a challenging and confronting style modelled by personal risk taking and a high level of self-disclosure.
2   Caring was found to be important, offering support, affection, praise, protection, warmth, acceptance, genuineness and concern.
3   Meaning-making was very important: explaining, clarifying, interpreting, and providing a cognitive framework for modelling change, translating feelings and experiences into ideas.
4   The executive functions of setting limits, rules, goals, managing time, pacing, stopping, interceding and suggesting procedures were important.

Whereas outcome was positively and linearly correlated with the amount of caring and meaning making from the leader, emotional stimulation and exerting executive functions had a curvilinear relationship to outcome such that too little or too much impacted on outcome. Caring and meaning making were both necessary for success, neither alone being sufficient. Regarding meaning making, it was the *process* of explanation that proved to be significant. Successful outcomes required the leader to enable participants to integrate their experiences cognitively and draw insights and general principles from it (Yalom and Leszcz 2005: 536–7).

For any team to be successful you need more than the two roles of leader and follower. Further specialisations need to emerge from the subliminal jousting to fill the vacuum. The types of role needed to optimise team success have been studied at Henley Management College over many years under the direction of Meredith Belbin. Belbin and colleagues studied many management teams constructed to assess what personal qualities and roles need to be represented in the team. Nine roles were defined during the course of their research; these are positioned arbitrarily in relation to the type of cerebral function most characteristic of the role (see Figure 23.1).

Readers unfamiliar with the descriptions of the different team roles in the Belbin model are referred to their website (www.belbin.com), where a list of team role descriptions is available. In Figure 23.1 the term 'Innovator' has been used to replace the Belbin term 'Plant' and the original Belbin term 'Chairman' has been used instead of their more recent use of the term 'Coordinator'. Their online self-assessment questionnaire helps to identify

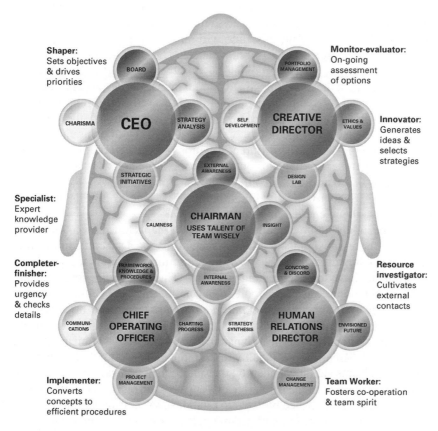

Figure 23.1 Belbin team roles aligned with cerebral functions.

preferred team role(s). The similarity of these roles to the functions of various parts of the cerebral hemisphere is striking. What the Belbin researchers seems to be saying is that you need a full complement of cerebral functions in order to optimise the chances for team success (Belbin 2010). One way or another you need to have all of your cerebral bases covered, to an appropriate depth, to form an optimal team mindset constellation.

Belbin's research indicated that the ideal size for a team is five or six members who are selected for complementary skills such that all the bases are covered without overloading the logistics of interaction because of the necessity of turn taking in any discussion. Thus nine roles covered by five or six members should in theory fulfil the preconditions for success. Careful consideration needs to be given to the idea of combining the role of Chairman and Shaper. Such a combined role may constrain rather than facilitate team functioning as the Chairman is there to ensure that everyone feels adequately heard and to recognise anxiety levels in team members managing this into the optimal zone for coping and thriving on the Yerkes–Dodson curve (see Chaskalson 2011). A certain level of anxiety is needed to focus attention and some people thrive under pressure (within limits), becoming relaxed and unfocussed without it. But this zone will vary from person to person and according to dynamic personal circumstances. The Chairman should be able to support team members in moving beyond their comfort zone but not to the level at which the parasympathetic modulation of the amygdala's anxiety alert is replaced by sympathetic activation. In a well-performing team the Chairman modulates the degree of challenge according to the personal resources of each team member to enhance the chance of achieving a state of connection in which the different functions of the cerebral hemispheres of all team members are able to contribute to the formation of a 'super-mind', combining the range and depth of the thinking networks of the team members. A Shaper/CEO style is unlikely to be able to do this as it may compromise their 'challenging' team role.

It has become routine in many companies for teams to follow a traditional approach for organising team logistics such as having a schedule of meeting dates, pre-circulated agendas, post-meeting minutes and action points according to linear logical thinking processes. This may be fine for reviewing routine operational business progress and promoting peer review account-ability. However, for *innovation and adaptability* teams and organisations need to engage in interactions that are non-linear, involving positive and nega-tive feedback dynamics. Linear dynamics, according to Newtonian physics, assumes that there is proportionality in the input and the output of a 'system'. If the participants act independently, the sum of their contributions can be no greater than the sum of the parts. If teams engage with one another at a deeper level such as that described by *Ich–Du* relationships, non-linear unconscious thinking processes (deeply connected multiple parallel thinking processes) may operate, creating an entirely different dynamic as explained below.

High-performance team characteristics

High-performance business teams have been studied using non-linear complexity-based models to identify important factors contributing to success (Losada and Heaphy 2004). Sixty Strategic Business Unit (SBU) management teams each consisting of eight people were studied to evaluate how well they connected and interacted with each other. Verbal communication within the teams was analysed on three bipolar scales: positive feedback (e.g. supportive statements) versus negative feedback (e.g. discouraging statements), inquiry (exploring another position) versus advocacy (promoting one's own viewpoint) and 'self' orientation (speaking about one's self, group or company) versus 'other' orientation (referring to someone, a group or company not included in 'self'). The performance levels of the teams were rated according to profitability, customer satisfaction ratings and 360 degree evaluations. High ratings in all three measures corresponded to a high-performance team classification, whereas low performance ratings in all three corresponded to low-performance team classification with medium-performance teams falling in-between. Connectivity between team members was measured by looking at strong and sustained patterns of interlocked behaviour between team members called nexi (plural of nexus).

The results from this study revealed that the ratio of positive to negative feedback in high-performance teams was 5.625, that is, over five times more positive feedback was communicated than negative. In contrast, low-performance teams had a ratio of 0.375 positive to negative feedback, that is, over twice as many negative comments were made compared to positive feedback. Medium-performance teams were associated with about twice as many positive feedback comments as negative. Low-performance teams made 20 times more self-advocacy statements, that is, stating their own position, than clarifying inquiries about other positions, and made self-referential statements 30 times more frequently than statements about other external people or organisations. In high-performance teams in both cases this was balanced. Medium performance teams fell in-between.

Regarding connectivity between team members, the average number of nexi for high-performance teams was 32 compared with 22 for medium performance teams and 18 for low-performance teams.

These results are compatible with the view that low-performing teams maintain subject to object relationships whereas high-performance teams progress to genuine subject to subject contact relationships, facilitating the formation of a *team mindset constellation.*

Non-linear dynamic modelling of these results enabled the researchers to examine interactions between the parameters measured, looking for types of attractor; attractors are like the geometric pattern created by a 'gravitational field', pulling behaviours into a particular kind of 'orbit' according to the interactions shaping the field or cultural milieu. Different types of attractor describe the different geometrical shapes of an orbital path between two or more 'bodies' in relationship and therefore degrees of constraint on behaviour and freedom to think. When applied to team dynamics we could call an attractor a descriptor of the *geometry of thinking* permitted by group interactive dynamics. In other words, this type of dynamic modelling identifies whether the interaction between team members is likely to exceed the sum of their individual contributions, reflecting synergistic and coordinated output from the parallel processing of multiple minds and their multiple functions.

The most rigid 'attractor' in such a dynamic model is known as a *fixed point-attractor*: this may be thought of as the geometric dynamic of a marble rolling around in a semi-spherical basin. In the absence of an external driving force, the marble will eventually spiral towards a fixed point at the bottom of the basin.

Figures 23.2 and 23.3 illustrate the expanse of the *thinking geometry* that develops in teams as interactions oscillate between 'self' orientation and 'other' orientation and more positive/supportive interactions with others

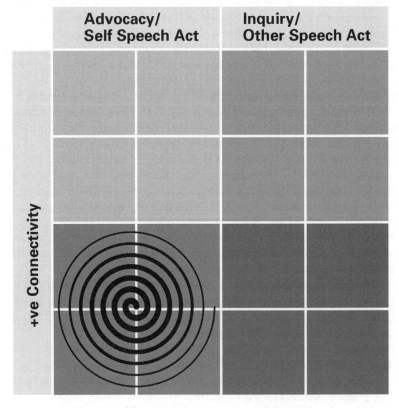

Figure 23.2 Likely pattern of 'point-attractor' thinking geometry to emerge from self-focused, poorly connected team members, resulting in poor performance.

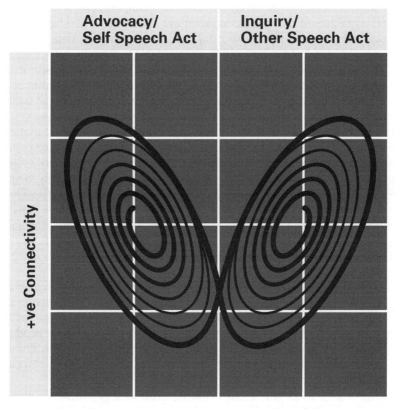

Figure 23.3 Likely pattern of 'strange-attractor' thinking geometry to emerge from balanced self–other perspectives and well-connected team members, resulting in high performance.

(upper half of chart) or more negative/unsupportive interactions with others (lower part of chart) across the four quadrants of what is known as 'phase space'.

In low-performance teams (Figure 23.2) the geometry of thinking is restricted to one quadrant of phase space, the lower left, constrained by negativity and self-orientation. This dynamic pattern is consistent with fixed point-attractor dynamics.

In contrast to the restricted orbital dynamic seen in low-performance teams, Losada and Heaphy (2004) observed that, when positive feedback is stronger than negative feedback in a team and a more balanced perspective was taken regarding self–other positions or advocacy and inquiry statements, the dynamic pattern over time indicated that a much more flexible attractor was operating, producing a 'strange' geometric shape known as a *strange-attractor*.

In between the rigid orbital dynamics of the point-attractor and the flexible orbital dynamics of the strange-attractor are a relatively rigid limit-cycle or periodic attractor and the not so rigid limit-torus attractor. Mid-performing teams in the study of Losada and Heaphy (2004) eventually settled into the dynamics of a limit-cycle attractor as there was insufficient positivity and connectivity in their interactions 'to escape the entropic gravitational pull of negativity' (Losada and Heaphy 2004: 762) in order to achieve strange-attractor dynamics.

Health is associated with strange-attractor dynamics: 'Chaotic dynamics appear to underlie the variability and adaptability necessary for responding to a fluctuating environment' (Goldberger and Rigney 1990: 30) and 'systems, which stay constantly poised between order and disorder, exhibit the most prolific, complex and continuous change' (Brown and Eisenhardt 1997: 29), whereas disease can be thought of as the onset of rigid dynamics. A metaphor for life *at the edge of chaos* is the human heartbeat, stable and unstable at the same time but adapting to conditions and maintaining vitality.

The conclusions from this section are as follows:

- 'Teams' in which participants fail to connect with each other because of maintaining their 'self' view, advocating only their own position and expressing predominantly negative feedback produce interactions described by point-attractor dynamics in which nothing new is produced, the sum of the output being no greater than the individual parts. Thinking is constrained by self-boundary concepts generated by the parietal cortex for spatial orientation.
- High ratios of positivity to negativity (up to a point; some negative feedback is needed for grounding the team) and high levels of connectivity between team members (strong and sustained patterns of interlocked behaviours indicative of a process of mutual influence) enable flexible dynamics in which the gravitational pull of the thinking pattern changes, creating new ideas and performance levels greater than the sum of the parts. Without self-imposed boundary limitations and limbic defences the output of multiple neuronal networks in different individuals synchronises to achieve a more expansive thinking geometry from which creative solutions are likely to emerge.
- At the behavioural level this positivity is believed to be associated with more approach rather than avoidance behaviour.

Positivity in teams appears to encourage approach behaviours favouring experiential learning so that internal models can be created, tested and fine-tuned (Frederickson and Losada 2005). In discussing their results and similar findings from studies of successful marriages (Gottman 1994), Frederickson and Losada concluded that a positivity ratio above 2.9 is associated with flourishing rather than languishing. At a ratio of 11.6 the complex dynamics of flourishing was found to show first signs of disintegration as without appropriate negativity behavioural patterns 'calcify'. Group bonding activities that promote the release of bonding neurochemicals such as oxytocin are likely to further improve connectivity within teams. Thus skin-to-skin contact in the form of shaking hands, and embracing (hugging) may be more than rituals or niceties. Anecdotal evidence supports that such bonding activities aid problem-solving capability possibly by increasing the sense of a secure base so that fewer mental resources are taken up with defence monitoring and thus more becomes available for problem solving. Mindfulness skills to monitor and direct thinking geometry are theoretically likely to facilitate the broadening of thinking geometry by aiding the shift from bounded spatial self-metaphors to unbounded temporal metaphors.

Creative process

Positivity and interconnection within a team seem to be essential prerequisites for high-performance teamwork but what is the process that such a team should follow if they are to take advantage of the highly connected parallel processing capability enabled by complex team mindset thinking dynamics? Such dynamics may be essential for solving complex problems by teams. One of the first models of the creative process, which drew on insights of the mathematician Henri Poincaré, was a five-stage model proposed by Graham Wallas in 1926. The stages of the creative process that he described were:

- preparation: immersing oneself in the nature of the problem to be explored and considering it from multiple perspectives;
- incubation: allowing the information from the preparation phase to be processed by the parallel processing of the unconscious mind;
- intimation: getting a feeling that a solution is imminent;
- illumination: the creative idea springs forward into conscious awareness;
- verification: the idea is subjected to scrutiny by conscious and rational mental processes.

These phases have been debated as to their validity but in essence the model remains useful and the nature of what is going on in the 'incubation phase' has been subject to some recent helpful research. Sleep, or in particular rapid-eye-movement dream sleep (REM sleep) seems to be particularly effective in facilitating creativity if it is preceded by priming. The researchers proposed that during REM sleep high levels of acetylcholine in the hippocampus suppress feedback to the cerebral cortex, allowing the cerebral cortex to 'reorganize associative hierarchies ... We propose that REM sleep is important for assimilating new information into past experience to create a richer network of associations for future use' (Cai *et al.* 2009: 10,133). Concluding their article, the authors quoted the recommendation 'Let us learn to dream' from Friedrich August Kekulé, the Nobel Laureate who worked out the ring structure for benzene following a dream in which a snake grabbed its own tail.

In reviewing the research surrounding the neurological processes involved in creativity and insight, Dietrich and Kanso (2010) noted that in order for insight to arise the executive functions of the frontal cortex need to back off for a while and let deeper connected brain areas process the information and relationships between data. They referred to this as '*hypofrontality*' which appears to be necessary for insight to arise. Essentially, it seems that the visual and verbal working memories that consciously process very limited amounts of information should not get involved too early on in the creative process and, as mentioned above, suppression of memorised associations between data from past experience during REM sleep may help to see relationships in a new light.

Drawing from this research it is suggested that creative problem solving in a team is likely to benefit from the following:

*   a well-constituted team with all cerebral bases collectively covered with as much depth (expertise) as possible, capable of looking at issues from multiple perspectives and open to diverse views;
*   a Chairman capable of guiding the team so that all perspectives are adequately considered during a preparation phase, encouraging authentic and grounded positivity with a good balance of advocacy and inquiry, self-orientation and other-orientation. Emotional activation, caring, meaning attribution and executive guidance are all important factors for success;
*   a sufficient period of time for the knowledge about the issue being considered to be 'incubated'. The more deeply embedded the knowledge, the greater the chance of 'flow' as various functions seamlessly interact together. This should include periods of REM sleep. Team members are recommended to keep a notepad close to where they sleep to jot down images as soon as they wake up;
*   the ability to grasp the significance of metaphors occurring in dreams or while awake and sharing these metaphors with team members in a positive way to encourage cross-fertilisation of ideas from non-linear thinking and imagination;
*   the ability to evaluate the resulting insights and hone them into practical proposals for communicating to others.

The working memories in the frontal cortex should only come into play towards the end of the process to select from a limited number of creative proposals. Conscious evaluation and practical proposals for implementation of creative ideas should not enter into team members' thinking too soon.

Team chairmanship

It is important to keep in mind that although the research conducted by Losada and Heaphy (2004) models complexity, it is only looking at the interaction of a few carefully selected parameters related to the SEEKING motivational system for approach and avoidance, which as we know is influenced by primary attachment pattern, positive optimistic outlook conditioned by left-frontal hemisphere perspectives, and resonance with others involving mirror neuron functioning to reciprocally identify intentions. Many other aspects of team interaction influence team dynamics and a competent Chairman needs to be alert to these dynamics too.

Any aspect from the full spectrum of psychological undercurrents is likely to emerge at different stages of a team's development. Transactional Analysis and the Gestalt interruptions to contact mentioned earlier provide models to help notice what psychological influences are at large. In addition, sibling rivalry may operate in covert ways such as if a team member calculates that the initially appointed leader is likely to fail and engages in a few Machiavellian-style interventions to assist with his demise. Freudian defences may emerge in team dynamics and the games made apparent by Transactional Analysis may be played. The ACC and hippocampus may call up patterns from past memories, triggering anxiety, and provide material for transferring a past 'persona' onto one of the participants in the team. Transferences onto the team leader derived from past experience with authority figures such as parents is common. Disowned characteristics of one team member may be projected onto another who may identify with the projection, giving rise to a whole sub-dynamic played out within the team. This potentially introduces misleading thinking and behaviour into group dynamics.

Internal harmony and management of discord are important areas for modulation in order to improve the overall performance of any organisation including one's self-organisation. Those who have experienced disharmony in the past may subconsciously recall such memories increasing their sensitivity to the early signals portending to growing discord. In any group, any such individual will tend to be the first to notice when relationships are not developing well. The Chairman needs to be aware of those whose antennae are most sensitive to a particular type of dynamic, acknowledging this and managing the team accordingly. Anxiety levels, if they exceed parasympathetic controllable levels, may impede the cerebral functioning of the team and risk regressing the team towards Bion's basic assumptions via emotional contagion, so that no real work gets done.

If a participant's compassion was provoked in their early life, for example, having concern for the well-being of a caring mother who seemed to have troubles of her own, then such an individual may be predisposed to rescuing those they perceive as being vulnerable, wanting to act as if in a protective parental role. They may develop a lifetime tendency to put the needs of others before their own and gain meaning in relationships by helping perceived 'victims'. When someone who does feel rather overwhelmed and inadequate comes onto the scene and sounds as if they need help (appealing using a particular tonal vocal quality), any predisposed rescuer can unwittingly become enmeshed in a triangular subliminal game, particularly if the victim identifies some persecutor as being involved. The classic Karpman Drama Triangle is a subliminal power game in which someone who perceives himself or herself to be powerless considers a person that they perceive to be in a position of power to be persecuting them and recruits someone they believe will look after them and rescue them from the persecutor. If this does not work the victim may blame the rescuer, as a child may blame the parent, and even switch to persecuting the rescuer who may respond by hiding behind their vulnerabilities, thus becoming the victim. The switching of roles in this subliminal game makes a fascinating drama that unfolds owing to mirror-neuron mediated subconscious undercurrents, but is not usually helpful for team performance. To break the pattern, the rescuer must guard against colluding with someone who does not take responsibility for themselves. The person perceived as having power needs to be encouraged to explicitly state where they stand in adult to adult conversation and the victim needs to own their vulnerability and take responsibility for themselves.

Such subliminal patterns of behaviour can often be seen in the Boardroom in the form of power politics (possibly linked to sibling rivalry), playing to the gallery and group-think dynamics owing to emotional contagion. In the absence of a sufficiently experienced Chairman, bringing a psychologically trained team coach into the team can help shift the dynamics in a more positive direction.

It is important in any team that when the team work is about to come to an end a process of closure takes place to review and acknowledge what has taken place within the team and the progress made. A sense of completion is important as unfinished business remains in the subconscious, taking up resources (likely to include hippocampal rapid access memory), thereby limiting future performance capacity. One way or another the leader's closing responsibility includes tying up loose ends, wrapping up the team's production into a report or presentation, acknowledging the contributions and learning acquired on the journey, and 'parking' the project in the archive. This corresponds to the fifth stage in Tuckman's model, added in 1977, called *adjourning*.

Coaching practice

Coaches working with teams may wish to consider asking clients the following:

- Has the team formed a well-constellated team mindset in terms of having all the bases covered to the necessary depth?
- Is the geometry of thinking flowing well around the constellation?
- Has there been sufficient time allowed for information loading and incubation?
- If it is not flowing well, what is impeding it? Are attachment/'Freudian'/Gestalt/TA/other psychological explanations useful for understanding blockages?
- Is the Chairman able to recognise and manage these processes?
- Does the team capture its dreams and work with metaphors?
- What mindfulness exercises might help?

Chapter 24

Larger constellations

A corporation is a complex interaction of many individual relationships over time, linked by a sense of a collective purpose. It is therefore dynamic and constantly changing, influenced by the social and environmental trends in the places where it operates. Companies will tend to have an espoused culture and a 'subconscious' culture, strongly influenced by its history and lived values. Individuals will tend to develop internal working models of 'self' shaped by the type of culture they experience in the workplace. It may be useful therefore to review a synthesis of some of the descriptions of different types of organisational culture, drawing on the models offered by Roger Harrison (Harrison 1972; Kakabadse and Kakabadse 1999) and the metaphors developed by Gareth Morgan (Morgan 2006) and Charles Handy (Handy 2007). Although we will consider a single culture concept we should remain mindful that within large organisations mixed cultures are often apparent. Once we have some idea of the type of culture our client operates in, constellation techniques in which key people in the organisation are represented in a relational field are likely to be very helpful for exploring ways of changing interpersonal dynamics (Horn and Brick 2005).

The power or club culture of 'Zeus' led organisations

A culture in which the vertical dimension is dominant so that a 'powerful' individual or group of individuals dominate decision making is the power culture. For those at the top it may be an exciting place to work, appealing to their archaic sense of grandiosity. For the majority of the organisation it may be perceived as exciting for those in favour and threatening for those who are not. Power cultures manipulate individuals through the psychology of inclusion or exclusion, echoing competitive sibling rivalry for parental attention and approval. Decisions are fast, weaknesses hidden and mistakes punished. In many ways, such a culture resembles the metaphor suggested by Gareth Morgan in which the organisation is an instrument of domination. Domination may be on the basis of a highly charismatic leader, a strong patriarchal or feudal

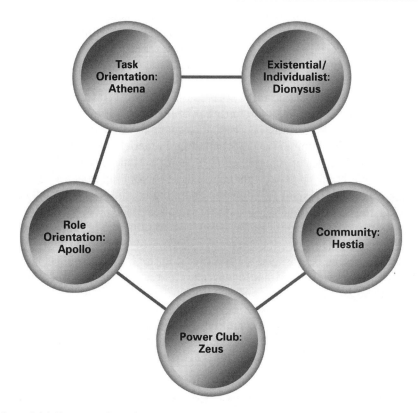

Figure 24.1 Five metaphors for organisational culture representing different thinking style preferences.

tradition, or the rational–legal bureaucracy used to give a ruler legal legiti-macy. It seems that such cultures are dominated by fundamental limbic and visceral drives dependent upon staff deference with high levels of competition and challenge. The FEAR/Anxiety and LUST/Sexual motivational systems often seem to be utilised by managers with such practices as 'rank and yank', firing the bottom 10 per cent of managers each year and richly rewarding the top 20 per cent of managers. It is a command-and-control model that Charles Handy personifies with the Greek god Zeus who he represents as a patriarchal, impulsive individual, often benevolent and possessing much charisma, who sits as a spider in the middle of a web. The culture is also called the club culture in which an inner circle rules the organisation.

The role culture of Apollo style organisations

In contrast to the power culture, in a role culture personal displays of power are not encouraged and the organisation is run according to formal definitions of roles, procedures, rules, hierarchical structures and bureaucratic procedures. The vertical top-down power structure is still dominant but the system is driven by procedures and roles constructed according to a particular structural configuration. Decisions are slow, change resisted and enthusiasm for new initiatives low. Morgan used the metaphor of organisations as machines to describe such cultures. It evolved from the Prussian military machine style of organisation initiated by Frederick the Great (1712–1786), ruler of Prussia. These ideas were developed further by many organisation development experts including Frederick Taylor (1856–1915), an American engineer who called it 'Scientific Management'. It could be said to be a highly rear-left-quadrant biased cerebral approach which may work efficiently in stable predictable operating conditions, repeatedly producing the same products or services. Charles Handy describes the role culture using the metaphor of the Greek god Apollo, god of order and rules. It is a secure place to work but may be experienced as boring (Handy 2007). This culture has been successfully utilised in the fast-food industry where tasks are straightforward and consistency is required in a stable environment (Morgan 2006). Such a style is not designed for innovation and can result in a 'mindless' unquestioning form of dehumanisation. As in the power culture, creative thinking capability will need to be imported into the company when the environment changes and adaptation is needed in order to survive.

The task culture of Athena led organisations

Two types of task culture seem to be apparent. The first relates to organisations in which tasks require focussed lines of reasoning with a clear short-term target such as many sales and marketing organisations. Here a culture develops in which there is much more freedom to operate in an autonomous way than is the case in the role culture or power culture, provided results are forthcoming. Sales teams rely on functions of the left-frontal cortex for developing charismatic selling skills involving persuasive use of language and clear lines of reasoning with their customers. There is competition between members of the sales 'team' who usually are supported by management and by each other to a limited extent but function as individuals hunting their prey as lone wolves rather than in a pack.

A second type of task culture is seen in organisations focussed on working on solving problems that often require genuine teamwork and high levels of professional expertise. Unlike the rigid role culture, a task culture is flexible and adaptable as teams can be formed and reformed according to need. In this culture the horizontal networked relational dimension may be more dominant than the vertical power structure and often a matrix organisation links the two. Power often exists at the interstices of the matrix rather than at the top. Tension between the vertical and horizontal dimensions is likely and has to be carefully managed to protect the motivation of both dimensions. Bureaucratic procedures, restrictive roles and viscerally driven behaviour are less prominent than in previous models. Charles Handy personifies this culture with the Greek warrior goddess Athena, fostering youth, energy and creativity. Such cultures recognise expertise as being most important, rather than age or length of service, and tend to employ many PhDs. Gareth Morgan uses the metaphor of an organism to describe such a culture, pointing out that such cultures are apparent in high-tech firms such as those in the aerospace and microelectronics industries. These cultures provide an environment in which professionals can follow and develop their own professional interests within the constraints set by the organisation. When trying to solve complex problems, right-frontal cortex multiple solution matrix capabilities are particularly valuable, drawing upon systems theory and contingency theory rather than using linear approaches for problem solving (Morgan 2006). In this second form of task culture, cooperation is more likely to arise as a means for solving complex problems, as collaboration may be necessary to generate new insights. Right cortical functions are particularly adept at understanding the interrelationship between the organisation and the environment and generating alternative ways of seeing innovative possibilities for change.

The existentialist culture of Dionysus

A fourth organisational culture has been described by Charles Handy which he called the existential culture and which he personified with the Greek god Dionysus. This culture is based on the philosophy that we shape our own destiny. Whereas in the previous cultural models the individual within an organisation is subordinate to the organisation, in an existentialist culture the organisation exists to help the individual to realise his or her purpose. This is the culture preferred by professionals who may agree to form cost-sharing partnerships such as lawyers or dentists or coaching consultants for example. Handy describes a 'growing band of new professionals' as being individuals who see themselves as independent professionals, temporarily loaning their talents to organisations. Management of such individuals can only be done by consent and requires negotiation. Such a culture may appeal to right-frontal dominant cortical thinkers who are not so task focussed but who consider possibilities from a much broader perspective. Morgan refers to such organisations using a 'Flux and Transformation' metaphor. Using the speciality of the frontal-right cerebral modes, the thinking processes here are not necessarily focussed upon abstracted short-term tasks, but concerned with continuous patterns and flow and transformations.

The person-driven culture of Hestia

Organisations that exist with the primary purpose of providing services to members of the organisation and function by mutual consent have been called person-driven cultures in which there is much personal warmth and consideration for each other (Kakabadse and Kakabadse 1999: 75). Here, the horizontal dimension is dominant and the vertical dimension facilitative for the organisation. Decisions are slow and reached by consensus. The community is more important than the individual. In terms of Greek Olympian gods, this culture is best represented by Hestia whose name means home and hearth and is identified with food, domesticity and community. Hestia was not a confrontational goddess, often giving up her seat to Dionysus to avoid confrontations with other 'gods'. Such a culture is likely to appeal to those wanting the warmth and the support of a community, such as community-based cooperatives in which the rear-right quadrant may be the predominant thinking mode. Gareth Morgan seems to describe such an organisation using the metaphor of a brain. But by invoking Karl Pribram's theory of the holographic brain (Morgan 2006: 73), and the Japanese concepts of *Kaizen* (continuous improvement e.g. TQM) and *Ringi* (collective decision making by exploring premises from multiple points of view, Morgan 2006: 94), it appears that Morgan is addressing right-rear quadrant and 'Chairman' functions rather than the whole brain. The practice of *Ringi* in Japanese companies in which draft proposals for any new policy are circulated to a range of managers illustrates a process for taking multiple perspectives.

National cultures

In the same way that individuals or companies can be viewed as having acquired predispositions and thinking tendencies, the same may be said for nations. Geert Hofstede and Gert Jan Hofstede conducted one of the largest surveys of national culture involving 74 countries based on data accrued from employees of the international computer company IBM during the 1970s. Further research has been subsequently conducted and reported (Hofstede and Hofstede 2005). In this book the authors suggested that the 'sources of one's mental programs lie within the social environments in which one grew up and collected one's life experience' (2005: 3). They called this sort of mental software *culture* with broader usage than when used by sociologists or anthropologists. Ultimately, five distinct cultural dimensions were delineated: power distance; collectivism versus individualism; femininity versus masculinity (assertiveness); uncertainty avoidance and long-term orientation (see Figure 24.2).

Power distance relates to the degree of dependence between a 'superior' and 'subordinate'. In countries where there is a large power distance, such as China or Russia, subordinates either prefer a form of dependence

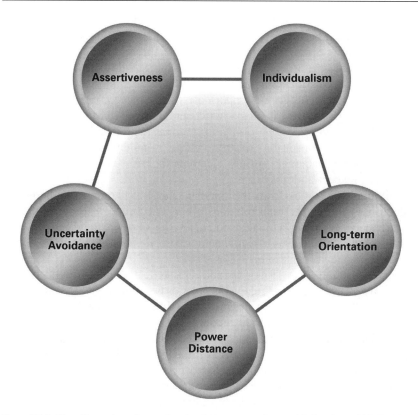

Figure 24.2 Five dimensions for national cultures according to Hofstede and Hofstede (2005).

conferring autocratic or paternalistic aspects onto their superior (as in the Zeus model of power or club culture in organisations) or reject this completely in a form of counter-dependence. As with the organisational model, the metaphor of a spider sitting in a web of power relationships seems to apply to high power distance cultures and unless one is a member of the inner circle, one's personal influence is very limited.

Mark Epstein noted that the 'Eastern self is enmeshed in a web of family, hierarchy, caste or other group expectations from which the only escape is often spiritual practice' (Epstein 1996: 176). Epstein observed that the Eastern practice of meditation is motivated by the same need of finding one's 'self' as it often is in the West, but that the starting positions are opposite. Rather than being enmeshed and 'connected' to the collective, in the West the feeling can often be more related to feeling alone and isolated. Hofstede and Hofstede found a negative correlation between power distance and individualism. Western countries scored very low on power distance and very high on individualism. A hierarchical structure and respect for parents and elders is common in countries with high power distance. China is an example of a high power distance country and one of the important influences on Chinese culture is Confucianism which holds that stability of society is based on an unequal relationship between people. Five important hierarchical relationships are held to be important: ruler–subject, father–son, older brother–younger brother, husband–wife, senior friend–junior friend (Lewis 2006: 487). Privileges *and* obligations come with the higher position. Collectivism and consensus are strong although policy may be determined by an invisible leadership group. Keeping face is very important as are politeness, respect and hospitality.

Individualism comes from the opposite cultural paradigm. Whereas in collectivist cultures personal relationships are accorded with more importance than tasks, in individualist countries the opposite tends to be true. Relationships with others are relatively loose in individualist cultures, whereas innovation tends to be stronger.

The dimension that Hofstede and Hofstede called masculinity and femininity creates much confusion because, as they acknowledge, these roles are culturally determined. In practice, this dimension measures assertiveness and material success versus tenderness and quality of life. Among the most assertive countries are Japan, Austria, Italy, Mexico, Ireland, China, Germany, the UK, the USA and Australia. Among the least assertive are Finland, Denmark, the Netherlands, Norway and Sweden. Hofstede and Hofstede noted that 'feminine' cultures are more likely in colder climates, suggesting that an equal partnership between men and women improves survival chances in such environments. It was also noted that 'masculine' assertiveness decreases with age.

Uncertainty can lead to anxiety and some countries develop cultures with a strong tendency to avoid uncertainty by introducing rules, regulations and other control measures. *Uncertainty avoidance was defined as the extent to which members of a culture feel threatened by ambiguous or unknown situations.* This was found to be high in Greece, Portugal, Uruguay, Japan, Peru and Argentina, and fairly high in France and Spain. In contrast, the USA, India, Malaysia, the UK, Ireland, China, Sweden and Denmark all had low scores regarding uncertainty avoidance. Uncertainty avoidance cultures tend to have an emotional need for developing more formal laws and informal rules and prefer structured environments in which people follow a clear process compared to other cultures. This reduces anxiety levels and is ideal for manufacturing where following repetitive processes consistently is required. In contrast, cultures with a low need to avoid uncertainty find rules and constraint to be the cause of emotional issues.

The final dimension, long-term orientation, was defined as: '*the fostering of virtues oriented towards future rewards – in particular, perseverance and thrift*'. East Asian countries dominated the long-term orientation preference with China in the lead position. In contrast, English speaking countries tended to dominate the other end of the spectrum, focussing on short-term orientation with a particular focus on 'the bottom-line', that is, short-term profits (Hofstede and Hofstede 2005: 219). The importance of profits ten years from now combined with the unimportance of this year's profits was significantly correlated to long-term orientation. The main values associated with long-term orientation included learning, honesty, adaptation, account-ability and self-discipline, with people investing in long-term personal networks of relationships.

Hofstede and Hofstede's research indicates that the culture that one grows up in influences the nature of the individual mind by skewing the probability of developing a particular predisposition. These five dimensions may be useful as a guide when engaging with cultural perspectives at a general level and echo to some degree the predispositions seen within organisations and individuals, possibly reflecting preferential development of certain neural networks. At the individual level, preferences and predispositions need to be specifically assessed as all types of predispositions will be represented to some extent in any collective. As globalisation proceeds, such national predispositions may diminish but for the moment the differences and diversity provide a kaleidoscope of differently nuanced functional capabilities for creative global problem solving. Coaches may wish to explore the extent to which any of these predispositions apply to their clients and tailor programmes accordingly.

Part 5

Unlocking our potential

Part 5 considers how improving our understanding of the mind may maximise our potential for creativity and problem solving and enhance the future development of the coaching profession.

Chapter 25

Demographic shifts and changing paradigms

The global population has increased from 3 billion in 1960 to 7 billion in 2012 and is heading towards 9 billion by 2050. Such a tripling of the world's population within a 90 year period is inevitably likely to place an enormous burden on the resources available to sustain the population and significant changes to the fabric of society may be anticipated. During such a rapid inflationary phase there is likely to be significant differentiation as different groups of people attempt to meet their needs in different ways. We may anticipate a very dynamic time with increased interaction and turbulence. If we are able to relate to each other at a human level, subject to subject rather than subject to object, this could be a very creative period in which the growing diversity and connectivity create conditions promoting extensive and intricate geometries of thinking. This requires refining our skills for promoting a meeting of minds.

Our Western-world mindset may be characterised by a preference for analytical inquiry prompting a tendency towards splitting things into component parts, analysing them and reconstructing them to improve their function. Our logical, linear thought processes have forged us ahead with spectacular technological innovation through in-depth scientific knowledge. Developing and using such skills has enabled our industrial revolutionary path in which we moved away from our close relationship with the land and our interrelationship with the complexities of nature to produce highly specified and consistent 'objects' to be traded from which we were able to derive wealth and surplus capital. Through industrialised production of desirable objects and competition much progress has been made in wealth creation as industrialised nations, particularly in the Western world, traded internationally with an underlying tendency towards domination. In so doing we have reinforced the object-based spatial metaphor of ourselves and our world in preference to reinforcing our interrelated temporal metaphor (flowing patterns) of ourselves and our world. But things are changing as the Eastern world integrates the Western mindset into its insightful inter-connected collectivist world view. As we may have noticed at the individual, organisational and national levels, the 'Eastern' mindset is characterised as having a stronger orientation towards seeing longer-term patterns of flow and relationships than the stereotypical 'Western' mindset. Neither mindset is innately superior to the other, being most likely polarities on a continuum. It seems likely that in order to solve the major complex problems that are emerging on the global horizon we will need to draw upon a full range of cognitive thinking functions developed to the deepest levels available and integrate the output in an interactive global creative process.

If we are unable to nurture a global meeting of minds, we risk fragmenting social cohesion and regressing to more primitive basic instincts. The complexity sciences suggest that there is a fine line between too much cohesion in a complex organisation with the risk of stagnation and decay versus too little cohesion with the risk of fragmentation and disintegration. The question posed is where is the edge of chaos? This is the place where full and vibrant life is truly lived, where we escape the zone of stagnation without entering the zone of disintegration.

A metaphor may help here. Imagine that you are a fisherman living in a village near a river close to a waterfall. The village is not directly on the banks of the river but set back behind a mangrove swamp. The best fish are to be caught, not near the swampy waters around the shore but out in the fresher flowing bubbling water in the middle of the river. If the fishermen do not venture far from the river bank they are likely to find small poorly developed fish with little nutritious value. Such a diet in the village leads to lethargy and stagnation. Venturing out into the middle of the river carries the risk of getting caught in turbulent currents. Your boat may be swept towards the top of the waterfall. Yet that is where the prized fish are to be found. How far out from the safety of the river bank should the fishermen go before crossing the edge of chaos?

This balance between stability and instability, integration and differentiation, cohesion and fragmentation is the balance all leaders of organisations try to find so that their organisations flourish rather than languish. Mindfulness practices offer a promising way of helping to determine where the point of balance may be.

In the inflationary phase of an expanding complex 'organisation', increasing diversity is likely. We see this in the world we live in today with multicultural and alternative lifestyles emerging to create colourful perspectives. But for this expanding diversity not to fragment, forces for cohesion need to be sufficient to prevent falling over the edge. We will increasingly need promoters of cohesion able to catalyse a meeting of minds; hubs around whom diverse teams can coalesce to find creative common ground. Such individuals are likely to have substantial and varied life experience and skills to bring people and their views together, synthesising insights from seeming polar opposites.

In Eastern cultures this role of providing cohesion and synthesis has often been fulfilled by 'elder statement' type roles. This has also been the case in many tribal cultures. Long-term vision and deep intuitive insight from years of insightful experience is needed to succeed in such a role. The Western world tends towards short-term thinking and objectification in order to achieve technological superiority, creating a very different leadership paradigm. Perhaps it is time for a synthesis of these contrasting leadership paradigms to emerge.

Luckily the current demographic changes, particularly in the West, are creating a growing pool of potential 'elder statesmen and women' with the potential for fulfilling a cohesive role as society expands. However, this may require a change in attitude towards senior members of the community, many of whom are often currently marginalised into retirement rather than remaining integrated within the social fabric.

Western organisations have yet to work out how to derive advantage from the post mid-life right hemisphere development surge with increased concern for unity and the long-term security of one's legacy. Those who have successfully derived these advantages, rather than remaining 'set in their ways' with fossilised IWMs, judgemental and possibly cantankerous, may be an unrecognised source capable of promoting cohesion and sustainability in organisations. Companies and social institutions are likely to benefit from extending the implementation of Mentors, Coaches and Panels of Senior Advisors if such roles are well supported with training, supervision and an understanding of the nature of the mind of individuals and cultures. HRD personnel familiar with the nature of the mind should be members of cor- porate management teams and capable of advising such teams on how to get the best from the collective minds available to the team. Mindfulness skills are likely to be highly beneficial in achieving a productive balance between creative diversity and social cohesion. If we can maintain sufficient cohesion and embrace diversity, our potential to synthesise new insights and realise creative solutions may become highly productive.

Chapter 26

Evolution of chairmanship

Over several millennia there has been a vast discussion on the nature of leadership. There are tens of thousands of books on the subject with many perspectives developed in different cultural climates. Today there is no shortage of leadership models with new ones emerging regularly. However, as the title of this section suggests, one area that has received insufficient attention in the past, but may play an essential role in the future is Chairmanship. The role of the Chairman is, and should be, entirely different to the role of the CEO in any organisation. The Chairman is not the driver of the organisation but the integrator-in-chief. He or she integrates the past of the organisation with the present and the future and ensures that all perspectives are respected. He or she has no operational role in the transactional business of the organisation but is intimately involved with the transformational currents buffeting the organisation and guiding its response. The Chairman appreciates all of the polarities and diversity within the organisation and externally, seeing how the interplay between multiple diverse perspectives provides creative opportunities for adaptive change, resonant with emergent society. The Chairman should not be a predominantly task focussed 'linear thinker' but capable of maintaining multiple paradoxical positions at the same time. The following attributes are likely to be essential for excellent Chairmen:

- an intuitive understanding of complexity theory and how multiple influences interact to shape any culture and emergent strategic views across time;
- an understanding of the conditions needed for multiple perspectives to come together to produce deeper insights by enabling connectivity in collective mindsets;
- being able to spot bifurcation points in the thinking dynamics and assessing how much nudging will be required to flip the thinking geometry into a 'strange-attractor' pattern;
- an understanding of the psychological processes within themselves, their teams, their organisation and society and how these can support or limit possibilities;

- an ability to create a holding environment in which team members feel sufficiently secure to express their feelings and vulnerabilities and the ability to reside in uncertainty without acting to resolve discomfort until conditions are right;
- deeply resonant personal relationships of the *Ich–Du* kind with all major influencers inside and outside of the organisation.

In essence such a person needs to have developed quiet wisdom through the integration of diverse life experiences to a transpersonal developmental level. On the basis of this level of integration, their powers of imagination will be strongly embodied and they will be able to disengage from imposed and established ways of thinking in order to explore uncharted territory. Re-engaging later with colleagues, Chairmen will be able to convey their insights using accessible metaphors. Mentors or coaches with the time and training to support the development of talented Chairmen may become essential for enabling many dynamic organisations to thrive.

Chapter 27

Evolution of coaching

Coaching is paradoxically a recently emerged 'profession' and yet it is as old as civilisation itself, for even leaders in ancient cultures consulted their oracles. The Oracle in the Temple of Apollo at Delphi was adept at asking questions so that their 'client' was in essence analysing themselves, drawing out the various perspectives from the jumble inside their minds. This is one of the basic methods of coaching: extracting the strands of the different threads of parallel thought processes and holding them up in a mirror so that the subject can see themselves more clearly and determine for themselves what path they should take. One may imagine an Ancient Greek commander visiting the Temple of Apollo at Delphi and being asked:

- What do you want? (What is your **G**oal?)
- What is happening now? (What is your **R**eality?)
- What could you do? (What are your **O**ptions?)
- What will you do? (What **W**ill you commit to doing?)

Here in essence is the basis for Sir John Whitmore's GROW model, published in *Coaching for Performance* in 1982. This could be viewed as the beginning of a coaching renaissance as far as management coaching is concerned, although sports coaching probably kicked things off. This renaissance is having an identity crisis. The editorial of the journal *Coaching: An International Journal of Theory, Research and Practice* in September 2009 reviewed a range of definitions for coaching, identifying two significantly different meanings (Bachkirova and Kauffman 2009). The first meaning held coaching as being a special type of conversation between two people. The second meaning held coaching as being a service or practice offered by a professional with a guaranteed quality ensured by his/her competencies. One year later Carol Kauffman stated that we are 'at a stage in our development where we can describe what we do as "technical eclecticism"'. She posed the question 'Do you know how to organise all the models, tools and techniques you use into some kind of coherent whole?' In her coherent whole, which she called the 'PERFECT' model (Physical;

Environmental; Relational; Feelings; Effective Thinking; Continuity of Past–Present–Future; Transcendent), neuroscience was cited as playing a part in the physical category (Kauffman 2010). Understanding the nature of the human mind was not mentioned at all, although all of the levels of her model relate to it in some way. For me, understanding the nature of the human mind provides a useful and relevant way of organising a coherent whole from the multitude of coaching approaches. To have any effect, all coaching interventions, whether coaching conversations or experiential role play, must impact upon the human mind; or, stated another way, the coach and his/her client co-create a dynamic process in which development is optimally facilitated through a meeting of minds. Focussing on the mind may help to resolve the 'eclectic' yet fragmented silo approach characterising the multiple empirically useful coaching models available, providing both diversity and cohesion.

Coaching draws on many strands of human endeavour. Neuroscience is one such strand but it cannot be considered the main one, for viewing the mind only through the lens of neuroscience carries with it the danger of objectifying components of the mind and confusing the 'black box of the television with the transmissions it is capable of revealing'. The mind is more about our transmissions than about how we transmit.

Objectification needs to be kept in balance as does the urge to provide cohesion by setting out procedures and processes to be followed rote fashion during coaching. In one of the more comprehensive coaching models, Integral Coaching Canada uses six 'lenses' for exploration with clients. This starts with the different perspectives gained from Ken Wilber's four quadrants model (view from inside the individual; view from outside the individual; view from inside the collective of which the individual is part; view from outside the collective of which the individual is part). The second lens considers levels of consciousness. The third lens considers six of Wilber's lines of development (cognitive, emotional, interpersonal, somatic, spiritual and moral). The fourth lens considers states of consciousness. The fifth lens considers gender type structures (Divine 2009). Finally, the fifth lens looks at assessments from the Westernised version of the Enneagram psychological model which was originally devised by Sufi mystics in Afghanistan and looks at intuitive 'type' preferences rather than cognitive 'type' preferences. Integral Coaching Canada's model is a comprehensive and highly structured approach that superimposes complex theoretical frameworks and models onto observations about the client and provides a prestructured development path with colour-coded target goals. This 'top-down' approach may be very useful when consistency, cohesion and structure are desired to aid assimilation into organisations, for example. In contrast, Gestalt/existential approaches aim to 'bracket' pre-existing frameworks and respond to arising events as they occur with clients in a co-creative and unstructured 'bottom-up' process. This may be preferred for strengthening individuality and diversity in populations when social acceptance issues are not of such concern. The 'framework free' Gestalt approach may, however, suffer by not recognising the fact that biological processes have their own frameworks and constraints. The aim of this book has been to synthesise a 'middle path', drawing upon the mind's innate ability to adapt, without superimposed direction, according to environmental conditions. Psychometric instruments conceived of in different environmental conditions may constrain the mind's ability to make appropriate adjustments according to one's own experience and perceptions. Psychometric tools are of benefit as experimental research instruments to explore the nature of the human mind but their overzealous use in daily coaching practice may not always be in the best interests of clients striving towards self-determined transformational change.

Familiarity with neuroscience, major psychological and developmental theories and the insights from thousands of years of introspective contemplation should help coaches to form hypotheses about what emerges in the arising process of coaching, helping to guide the selection of further interventions. This is subtly different from a top-down process of superimposing models upon observation, but rather aids informing a 'bottom-up' pattern recognition process. The process and the goals should then emerge from the client's innate personal characteristics and motivations if individuation is to be well supported. Finding the right balance is the art of successful coaching.

Looking ahead to where coaching itself may develop, one important aspect to keep in mind is diversity. Creativity requires diversity. Another important aspect to keep in mind is instability. Creativity requires instability too. If coaching were to become over standardised, systematised and proceduralised, as happens so often when emerging professions respond to the need to offer a consistent and predictable quality of service to their clients, it may threaten any goose capable of laying any sort of golden egg. Procedures, standardisation and evidence-based methodology are fine for role- or task-based organisations where stability and consistency rather than creativity are important. But where creativity is required, in order to be useful to clients as they confront a vast and diverse range of issues, coaches need to present an equally vast range of diverse means for addressing them. The means offered should not be restricted to only those that have been subject to research scrutiny, unless we really believe that we are now capable of framing comprehensive research questions, fully aware of the nature of creatively interacting human minds. No research can be framed without imposing some predetermined pattern of thought onto the object of the investigation. As is well recognised in science, no observer can study anything without influencing what is being studied. Coaching is still very much an art rather than a science but coaching methods should meet at least one of two important criteria:

1   Biological plausibility: the method should conform to what is known about how the mind functions; at least it should not contradict it.

2   Utility value and/or explanatory power: the method should be capable of achieving an intended end result without unexpected side effects or provide insights into the nature of the issue being addressed.

Assessing the appropriate means will be co-determined by the coach and the client through a dynamic interactive and fully informed process.

What will be important will be provision of a means for diagnosing the type of issue to be addressed and identifying a specialist or range of specialists who may offer innovative ways to work with clients in co-creating solutions. There may evolve a system of 'General Practice' coaches, having evidence of broad training, providing referrals to 'Consultant Coaches' with evidence of specialist training in particular areas. The latter 'Consultant Coaches' will need to have invested sufficiently in their own self-development to have gone beyond the level of any of the clients they wish to provide services for. A working knowledge of the nature of the mind is likely to play an important part in offering a professional service capable of delivery efficacy beyond the 'placebo' effect.

Just as it is within the pharmaceutical world, the world of coaching also needs to be aware of the reality of the 'placebo' effect. Simply by being present, actively listening and doing no harm, a coach can elicit a beneficial effect from being with his or her client. This has value, but is it maximally efficacious? As in the pharmaceutical world, understanding the nature of the target 'receptor' for your intervention is likely to be important for maximising efficacy and minimising side-effects.

To be more effective, coaches may need to become experts in the mind-management skills that their clients seek to develop. The ability to develop the integration function, the Chairman, through mindfulness practices may become particularly important. Understanding the geometry of thinking processes is also likely to be important so that the appropriate models are used according to the level of complexity involved. For example, the GROW model mentioned earlier is appropriate in top-down command-and-control situations in which there are organisation-wide cascading goals, objective-setting and appraisals following linear processes. Such an approach is likely to be useful in manufacturing industries and the fast-food industry where fast, efficient, stable, consistent and predictable output is required. Solution-focussed coaching methods may be appropriate in situations where a point-attractor dynamic is in operation, for example, all revolves around the EBIT margin or sales targets. However, such methods are likely to have limited effect in more complex dynamics where multiple parallel processing is required and 'out-of-the-box' thinking geometry is needed. When dealing with circumstances involving organisational development or R&D there is a need to become conversant with strange-attractor (chaotic attractor) models and complexity theory if the output is to exceed the sum of the parts and generate creative solutions. Working out how to promote connectivity between functions and generate states of 'flow' will be very important. Promoting the use of the imagination, interpreting bodily sensations, capturing images from dreams and exploring metaphors will also be important. Understanding the circumstances promoting or impeding such work will be necessary in order to unlock potential. Coaches will need to develop their minds as though they are finely tuned musical instruments encompassing their brain, body and environment. Some may learn to resonate like a Stradivarius.

Chapter 28

Certainty and uncertainty

There is a significant debate between scientists as to whether computers will be able, sooner or later, to emulate all of the functions of the human mind and satisfy the conditions of the Turing Test. Some experts argue that the biological processes that the brain uses invoke quantum mechanical principles: 'owing to its quantum character, the brain necessarily generates an amorphous mass of overlapping and conflicting templates for action' (Schwartz *et al.* 2004). This means the brain is quite capable of holding contradictory views and our intentional conscious mental efforts are able to shift unstable patterns of activity towards stable patterns, increasing our chances of achieving our intended outcomes. They further argue that quantum effects produce consciousness and that the mind is a quantum computer that cannot be emulated by classical computing machines. Uncertainty is inherent in any quantum phenomena so that outcomes may not be predictable. So far, nothing in the world of artificial intelligence or computing resembles the complexity of the human mind. For the moment at least it seems that the human mind has far more depth, complexity and mystery than we are capable of creating artificially. Any neuroscience-based insights need to be conveyed with an appreciation of the richness of what it is to be human.

Developments in the physical sciences and the mathematics of complexity have altered our understanding of our reality in the world. Has our quest to understand the nature of reality nearly concluded? We live at a time when great excitement has been generated by apparent mounting evidence for the existence of the Higgs Boson, the so-called 'God' particle providing the glue holding other fundamental subatomic particles together. We live at a time when scientists are proposing possibilities that sound mind-boggling and counterintuitive, such as the existence of 11 dimensions according to M-theory. Despite so many uncertainties about the basic fabric of our universe, we often act as if we know a great deal about our universe. Our urge for stability, predictability and certainty seems to exert much influence and our abstracting analytical minds seem to believe that our technology has taken us to the brink of being able to understand everything. Perhaps this healthy optimism is necessary so as not to become overwhelmed and depressed.

One of the greatest explorers of the mind, Carl Gustav Jung, commented in his memoirs that, in his opinion, in order to understand the complete picture of the psyche requires the existence of another dimension beyond those of space and time (Jung 1963). Today, physicists seem to have concluded that extra dimensions are needed to explain their observations too. If there are dimensions to our universe that are not yet apparent, then it is quite possible that entities that travel through such dimensions could convey aspects of our psyches that currently have no plausible explanation. Gradually, parapsychology, synchronicity, thanatology and psychokinesis may become more accepted by mainstream science (Grof and Bennett 1993). It would seem advisable to keep our minds open to such possibilities. We may one day begin to understand how the interaction of linear causality and non-linear causality may interact to structure and organise a quantum field to produce form according to the philosophy of dependent origination, or as the Zen Master Thich Nhat Hanh might put it, the phenomenon of inter-being. We may come to understand the notions of synchronicity and karma pointing us to the realisation that our fate, the fate of those around us and the environment are somewhat related and interdependent (Nhat Hanh 1991).

Chapter 29

Harmony and the human spirit

In 2010 Sir John Whitmore delivered a presentation on 'Sustainability and the Role of the Global Coaching Community' at the Association for Coaching's International Conference. Sir John offered a number of insightful reflections that found resonance with many members of the audience. He reflected that our quantitative outer knowledge has raced ahead of our qualitative inner wisdom. This gap, he said, is unsustainable and substantial transformations are required to restore balance. He believes our system of deferring to hierarchy is in decay and in need of replacement, fuelled by a growing imperative for self-responsibility. The 'Old World' he characterised as striving for growth, conforming to imposed rules backed by a sense of fear and a focus on quantity. The 'New World' he envisaged should be characterised by sustainability instead of growth, inner values rather than imposed rules, a platform of trust and a focus on quality. One assertion that took me by surprise was an assertion that competition between people is not an inevitable part of human life required in order to comply with Darwinian survival of the fittest ideas. Cooperation between people may in fact be our only viable survival strategy. In thinking about his presentation subsequently, I began to see the wisdom of such a statement. I had assumed that competitive Darwinian natural selection was necessary for human advancement. Implicit in adopting such an assumption, I later realised, was the fact that I had overlooked what it is to be fully human. Being a product of our super 'rationalised' world mindset that Max Weber warned us about, my mindset too had become more adept at abstracting reality, manipulating it and utilising objects in one way or another. Sitting each day behind a computer, dealing with facts, figures and verbal information threatening to swamp me with detail, it is easy to dissociate from residing occasionally in that deep tranquil formless space from which we can appreciate what it is to be human.

In pondering the dichotomy of competition versus cooperation I asked myself: why not both? As with the mind itself we do not benefit by sticking to one end of a polarity or the other. We need to balance both, finding the appropriate point between them according to the circumstances. Being human may well entail generating contradictory perspectives and holding paradoxical positions. In order to generate creative thinking dynamics, beyond the sum of the parts, competition and cooperation are needed together to co-create a dynamic creative tension. Presumably, the other cerebral polarities of stability and instability, integration and fragmentation need to be in a dynamic tension too, in order to generate optimal thinking dynamics.

To summarise, the balancing act that we need to achieve in order to create optimal thinking dynamics for generating sustainable solutions involves the left and right hemisphere-based polarities, forming a horizontal platform of cognitive perspective, and also the vertical polarity between the functions of integration and differentiation. This forms a diamond constellation represented in Figure 29.1. The upper pyramid, above the cognitive level, may be thought of as the area of spiritual integration, while the inverted pyramid below the cognitive level may be thought of as the area for developing an appreciation of our physicality and the diversity of nature. Our cognitive constructs are refined over time by the widening spiralling dialectic process of integration and differentiation, leading to ever more subtle understanding. Developing mindfulness of the dynamic constellations within this diamond shaped developmental arena may facilitate the creation of expert teams capable of generating sustainable solutions, resulting in major transformational change.

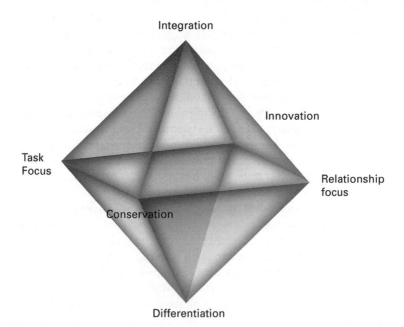

Figure 29.1 The diamond model for polar exploration: how far along each axis does your experience extend?

In looking for an example of where competition and cooperation seem to be in a dynamic tension together with stability and instability I alighted on the spirit generated during the Thirtieth Olympiad at the London 2012 Olympic Games. Before the Games there was considerable anxiety concerning whether sufficient stability could be maintained throughout the period of the Games. Threats to stability came from the failure of security contractors to deliver services, and possible terrorist security threats. The transportation system was expected to be stretched to, or even beyond its limits. Anxious defensive comments and behaviours were clearly observable during the run-up to the Games. Would Britain be able to maintain its face to the rest of the world or would this fragile stability start to fragment? Would our athletes be able to perform creditably as the world focussed in on the competition? Would the overall cultural experience go down well at home and abroad? Many uncertainties filled the air. Surely, here was an example of the dynamic tension between stability and instability; between the need for competition to drive performance and the need for cooperation to facilitate it?

The Opening Ceremony got off to an excellent start with Danny Boyle highlighting the multicultural diversity and shared values that shape modern Britain: differentiation and integration in dynamic tension. Diversity, shared values and experiences looking inward and outward, together with 70,000 volunteers promoting positivity and connectivity. Are these not essential factors for generating high performance? Strange-attractor dynamics indeed! In this atmosphere of large numbers of people interacting with athletes from all over the world during 17 intense days in which both competition and cooperation seemed to be in such abundant supply, can it be said that conditions were ideal for generating performance levels beyond the sum of the parts? Within each athlete the vertical 'flow' achieved through the functions of brain and body in synchrony working together seemed to commune with the horizontal transpersonal mindset of the spectators to create a 'superflow' in which ordinary performance levels were transcended. Some athletes such as Mo Farah (Team GB) and Galen Rupp (Team USA) seemed to be engaged in a synthesis of competition and cooperation by training together and pacing each other to take gold and silver medals in the 10,000m respectively. And this whole dynamic was repeated a few weeks later in the Paralympics. The results seem to speak for themselves, showing how, with the right conditions, the human spirit is able to achieve amazing levels of performance. Can we imagine such transpersonal dynamics at an Android Olympics? Could machines ever replicate such spirit?

I leave you to ponder this and other experiences you may have had in which creativity emerged from holding the dynamic tension of stability and instability, competition and cooperation, and differentiation and integration in hand. Perhaps NASA's Apollo space programme putting man on the moon or creation of the International Space Station provide other examples of where the paradoxical dynamic of competition with cooperation, stability with instability and differentiation with integration enables us to live life at the edge of chaos where we can truly excel? These are large-scale examples and perhaps you can bring to mind that essence, like the true Olympic spirit, that has at some time touched your life? Can you liberate this spirit in your clients that over the millennia has fuelled the highest levels of human achievement?

Chapter 30

Final thought

As we progress further into the twenty-first century we will face many complex challenges that will stretch our powers of creativity. Let us end by imagining ourselves to be asleep and experiencing a dream (assuming you've managed to stay awake to this last, refreshingly short, chapter of the book). In this dream you have just been appointed by the highest authority, the cosmic Chairman, to be the Global Project Manager charged with solving all the sustainability problems of the twenty-first century. You did not apply for this position, so you say to the Chairman:

GPM: 'I don't have the ability to solve all of the problems that are emerging today. They are too complex and change too quickly for solutions to be developed. What should I do?'

Chairman: 'You have a brain containing 100 billion neurones, each of which can be connected with up to 10,000 other neurons in the most deeply connected, flexible, parallel-processing, problem-solving creation in the entire universe. You have another 7 billion of these problem-solving creations on your planet already. How many more do you think you need in order to solve your problems?'

GPM: 'Oh, please, no more Mr Chairman. I just need the owner's manual!'

Welcome to the human mind: the most complex, malleable, intricate and subtle creation that you regularly encounter, and the greatest of all privileges to work with!

Glossary of terms

Agency As in 'self-agency': an ability to decide upon the effect you want to produce.

A priori Formed previously/already existing.

Archetype Archaic/primordial type of role model.

Attachment A type of bonding or emotional tie between two people such as a mother and her infant. In John Bowlby's Attachment Theory the type of attachment may be described as secure, insecure/avoidant, ambivalent or disorganised.

Attractor In Chaos Theory, a point or collection of points around which dynamic activity is organised. If it is a single point it is said to create 'point-attractor' dynamics that most severely limits the range of activity; in contrast, 'strange-attractor' dynamics around multiple points produces more creative dynamic patterns.

Attunement A state of congruence between the emotional states of two individuals.

Autonomy Independent or self-directed.

Basic assumptions In Wilfred Bion's theory of group dynamics certain situations such as high anxiety levels may generate an emotional group state in which the growth and development of the team is halted and behaviour regresses to 'basic assumptions' involving dependence on a selected leader or a pair of individuals or flight/fight behaviour.

Butterfly effect A dynamic situation in which small differences in initial starting conditions lead to huge differences at a later point in time.

Coaching An interaction between two people with the aim of enhancing the self-awareness and self-directed abilities of the person(s) being coached.

Cognitive dissonance A state in which two simultaneously held models for a particular behaviour conflict, causing discomforting uncertainty.

Cognitivism Psychological theory in which it is believed that the mind forms accurate representations (mental models) of the external world.

Complexity Sciences Branch of mathematical sciences concerned with non-linear dynamic interactions which provides metaphors for understanding complex biological processes.

Confluence   Situation in which two individuals share the same state of mind and are as 'one'.

Constellations   A representation of a collection of interrelated dynamic systems, e.g. persons interacting together which may be modelled using neutral volunteers to explore different scenarios.

Constructivism   Psychological theory in which it is believed that the mind is highly selective in choosing what it pays attention to and by directing this selective process creates its own reality.

Contagion   The transmission of an emotional state of mind from one person to another via activation of the mirror neuron system evoking a recognised empathetic emotional response.

Core values   Things that are important to you in life and worth passionately defending.

Decentring   In mindfulness practices, moving the focus of awareness away from the inner narrative-generating default network out towards the sensory areas of the cerebral cortex.

Default network   Network of neurons in the central midline of the cerebral cortex which become active during a 'downtime' for other activities and are engaged in weaving your experiences into a narrative/story.

Dialectic   Form of reasoning in which contradictions (polar opposites) are transcended through logical argument, resulting in a unity that itself contains 'higher level' contradictions.

Edge of chaos   Concept within complexity sciences in which structural frameworks providing control and predictability are removed sufficiently to enable new adaptive changes to occur without fragmentation into total chaos.

Epigenetic   Processes modifying the products of genetic transcription 'downstream', i.e. not the immediate result of decoding genes but subsequent modifications.

Emotional intelligence   Ability to self-regulate emotional influences (as distinct from cognitive intelligence: thinking ability).

Empiricism   Philosophical view that all knowledge comes from our experience of sensory information.

Executive attention   The process of noting the mental activity most influential in determining how the decision making in the frontal cerebral cortical areas is likely to operate.

Explicit memories   Memories that can be consciously recalled in everyday circumstances.

Feeling   In Jungian MBTI psychometric categories, this 'type' means reflective evaluation rather than emotional affect.

Fixed Gestalts   Behaviours that have become engrained through repetitive use of particular neural pathways.

Fractal   Patterns generated according to mathematical principles associated with chaos theory that exhibit similar (strictly self-similar or statistically self-similar) recurring features at different levels of resolution.

Frameworks   Mental construct used to provide rapid evaluation of the likely meaning of sensory input.

Framing   Selection of a framework of interpreting likely meaning of a situation or experience.

Geometry of thinking   Expanse of neural territory (number and depth of specialist functions) covered in a thought process.

Gestalt   German term meaning dynamic 'form' or emerging pattern.

Group think   Type of confluence in which members of a group use the same limited geometry of thinking to evaluate a situation rather than considering diverse perspectives.

Holonomic brain   Theory supported by Dr Karl Pribram in which the brain stores memories according to holographic principles so that, as with fractals, any part of the memory contains the template for the whole pattern. In this way different parts of the brain have access to the template for the whole brain.

Hypofrontality   Process in which the influence of the Executive Attention centres in the frontal cerebral cortex is limited in order for a more creative process to emerge analogous to an edge-of-chaos effect.

Image schemas   Primitive form of internal representation of external spatial concepts such as UP–DOWN, PART–WHOLE etc. created very early in life before complex symbolic representations are stored, proposed by Jean Mandler.

Implicit memory   Memories that cannot be consciously recalled in normal circumstances.

Internal working model (IWM)   Concept introduced by John Bowlby to move the original idea of 'internal objects' towards a model more compatible with cognitive science in which complex information representing an external object is stored implicitly as an internal model.

Introjects   Anything from the external world that we take 'on board' and incorporate within ourselves is said to be an introject. In psychology this tends to mean ideas or rules as to how one should behave.

Intuition   An influence on the thinking process resulting from complex evaluations of past experiences rather than an analysis of abstracted facts.

Kaizen   Japanese management concept to encourage continuous improvement in the workplace.

Limbic system   A collection of parts of the brain specialised in relating the behaviour of an individual to the circumstances in the environment influenced by past experience. It functions therefore on the edge or border of the internal and external world (Latin *limbus*: border or edge).

Mentalisation   The capacity to relate to the mental states of other individuals. This is also related to the notion expressed in the 'Theory of Mind'.

Metacognition   Awareness of one's own thinking and the cognitive factors influencing that thinking.

Metaphor   A linguistic device used to express a complex abstract idea using an analogy from everyday experience that is easier to grasp yet potentially misleading.

Mindfulness   A state of being aware of being fully present in the 'here-and-now', keenly noticing what is occurring internally and externally.

Mind-mapping Technique of charting graphically a 'train of thought' often not linear.

Mirror neurons   A network of neurons sensitive to observing the goal-directed behaviour of others that serve to bridge external observation and internal activation of emulating functions.

Mirroring   Emulation/imitation of the behaviour of another person.

M-Theory   Theory concerning subatomic particle physics encompassing 'String' and 'Super-String' theory which postulates the possible existence of up to 11 dimensions to the universe of which we are so far only cognisant of four.

Narcissism   From the ancient Greek myth of the beautiful young man who fell in love with himself (his own reflection); within management, narcissism, in its extreme reactive form, has come to mean a state of self-centred grandiosity, over-inflated sense of self-importance, envy and exploitation of others. A constructive form of narcissism may be important for fuelling the self-belief necessary to become inspiring transformational leaders capable of realising paradigm shifts.

Neuroplasticity   Ability of neural networks and connections to reconfigure themselves in order to adapt to emerging needs. Flexibility is particularly needed early in life and at times of major change such as preparing to leave the parental home and become more independent, and during the 'mid-life' crisis of purpose but in principle cognitive models can be reconfigured throughout life.

Oedipus complex   Ancient Greek myth of a young man who unwittingly killed his father and made love to his mother used by Sigmund Freud as a metaphor for the sexual attraction and attention-seeking behaviour that a child may develop towards the opposite sex parent with a sense of rivalry with the same sex parent.

Payoff   Concept in Transactional Analysis in which a person generates a script/story for themselves early in life with a particular end result or 'pay-off', that has the potential to become a self-fulfilling prophecy as they organise their life according to the script.

Personification   Act of assuming the behaviour and characteristics of someone or particular aspects of someone including one's self.

Point-attractor   A focal point of attention or 'gravitational pull' around which a dynamic system (e.g. a cyclonic weather system) may orient. If there are multiple focal points of attention causing competing 'gravitational pulls', more complex dynamics are likely to be observed. In business teams a profit target may act as a point-attractor limiting the scope of team behaviour. If a balanced scorecard is used more complex behaviours would be expected.

Projection   Act of ascribing a particular aspect of one's own personality onto someone else because it is not consciously accepted as part of one's self. If this relates to an attribute that is disliked, this operates as a self-protection mechanism against guilt as one can then condemn someone else rather than feel guilty oneself. If this relates to an attribute that is liked, the reason why one discounts oneself and praises another is an interesting line of enquiry.

Quantum theory   Theory from subatomic particle physics in which the principle of uncertainty operates such that when considering, for example, the likely outcome of neural pathway activity, the outcome is beyond prediction with certainty and is better assessed in terms of probabilities. This may explain why human behaviour is fundamentally unpredictable, providing creative possibilities.

Rapid-eye-movement (REM) sleep   Dream sleep in which the eyes may move rapidly. This may be associated with a form of mental processing of experiences using interpretive frameworks different from the ones usually used to aid creativity.

Rationalist   Someone such as the Ancient Greek philosopher Parmenides who believes that absolute truth can be achieved through reasoning relying on a priori knowledge rather than sensory input (the opposite of an empiricist's position). Such philosophical perspectives are relevant for informing our thinking about how we come to know things and learn.

Relativity   A general principle that contends that all events/entities have meaning only with respect to their relationship to other events/entities; thus, contexts and relationships need to be considered in order to understand events/entities properly.

Resting state networks   Networks of neurons that become active when task focussed or other purposeful activities are disengaged, e.g. the default network.

Retroflection   Act of doing to oneself something that would normally be expected to involve another, such as blaming oneself for something for which someone else was responsible or providing self-support when support from another is needed but not forthcoming. The former is potentially destructive, whereas the latter is potentially necessary.

Ringi   Japanese term for a decision-making process that examines proposals from multiple points of view considering values, premises, consequences and details until all likely scenarios are fully understood and an agreed-upon position is reached that satisfies critical concerns. Ethical decisions for example involve such a process.

Safe haven   Place where one has access to a trusted individual who provides psychological support, comfort, protection and sense of security.

Schemas   Frameworks used to organise experiences in order to derive likely meaning.

Script   Concept proposed in Transactional Analysis that holds that human beings have a propensity early on in life to construct stories about how their future may unfold. The early life experiences shaping these scripts may be detrimental to personal growth and development, and in order to escape any self-fulfilling prophecy therapeutic interventions may be necessary.

Secure attachment   Form of psychological attachment to another person who provides a safe haven, secure base and the conditions for growth and development.

Secure base   Reliable psychological support foundation enabling one to have sufficient confidence for sustained exploration, risk-taking behaviour and self-expansion.

Self-agency   see Agency.

Self-directed neuroplasticity remodelling   Proposal that the connections made between neurons involved in providing behavioural models, for example, are susceptible to conscious intervention through mindfulness practices enabling such things as anxiety to be better controlled.

Self-referential   Concerning or referring to one's self.

Sensing   In MBTI terms a meta-function concerned with drawing upon information from the environment and interpreting this information using well-established frameworks.

Strange-attractor   A concept from the complexity sciences and chaos theory in which a particular type of attractor complex creates a 'strange' or unusual dynamic effect. A person can be a 'strange-attractor' having a broad understanding of many diverse areas such that they are able to increase the geometry of thinking in any group, potentially leading to new insights and creative ideas.

Tabula rasa   Latin term meaning 'blank' or erased slate used to convey the notion that we are born with no a priori knowledge; thus, knowledge comes from experience and perception.

Theory of Mind   Theory that holds that by interpreting observations of someone's goal-oriented behaviour we are able to know the intentions that they have in mind.

Transactional Analysis   A theory relating to influences on the formation of personality resulting from interactions with other people, providing methods to promote growth and development. The originator of the theory was Eric Berne.

Transformational change   A process in which the cognitive frameworks used to interpret information and make decisions are replaced with new frameworks as a result of double-loop learning and the impact of new insights. Significant changes in the way in which one perceives and interacts with the world then result.

Unconditional positive regard   A concept from Person Centred psychological theory such as that proposed by Carl Rogers in which the attitude
one (e.g. a coach) adopts towards another (e.g. a client) is not conditioned
by personal biases, prejudices, philosophical or religious positions etc.,
but infused with profound respect for another fellow human being on
their journey through life.

Values   Principles held in such high regard that they are worth defending
passionately.

Verbal working memory   A function of the (often left-biased) prefrontal
cortex with limited capacity for evaluating proposals containing a small
number of conceptual ideas using predominantly verbally conditioned
linear logical reasoning.

Visual working memory   A function of the (often right-biased) prefrontal
cortex with limited capacity for evaluating proposals containing a small
number of conceptual ideas using predominantly visually conditioned
non-linear intuitive reasoning.

Bibliography

Alschuler, L.R. (2008) 'Jung and politics', in: P. Young-Eisendrath and T. Dawson (eds) *The Cambridge Companion to Jung* (pp. 299–313). Cambridge: Cambridge University Press.

Ammaniti, M., Nicholais, G. and Speranza, A.M. (2007) 'Attachment and sexuality during adolescence', in: D. Diamond, S.J. Blatt and J.D. Lichtenberg (eds) *Attachment and Sexuality* (pp. 79–105). New York: The Analytic Press.

Anālayo (2003) *Satipaṭṭhāna. The Direct Path to Realisation*. Cambridge: Windhorse.

Bachirova, T. and Kauffman, C. (2009) 'Coaching as a method for joining up the dots: an interview with Michael Cavanagh', *Coaching: An International Journal of Theory, Research and Practice*, 2 (2), 106–116.

Baressi, J. (2002) 'From "The thought is the thinker" to "the voice is the speaker"', *Theory and Psychology*, 12 (2), 237–250.

Beck, D.E. and Cowan, C.C. (2006) *Spiral Dynamics*. Malden, MA and Oxford: Blackwell Publishing.

Beisser, A.R. (1970) 'The paradoxical theory of change', in: J. Fagan and I.L. Shepherd (eds) *Gestalt Therapy Now: Theory, techniques, applications* (pp. 88–92). Harmondsworth: Penguin.

Belbin, R.M. (2010) *Management Teams: Why they succeed or fail*. Oxford: Elsevier.

Bentley, T.J. (2000) 'Gestalt in the Boardroom', *Gestalt Review*, 4 (3), 176–193.

Benziger, K. (2009) *Thriving in Mind: The art and science of using your whole brain*. Carbondale, IL: Benziger Org.

Berne, E. (1964) *Games People Play*. London: Penguin Books.

Bion, W.R. (1968) *Experiences in Groups*. London: Tavistock Publications.

Bléandonu, G. (1994) *Wilfred Bion: His life and works 1897–1979*. New York: Other Press.

Bluckert, P. (2006) *Psychological Dimensions of Executive Coaching*. Maidenhead: McGraw-Hill.

Bolen, J.S. (1989) *Gods in Everyman*. New York: Harper and Row.

Bostock, D. (1995) 'Plato', in: T. Honderich (ed.) *The Oxford Companion to Philosophy* (p. 684). Oxford: Oxford University Press.

Brown, B.C. (2011) 'Conscious leadership for sustainability: How leaders with late-stage action logics design and engage in sustainability initiatives'. Unpublished PhD Thesis, Fielding Graduate University, Santa Barbara, CA. Available at: http://integralthinkers.com/wp-content/uploads/Brown_2011_Conscious-leadership-for-sustainability_Full-dissertation_v491.pdf (accessed 13 Nov 2012).

Brown, S.L. and Eisenhardt. K.M. (1997) 'The art of continuous change: Linking complexity theory and time-paced evolution in relentlessly shifting organizations', *Administrative Science Quarterly*, *42* (1), 1–34.

Buber, M. (1923) *Ich und Du*. Guetersloh (reprinted 1974): Guetersloher Verlagshaus.

Cai, D.J., Mednick, S.A., Harrison, E.M., Kanady, J.C. and Mednick, S.C. (2009) 'REM, not incubation, improves creativity by priming associative networks', *Proceedings of the National Academy of Sciences*, *106*, (25), 10130–10134.

Car, S., Cooke, B., Harris, L. and Kendall, B. (2008) 'Coaching with MBTI', in: J. Passmore (ed.) *Psychometrics in Coaching* (pp. 47–62). London: Kogan Page.

Chaskalson, M. (2011) *The Mindful Workplace*. Chichester: John Wiley & Sons.

Clarkson, P. (2004) *Gestalt Counselling in Action*. London: Sage Publications.

Clarkson, P. and Mackewn, J. (1993) *Fritz Perls*. London: Sage Publications.

Cobb, R.J. and Davila, J. (2009) 'Internal working models and change', in: J.H. Obegi and E. Berant (eds) *Attachment Theory and Research in Clinical Work in Adults* (pp. 209–233). New York: The Guilford Press.

Combs, A. (2009) *Consciousness Explained Better*. New York: Paragon House.

Cozolino, L. (2006) *The Neuroscience of Human Relationships*. New York and London: W.W. Norton & Co.

Crane, R. (2008) *Mindfulness-Based Cognitive Therapy*. London: Routledge.

Csíkszentmihályi, M. (1991) *Flow: The psychology of optimum experience*. New York: Harper Perennial.

Damasio, A. (2012) *Self Comes to Mind: Constructing the conscious brain*, New York: Vintage.

De Board, R. (1978) *The Psychoanalysis of Organizations*. Hove and New York: Routledge.

Diamond, A. (2009) 'The interplay of biology and the environment broadly defined', *Developmental Psychology*, *45* (1), 1–8.

Diamond, D. and Blatt, S.J. (2007) 'Introduction', in: D. Diamond, S.J. Blatt and J.D. Lichtenberg (eds) *Attachment and Sexuality* (pp. 1–26). New York: The Analytic Press.

Dietrich, A. (2004) 'Neurocognitive mechanisms underlying the experience of flow', *Consciousness and Cognition*, *13*, 746–761.

Dietrich, A. and Kanso, R. (2010) 'A review of EEG, ERP, and neuroimaging studies of creativity and insight', *Psychological Bulletin*, *136* (5), 822–848.

Divine, L. (2009) 'A unique view into you', *Journal of Integral Theory and Practice*, *4* (1), 41–67.

Douglas, C. (2008) 'The historical context of analytical psychology', in: P. Young-Eisendrath and T. Dawson (eds) *The Cambridge Companion to Jung* (2nd edn) (pp. 19–38). Cambridge: Cambridge University Press.

Eagle, M. (2007) 'Attachment and sexuality', in: D. Diamond, S.J. Blatt and J.D. Lichtenberg (eds) *Attachment and Sexuality* (pp. 27–51). New York: The Analytic Press.

Ebenstein, W. and Ebenstein, A. (2000) *Great Political Thinkers* (6th edn). Belmont, CA: Thomson Wadsworth.

Eckman, P. and Rosenberg, E.L. (2005) *What the Face Reveals*. Oxford and New York: Oxford University Press.

Epstein, M. (1996) *Thoughts without a Thinker*. London: Duckworth.

Epstein, M. (2007) *Psychotherapy without the Self*. New Haven, CT and London: Yale University Press.

Erikson, E.H. (1959) 'Identity and the life cycle', *Psychological Issues*, *1*, 1–171.

Farb, N.A.S., Segal, Z.V., Mayberg, H.,Bean, J., McKeon, D., Fatima, Z. and Anderson, A.K. (2007) 'Attending to the present: Mindfulness meditation reveals distinct neural modes of self-reference', *Social Cognitive & Affective Neuroscience (SCAN)*, *2*, 313–322.

Fisher, D., Rooke, D. and Torbert, B. (2003) *Personal and Organisational Transformations through Action Inquiry* (4th edn) London: Edge/Work Press.

Fonagy, P. and Luyten, P. (2009) 'A developmental, mentalization-based approach to the understanding and treatment of borderline personality disorder', *Development and Psychopathology*, *21*, 1355–1381.

Frederickson, B.L. and Losada, M.F. (2005) 'Positive affect and the complex dynamics of human flourishing', *American Psychologist*, *60*, (7) 678–686.

Gallese, V., Fariga, L., Fogassi, L. and Rizzolatti, G. (1996) 'Action recognition in the pre-motor cortex', *Brain*, *119*, 593–609.

Gardner, H. (1983) *Frames of Mind: The theory of multiple intelligences*. New York: Basic Books.

Gaulthier, D. (1986) *Morals by Agreement*. Oxford: Oxford University Press.

Gay, P. (2006) *Freud: A life for our time*. London: Max Press.

Gazzaniga, M. (2012) *Who's in Charge?*. London: Robinson.

Gendlin, E.T. (2003) *Focusing* (25th anniversary edn). London: Rider.

George, W.W. (2012) 'Mindfulness helps you become a better leader', *Harvard Business Review Blog*, 26 October 2012. Available at: http://blogs.hbr.org/ hbsfaculty/2012/10/mindfulness-helps-you-become-a.html (accessed 19 November 2012).

Goldberger, A.L. and Rigney, D.R. (1990) 'Sudden death is not chaos', in: S. Krasner (ed.) *The Ubiquity of Chaos* (pp. 23–34), Washington, DC: American Association for the Advancement of Science.

Goleman, D. (1995) *Emotional Intelligence*. London: Bloomsbury Publishing Plc.

Goleman, D. (2000) 'Leadership that gets results', *Harvard Business Review*, March–April, 78–90.

Gomez, L. (1997) *An Introduction to Object Relations*. London: Free Association Books.

Goncalo, J.A. and Staw, B.M. (2006) 'Individualism–collectivism and group creativity', *Organizational Behavior and Human Decision Processes*, *100*, 96–109.

Gottman, J.M. (1994) *What Predicts Divorce? The relationship between marital processes and marital outcomes*. Hillsdale, NJ: Erlbaum.

Gould, S.J. (1977) *Ontogeny and Phylogeny*. Cambridge, MA: Belknap Press of Harvard University.

Grof, S. and Bennett, H.Z. (1993) *The Holotropic Mind*. New York: HarperCollins.

Gyatso, T. and Goleman, D. (2003) *Destructive Emotions and How We Can Overcome Them*. London: Bloomsbury Publishing Plc.

Hadamard, J. (1945) *The Psychology of Invention in the Mathematical Field*. Princeton, NJ: Princeton University Press.

Haier, R.J. and Jung, R.E. (2008) 'Brain imaging studies of intelligence and creativity: What is the picture for education?', *Roeper Review*, *30*, 171–180.

Handy, C. (2007) *Gods of Management* (4th edn). London: Souvenir Press.

Harrison, R. (1972) 'Understanding your organization's character', *Harvard Business Review*, *15* (3), 119–128.

Hawkins, P. (2011) *Leadership Team Coaching*. London and Philadelphia, PA: Kogan Page.

Herrmann, N. (1996) *The Whole Brain Business Book*. New York: McGraw-Hill.

Hiatt, J.M. (2006) *ADKAR: A model for change in business, government and our community*. Loveland, CO: Prosci Learning Center Publications.

Hofstede, G. and Hofstede, G.J. (2005) *Cultures and Organisations: Software of the mind* (2nd edn). New York: McGraw-Hill.

Holmes, J. (2007) 'Sense and Sensuality: Hedonic intersubjectivity and the erotic imagination', in: D. Diamond, S.J. Blatt and J.D. Lichtenberg (eds) *Attachment and Sexuality*. New York: The Analytic Press.

Horn, K.P. and Brick, R. (2005) *Invisible Dynamics*. Heidelberg: Carl-Auer Verlag.

Jacobs, L., Philippson, P. and Wheeler, G. (2007) 'Self, subject and intersubjectivity: Gestalt therapists reply to questions from the editors and from Daniel Stern and Michael Mahoney', *Studies in Gestalt Therapy*, *1* (1), 13–38.

Jarvis, J., Lane, D.A. and Fillery-Travis, A. (2006) *The Case for Coaching: Making evidence-based decisions on coaching*. London: Chartered Institute of Personnel and Development.

Joines, V. and Stewart, I. (2002) *Personality Adaptations*, Nottingham and Chapel Hill, NC: Lifespace Publishing.

Jung, C.G. (1959) *The Archetypes and the Collective Unconscious* (2nd edn, 1990 reprint). Hove: Routledge.

Jung, C.G. (1963) *Memories, Dreams, Reflections* (reprinted 1995). London: Fontana Press.

Jung, C.G. (1995) *Jung on the East*. J.J. Clarke (ed.). London: Routledge.

Kakabadse, A. and Kakabadse, N. (1999) *Essence of Leadership*. London: International Thomson Business Press.

Karmiloff-Smith, A. (2008) 'Nativism versus neuroconstructivism: Re-thinking the study of developmental disorders', *Developmental Psychology*, *45* (1), 56–63.

Karpman, S. (1968) 'Fairy tales and script drama analysis', *Transactional Analysis Bulletin*, *726*, 39–43.

Kauffman, C. (2010) 'The last word: How to move from good to great coaching by drawing on the full range of what you know', *Coaching: An International Journal of Theory, Research and Practice*, *3*, (2), 87–98.

Kets de Vries, M. (2006) *The Leader on the Couch*. Chichester and San Francisco, CA: Jossey-Bass.

Knox, J. (2003) *Archetype, Attachment, Analysis: Jungian psychology and the emergent mind*. Hove: Routledge.

Knox, J. (2011) *Self-Agency in Psychotherapy: Attachment, autonomy and intimacy*. New York and London: W.W. Norton & Co.

Kurzweil, R. (2005) *The Singularity Is Near*. London: Duckworth & Co.

Lane, R.D., Waldstein, S.R., Chesney, M.A., Jennings, R., Lovallo, W.R., Kozel, P.J., Rose, R.M., Drossman, D.A., Schneiderman, N., Thayer, J.F. and Cameron, O.G. (2009) 'The rebirth of neuroscience in psychosomatic medicine, Parts 1 and 2', *Psychosomatic Medicine*, *71*, 117–215.

Lewis, R.D. (2006) *When Cultures Collide* (3rd edn). Boston, MA: Nicholas Brealey Int.

Lichtenberg, J.D. (1989) *Psychoanalysis and Motivation*. Hillsdale, NJ: Analytic Press.

Lichtenberg, J.D. (2007) 'A discussion of eight essays that propel attachment and sexual theories into the 21st century', in: D. Diamond, S.J. Blatt and J.D. Lichtenberg (eds), *Attachment and Sexuality* (pp. 237–261). New York: The Analytic Press.

Loevinger, J. (1976) *Ego Development*. San Francisco, CA: Jossey-Bass.

Lombardo, M.M. and Eichinger, R.W. (2004) *FYI For Your Improvement* (4th edn). Minneapolis, MN: Lominger Int.

Losada, M. and Heaphy, E. (2004) 'The role of positivity and connectivity in the performance of business teams', *American Behavioral Scientist*, *47* (6), 740–765.

McGilchrist, I. (2009) *The Master and his Emissary*. London and New Haven, CT: Yale University Press.

McGrath, R.G. and MacMillan, I. (2000) *The Entrepreneurial Mindset*. Boston, MA: Harvard Business School Press.

Mandler, J. (1992) 'How to build a baby: II. Conceptual primitives', *Psychological Review*, *99*, 587–604.

Mikulincer, M. and Shaver, P.R. (2007) 'A behavioural systems perspective on the psychodynamics of attachment and sexuality', in: D. Diamond, S.J. Blatt and J.D. Lichtenberg (eds) *Attachment and Sexuality* (pp. 51–78). New York: The Analytic Press.

Modinos, G., Ormel, J. and Aleman, A. (2009) 'Activation of anterior insula during self-reflection', *PLoS ONE*, *4* (2), e4618.

Moore, K.L. and Persaud, T.V.N. (1998) *Before We Are Born: Essentials of embryology and birth defects*. Philadelphia, PA: W.B. Saunders.

Moore, R.L. (2003) *Facing the Dragon: Confronting personal and spiritual grandiosity*. Wilmette, IL: Chiron Publications.

Morgan, G. (2006) *Images of Organization*. Thousand Oaks, CA: Sage Publications.

Nardi, D. (2011) *Neuroscience of Personality*. Los Angeles, CA: Radiance House.

Nataraja, S. (2008) *The Blissful Brain: Neuroscience and proof of the power of meditation*. London: Gaia Octopus Publishing.

Nelson-Jones, R. (2000) *Six Key Approaches to Counselling and Therapy*. London: Sage.

Nevis, E.C. (2005) *Organizational Consulting: A Gestalt approach*. Santa Cruz, CA: Gestalt Press.

Nhat Hanh, T. (1987) *The Miracle of Mindfulness*. London: Rider.

Ochsner, K.N., Bunge, S.A., Gross, J.J., Gabrieli, J.D.E., (2002) 'Rethinking feelings: An fMRI study of the cognitive regulation of emotion', *Journal of Cognitive Neuroscience*, *14*, 1215–1229.

Ogawa, J.R, Sroufe, L.A., Weinfeld, N.S., Carlson, E.A. and Egeland, B. (1997) 'Development and the fragmented self: Longitudinal study of dissociative symptomatology in a non-clinical sample', *Development and Psychopathology*, *9*, 855–880.

Ogden, P. (2009) 'Emotion, mindfulness and movement', in: D. Fosha, D.J. Siegel and M.F. Soloman (eds) *The Healing Power of Emotion* (pp. 204–231). New York: W.W. Norton & Co.

Panksepp, J. (2009) 'Brain emotional systems and qualities of mental life', in: D. Fosha, D.J. Siegel and M.F. Soloman (eds) *The Healing Power of Emotion* (pp. 1–26). New York: W.W. Norton & Co.

Passmore, J. (2010) *Excellence in Coaching*. London and Philadelphia, PA: Kogan Page.

Peltier, B. (2001) *The Psychology of Executive Coaching*. Oxford and New York: Routledge.

Penrose, R. (1990) *The Emperor's New Mind*, London: Vintage.

Perls, F., Hefferline, R.F. and Goodman, P. (1951) *Gestalt Therapy* (reprinted 2006). London: The Souvenir Press.

Pfeffer, J. (2010) 'Business and the spirit', in: R.A. Giacalone and C.L. Jurkiewicz (eds) *The Handbook of Workplace Spirituality and Organizational Performance* (2nd edn) (pp. 27–43). Armonk, NY: M.E. Sharpe.

Pillay, S.S. (2011) *Your Brain and Business*. Upper Saddle River, NJ: FT Press.

Porges, S. (2009) 'Reciprocal influences between body and brain in the perception and expression of affect: A polyvagal perspective', in: D. Fosha, D.J. Siegel and M.F. Soloman (eds) *The Healing Power of Emotion* (pp. 27–54). New York: W.W. Norton & Co.

Povinelli, D.J. and Preuss, T.M. (1995) 'Theory of mind: Evolutionary history of a cognitive specialisation', *Trends in Neurosciences*, *18*, 418–424.

Prempak, D. and Woodruff, G. (1978) 'Does the chimpanzee have a theory of mind?', *Behavioral and Brain Sciences*, *4*, 515–526.

Rawls, J. (1996) *Political Liberalism*. New York: Columbia University Press.

Rock, D. (2009) *Your Brain at Work*. New York: Harper Collins Publishers.

Rock, D. and Page, L.J. (2009) *Coaching with the Brain in Mind*. Hoboken, NJ: John Wiley & Sons.

Rowan, J. (2005) *The Transpersonal* (2nd edn). Hove: Routledge.

Rowan, J. (2010) *Personification*. London and New York: Routledge.

Scanlon, T.M. (2000) *What We Owe to Each Other*. Cambridge, MA and London: Harvard University Press.

Schore, A.N. (2009) 'Right brain affect regulation: An essential mechanism of development, trauma dissociation, and psychotherapy', in: D. Fosha, D.J. Siegel and M.F. Soloman (eds), *The Healing Power of Emotion* (pp. 112–144). New York: W.W. Norton & Co.

Schutz, L.E. (2005) 'Broad-perspective perceptual disorder of the right hemisphere', *Neuropsychology Review*, *15* (1), 11–27.

Schwartz, J.M. and Begley, S. (2002) *The Mind and the Brain: Neuroplasticity and the power of mental force*. New York: Harper Collins.

Schwartz, J.M., Stapp, H.P. and Beauregard, M. (2004) 'Quantum physics in neuroscience and psychology: A neurophysical model of mind-brain interaction', *Philosophical Transactions of the Royal Society of London, Series B: Biological Sciences*, *360*, 1309–1327.

Scruton, R. (1982) *Kant*. Oxford: Oxford University Press.

Segal, Z.V., Williams, J.M.G. and Teasdale, J.D. (2002) *Mindfulness-based Cognitive Therapy for Depression: A new approach to preventing relapse*. London: Guildford Press.

Shaver, P.R. and Mikulincer, M. (2009) 'An overview of adult attachment theory', in: J.H. Obegi and E. Berant (eds) *Attachment Theory and Research in Clinical Work in Adults* (pp. 17–45). New York: The Guilford Press.

Siedel, E.M., Satterthwaite, T.D., Eickhoff, S.B., Schneider, F., Gur, R.C., Wolf, D.H., Habel, U. and Derntl, B. (2012) 'Neural correlates of depressive realism – An fMRI study on causal attribution in depression', *Journal of Affective Disorders*, *138* (3), 268–276.

Siegel, D.J. (1999) *The Developing Mind*. New York: The Guilford Press.

Siegel, D.J. (2007) *The Mindful Brain*. New York: W.W. Norton & Co.

Sills, F. (2009) *Being and Becoming*. Berkeley, CA: North Atlantic Books.

Singer, P. (2005) 'Hegel, Georg Wilhelm Friedrich', in: T. Honderich (ed.) *The Oxford Companion to Philosophy* (p. 342). Oxford: Oxford University Press.

Smith, E.E. and Jonides, J. (1997) 'Working memory: A view from neuroimaging', *Cognitive Psychology*, *33*, 5–42.

Stacey, R.D. (2007) *Strategic Management and Organisational Dynamics: The challenge of complexity* (5th edn). Harlow: Pearson Education.

Stacey, R.D. (2012) *Tools and Techniques of Leadership and Management*. Abingdon: Routledge.

Stein, S.J. and Book, H.E. (2006) *The EQ Edge: Emotional intelligence and your success*. Mississauga, ON: Jossey-Bass.

Stern, D.N. (1995) *The Motherhood Constellation: A unified view of parent–infant psychotherapy*. London: Karnac Books.

Stern, D.N. (2000) *The Interpersonal World of the Infant: A view from psychoanalysis and development psychology* (2nd edn). New York: Basic Books.

Stewart, I. and Joines, V. (1987) *TA Today: A new introduction to transactional analysis*. Nottingham and Chapel Hill, NC: Lifespace Publishing.

Tarnas, R. (1991) *The Passion of the Western Mind*. New York: Ballantine Books.

Trevarthen, C. (2009) 'The functions of emotion in infancy', in: D. Fosha, D.J. Siegel and M.F. Soloman (eds) *The Healing Power of Emotion* (pp. 55–85). New York: W.W. Norton & Co.

Tzourio-Mazoyer, N., De Schonen, S., Crivello, F., Reutter, B. (2002) 'Neural correlates of women face processing by 2-month-old infants', *Neuroimage*, *15*, 454–61.

Wagner, U., Gais, S., Haider, H., Verleger, R. and Born, J. (2004) 'Sleep inspires insight', *Nature*, *427*, 352–355.

Ward, J. (2010) *The Student's Guide to Cognitive Neuroscience* (2nd edn). Hove: Psychology Press.

Welwood, J. (2000) *Towards a Psychology of Awakening*. Boston, MA: Shambala Publications.

Whitmore, J. (2002) *Coaching for Performance* (3rd edn). London: Nicholas Brealey Publishing.

Whitmore, J. and Einzig, H. (2010) 'Transpersonal coaching', in: J. Passmore (ed.) *Excellence in Coaching: The industry guide* (2nd edn) (pp. 119–134). London: Kogan Page.

Wilber, K. (2006) *Integral Spirituality*. Boston, MA: Shambala Publications.

Williams, M. and Penman, D. (2011) *Mindfulness: A practical guide to finding peace in a frantic world*. London: Piatkus.

Yalom, I.D., and Leszcz, M. (2005) *The Theory and Practice of Group Psychotherapy* (5th edn). New York: Basic Books.

Young-Eisendrath, P. and Dawson, T. (2008) *Jung* (2nd edn). Cambridge: Cambridge University Press.

Zahn, R., Moll, J., Paiva, M., Garrido, G., Krueger, F., Huey, E.D. and Grafman, J. (2009) 'The neural basis of human social values: Evidence from functional MRI', *Cerebral Cortex*, *19*, 276–283.

Index

basal ganglia 11, 15, 40, 66
basic assumptions mentality 67,
    112–113, 173–174
basic perinatal matrices (BPM) 127
Belbin, R.M. 165–166
Benziger, K. 12–13, 93
Berne, E. 144–145
beta-blockers 101
bias 25–26, 43
bifurcation points 190
biological motivational systems 82,
    104–110
Bion, W.R. 112–113, 173–174
blastocytes 130
blood pressure 100, 109
Boardroom function 20–23, 27, 29–30,
    38, 56
body language 27, 49, 52–53, 65, 113, 160
Bowlby, J. 83, 105–107, 125, 135
Boyle, D. 201
brainstorming 32, 57
Briggs, K.C. 12
Britain 4, 201
Broca, P. 45
Brodman areas 44/45 45
Buber, M. 157, 162
bullying 115, 146

calmness 61–65, 68, 71, 93, 101, 132
Care motivational system 106–107,
    113–114, 117, 130, 132–133,
    150–151
Cartesianism 123–124
causality 123, 198
central processing unit (CPU) 5
Centre for Ethics and Personal Values
    function 31, 35–37
Centre for Self-Development function
    31–33
cerebellum 66
cerebral cortex 3, 5–7, 44, 47, 51;
    balancing demands 81, 83, 85;
    constellations 73–75, 77; creativity
    134; emotional constellations 112;
    integration 67, 70; liberation 153;
    meta-functions 11–18; relationships
    56–57; self repertoire 86–88;
    teamwork 162, 165–166, 171–172
cerebrum 11
certainty 197–198
Chairman function 14–15, 17, 23, 34,
    57; constellations 72–77; evolution

190–191; integration 60–71; large
    constellations 180; role 203; self
    repertoire 90; teamwork 162, 166,
    172–175
change management/processes 57–59,
    95–96
chaos theory 6, 170, 188, 195, 202
charisma 27–28, 34, 73, 140, 176–178
charm 52, 140
charting progress 44–45
Chief Executive Officer (CEO) function
    15–17, 19–31, 33, 38–39, 51;
    comparison 190; relationships 56; self
    repertoire 89; socialisation 148;
    teamwork 162, 166
Chief Operating Officer (COO) function
    16, 40–48, 57, 69, 148, 162
childbirth 130, 133
China 180, 182–183
cingulate cortex 91–96
clinical conditions 132
club culture 176–177, 181
co-construction 126, 193, 195, 200
*Coaching: An International Journal of
    Theory, Research and Practice* 192
coaching practice 22–23, 25–30, 33–37,
    44–47, 52; constellations 75–76;
    defence services 103; emotional
    constellations 113, 115, 117–118;
    evolution of 192–196; integration
    64–65, 67–68, 71; library services 99;
    relationships 55–59; self repertoire
    88–89; socialisation 149; surveillance
    services 94; teamwork 174–175
coercive style 115
Cognitive Behavioural Therapy 126,
    128
cognitive dissonance 58, 92–93, 95, 117,
    132, 142, 147, 150
cognitive type preferences 193
cognitivism 125
collectivism 180, 182
Combs, A. 125
command-and-control model 177, 195
communication 45–46, 60, 145,
    158–159, 167
competency models 75–76
complementary transactions 144–145
complexity theory 6, 77, 83, 125, 131,
    170, 190, 196–197
computer assisted design (CAD) 47
concentration 68–69, 94